P9-DCJ-236

College of the Ouachitas

COLLEGE OF THE OUACHITAS
LIBRARY/LRC

3 9005 00035 3627

IMPERFECT JUSTICE

IMPERFECT JUSTICE

PROSECUTING CASEY ANTHONY

Jeff Ashton with Lisa Pulitzer

WM

WILLIAM MORROW
An Imprint of HarperCollins*Publishers*

College of the Ouachitas

IMPERFECT JUSTICE. Copyright © 2011 by Jeff Ashton. All rights reserved. Printed in the United States of America. No part of this book may be used or reproduced in any manner whatsoever without written permission except in the case of brief quotations embodied in critical articles and reviews. For information address HarperCollins Publishers, 10 East 53rd Street, New York, NY 10022.

Designed by Richard Oriolo

ISBN 978-0-06-212532-3

F
35
58
84
011

PROLOGUE

I hate the moment right before the verdict is read. It is my least favorite part of any trial, because someone in the room knows what the jury has decided and I don't. Although I have tried more than three hundred cases in my thirty years as a prosecutor, that moment never loses its impact, and this time was no different. Sitting between my two co-counsels in Courtroom 23A of the Orange County Courthouse, all I could do was watch as the jury filed in to hand down the last verdict of my career: the guilt or innocence of Casey Anthony.

The seven women and five men had been deliberating only thirteen hours over the previous two days and had not asked to review any of the jailhouse recordings of Casey's conversations with law enforcement or members of her family. It was very unusual for a jury, especially in a case like this, to fail to request something of the court. Even in minor cases, jurors customarily need clarification on legal issues important to the case. I never predict a jury verdict, but based on the quickness of their decision, I was confident that they would find the young mother guilty of first-degree murder, or manslaughter at the very least.

Prosecutors Linda Burdick and Frank George were seated on either side of me at the prosecutor's table. We had been summoned back to the courtroom a little after 1 P.M. that Tuesday, July 5, 2011, with the announcement that the verdict was in. I had returned to my office from lunch and had been back only five minutes when I got the call to report to the courtroom. We all felt the trial had gone well, but we were glad to have it over with. The proceedings had taken their toll on everybody.

Jose Baez, the lead defense attorney, hadn't arrived yet, but some of the other defense team lawyers were in their seats. Linda speculated that perhaps Baez was with Casey in the holding cell, which was in the basement of the twenty-three-story art deco courthouse in downtown Orlando. The judge had told the media that when there was a verdict, he would give them thirty minutes to be in their positions. Spectators who had waited hours the day before in the heat of a Florida summer to get one of the fifty gallery tickets were finally allowed into the air-conditioned comfort of the courthouse. They filed in to their assigned seats in time to see Baez arrive, wearing a brown suit and a paisley tie.

For my part, I was in a dark gray suit and one of my signature Jerry Garcia ties, which had become a hot topic in the media. Everything about this case was spun out and dissected by anyone who felt like weighing in. Despite the tragic death of a beautiful two-year-old girl, the story had become light, tawdry summer entertainment.

I may have been projecting, but when Casey arrived shortly thereafter, dressed like a schoolmarm, she looked grim and somber. In fact, her whole team looked unhappy. I hadn't seen her parents, George and Cindy Anthony, slip quietly into the back row of the gallery, but they had been trying to keep a low profile.

As the jurors filed in, Linda told Frank to see which one was holding the verdict form, the clue to who the foreman was. Frank whispered that it was "the coach," a juror originally from Pittsburgh who was a high school sports coach. Linda had particularly liked him during jury selection because the Pennsylvania city was her hometown. I knew the moment of reckoning was upon us as Judge Belvin Perry took his seat at the bench.

"I understand you have a verdict," he said, addressing the jury foreman.

The coach handed the forms to the court deputy, who folded them in half and handed them to the judge. Years earlier, there had been times when we could see the verdict before it reached the bench. If the deputy was holding the forms a certain way, we could see which box was checked, "guilty" or "not guilty," so the solution had been to fold the forms in half, prolonging those seconds of agony just a little bit more.

As much as I dread the anxiety of that single moment, the courtroom is in my blood. I love being a prosecutor. I love the work, the gamesmanship, and the theatrics. I love every aspect of the trial, from the performance to the public speaking. There's an aspect of a trial that is like being the director of a play. There is an art to the order and presentation of the witnesses, to the choice of the questions you ask, to understanding the effects the answers have on the jurors, and to interpreting the opposing counsel's responses. Ultimately, your preproduction and your opening moves can influence the outcome of a case.

I'm drawn in to the theatrics, but I always approach a trial with a sense of angst, as each one is fraught with variables and uncertainty. Will the witnesses show up? Will they testify as expected? I spend hours running through my mind every possible twist and turn the evidence may take based upon what the witnesses may say, what the other side may do, or how the court may rule on evidentiary issues in trial. I would not say that I plan every moment of the trial, or that anyone could, but I do try to anticipate every possibility and plan a response. It is sort of like playing chess with live pieces that can move on their own, and rules that may or may not be followed. The only certainty in a trial is that nothing will ever go as planned.

But once the jury enters the courtroom for the opening arguments, all of that dread disappears, and my juices start to flow. I relish being present in a trial. I imagine it to be much like what an athlete goes through before a game. My entire focus is on one thing. I particularly enjoy going up against an experienced attorney in front of a judge who knows the law. Only then are my skills supremely tested. Our judges do not use gavels, so our trial sessions begin with a simple "Please rise for the jury," our version of "Gentlemen, start your engines."

Having looked at these twelve jurors for as long as I had, I knew the

futility of trying to guess their decision. I didn't want to go through the
mental gymnastics of trying to read their faces. Still, I was confident in the
case we'd put together and how we'd presented it. My mind was ahead of
the verdict, already planning how to work the dates for the penalty phase.
I thought, with the first-degree murder conviction, we could start the arguments on Thursday. That would give the defense thirty-six hours to prepare
their mitigating factors. With the death penalty on the table, they might
need more time.

Judge Perry's face gave away nothing, although he seemed a little
aggressive with the verdict forms. There were nine pages altogether, seven
for each of the seven counts and two for special findings, in the event the
jury found Casey guilty. He made an unusual gesture with the third page.
After he laid it down, he picked it back up to review it one more time and
then put it down hard when he returned it to the pile. I didn't think much
of it. I just wanted to hear the verdict. To me, in light of the brevity of the
deliberations and the weeks of testimony, the outcome was obvious. It had
to be guilty.

At that moment, Judge Perry handed the verdict forms to the clerk and
asked the defendant to rise. I didn't give Casey much notice, staring instead
at the clerk. I always try to read the clerk's body language and eyes to detect
how far down the page she is reading. "Guilty" is always the choice at the
top of the page, with "not guilty" the lowest. This time, her eyes dropped
down the whole page, not a good sign.

"As to Count One, murder in the first degree, we find the defendant
not guilty," she said.

I was stunned, numb, like the feeling a millisecond after an automo-
bile accident when intellectually you know something just happened, but
emotionally it's too surreal to comprehend. When I heard "not guilty" on
the second count, aggravated child abuse, I knew it was over. Count Three,
aggravated manslaughter, was going to be "not guilty" as well. If the jury
didn't believe Casey had committed even child abuse, they were not going
to find her guilty of anything.

Wow.

I could feel myself mouthing the word of disbelief, physically moving my lips and saying it, but not out loud. I stifled the urge to shake my head, even though that was what my body wanted to do. I did not want to demonstrate either approval or disapproval to the jury. To me, one of the most sacred rules of attorney decorum and respect is that you never demonstrate approval or disapproval of a jury's verdict.

If there were gasps in the courtroom, I didn't hear them. I don't even remember hearing the guilty verdicts on the misdemeanor counts. I am not even sure if I heard the "not guilty" verdict on Count Three. Linda, Frank, and I all just sat there. I knew that Linda would be an absolute iceberg. She was the consummate professional and kept her emotions to herself. I was completely in my own head.

I knew what was happening, but I don't remember processing it. It might be egotistical, but it never occurred to me that all twelve of those jurors, in that amount of time, could have rejected all that evidence. It had always been in our minds that they could find Casey guilty of second-degree murder or manslaughter, but a complete "not guilty"? *That* was shocking.

PART I

CHAPTER ONE

JOINING THE TEAM

The Daily News Café in Orlando is your typical lunch spot. Bustling, people shouting orders, good sandwiches—no matter the day, no matter the season, the counter is always packed and the food is always exactly what you need. Located on Magnolia Avenue just a block and a half from the courthouse, the Daily News has long been a staple for Orlando's lawyers, and so perhaps it was fitting that my good friend and colleague at the State Attorney's Office Linda Drane Burdick brought me there one hot day in August 2008 to talk about the case that currently had the entire legal community abuzz: the disappearance of a two-year-old girl named Caylee Marie Anthony.

The Daily News Café was always crowded at lunchtime, so Linda and I ordered at the counter and went to find a table, where we began to talk about the details discovered to date. She was the chief of the sex crimes/ child abuse unit, and as such, the Caylee Anthony case had been in her lap since the beginning. I, like everybody else in Orange County, Florida, had been following the story in the newspaper, and I knew the broad strokes, but there was a lot going on behind the scenes that I was unaware of.

Linda had been contacted about the case on July 16, 2008, as a result of the child's grandmother calling 911 to report Caylee missing. When the call came in, Caylee hadn't been seen in thirty-one days. The child's mother, Casey Anthony, told investigators that she had been working at Universal Studios, a local theme park, and Caylee had been staying with various friends and nannies, in particular a twenty-five-year-old woman named Zenaida Fernandez Gonzalez. According to Casey, she had dropped Caylee with the nanny on her way to work, but when she came back to get her, both of them were gone and the phone had been disconnected. She didn't report her daughter missing, but claimed that she had been searching for her ever since. However, nothing Casey had told the police since the 911 call had proved true. As if the lies weren't bad enough, there was forensic evidence from Casey's car that pointed not only to foul play, but to Casey's involvement.

In my thirty years as a prosecutor, I'd taken seventy homicide cases to trial; all but two had returned guilty verdicts. I'd also prosecuted twelve capital murder cases and won convictions in all of them. My record was solid, but it was only one of the reasons Linda asked me to lunch that day. In many of those convictions, the innovative use of forensic evidence was where I'd distinguished myself. I had renowned expertise in scientific evidence, and Linda thought my perspective and experience might be helpful.

As a prosecutor, I've always been interested in exploring how new scientific techniques could be used to convict guilty suspects. In 1987 I successfully prosecuted the first case in the world in which DNA evidence was used. A man by the name of Tommy Lee Andrews had climbed through a window and attacked a woman, slashing her with a box cutter and raping her repeatedly. Andrews left a fingerprint on the window screen where he'd entered the house, but since it was on the outside of the screen it was hard to connect it to the crime. To positively ID the attacker, DNA was collected from both semen in the rape kit and a sample of Andrews's blood, and it matched. The jury accepted the new science and found him guilty, and the judge sentenced him to prison. It was the kind of forensic evidence that was truly novel in a criminal case, and that perspective was precisely what Linda needed.

For weeks before our lunch, Linda had been hinting about my joining the prosecution team. I had mentored her since she'd joined the office in 1989. We had worked together on many cases in the past, including a cold case murder of a little girl that was solved by DNA. Linda was tough and intense, with a big heart. I called her the marshmallow hand grenade. Frank George, a ten-year veteran of the office, was already on board with her, but as this shaped up to be a homicide, Linda wanted me on the team, too. I was still the go-to man in forensics, and because the case against Casey Anthony was developing with only circumstantial evidence, forensics were going to be of critical importance.

The forensics at the forefront that day in August had to do with a nasty odor and a nine-inch hair, both of which had been found in the trunk of Casey's parents' Pontiac Sunfire, the car Casey had been driving the last time she was seen with Caylee. A cadaver dog had alerted on the area and reacted strongly when the trunk had been opened. Despite Casey's early story that Caylee had been kidnapped, it was beginning to look a lot like a homicide.

Linda told me about the work of Dr. Arpad Vass, a forensic anthropologist who was doing cutting-edge research in decomposition odor analysis. Dr. Vass had examined some of the evidence from the trunk, and Linda wanted me to call him to discuss his findings and see if his science could be admissible. Linda was hoping to bring me into this case, and morsels of forensics like this surely piqued my interest.

I was thrilled to be on Linda's short list, but before either of us could begin to plan anything, office politics had to be negotiated. In 2002 I'd been made a supervisor, leading the juvenile division of the State Attorney's Office. The assignment was supposed to have been a promotion, but I'd hated it. I missed trial work, and the following year I asked to return to the felony trial branch. Even though I had founded the homicide division in 1990, I was no longer a member of that department and could not move back. Instead, I was now tucked away in the trial division, even though I had twenty-eight years of service, an unblemished record, and a near-perfect conviction rate. After some difficulties with my supervisors, I'd earned an unwarranted reprimand and been informed I was not a team

player. I became an overpaid desk ornament, doing trials I was way over-
qualified for.

Part of the problem was that there were two distinct camps in our office:
those who wanted every case that came across our desks to go to trial and
those who wanted to be more discriminating. Those who thought that whoever got arrested should get prosecuted didn't like my vociferous objection to
that policy. I was of the belief that we should choose the crimes that warranted prosecution and prosecute them appropriately, without buckling to
public pressure. We shouldn't just rubber stamp what the people who had the
case before us had done; we needed to look at the merits of every case to determine if a crime had been committed before we prosecuted it. I honestly think
that State Attorney Lamar Lawson, who headed our whole office, agreed with
me, but the people below him supported the "prosecute all" philosophy.

Maybe I was too abrasive in my conviction and rubbed those on the
other side the wrong way. For whatever reason, my successful record as a
prosecutor seemed to have been overshadowed by my beliefs. The political
players in the office clearly wanted me buried, and so I was. Nevertheless,
the 120 trial lawyers on staff still held me in the highest regard, and most
important, one of those was Linda Drane Burdick.

FROM THE TIME I WAS eight years old, I'd had the makings of a lawyer.
When I was in fourth grade my grandmother and my great-aunt Thelma
were visiting us in Saint Petersburg. After a spirited discussion on some
topic, Thelma said to me, "You should be a lawyer."

"I think I'd like that," I responded. There weren't many cowboys in Florida, and my friends had already cornered the careers of firemen and cops.

I am a Florida boy, born and raised in the great Sunshine State. I was
delivered to Barbara and Richard Ashton on October 3, 1957, in Saint Petersburg, a west coast town on a peninsula between Tampa Bay and the Gulf of
Mexico. At the time, Saint Pete was a retirement mecca for Midwesterners,
so my family didn't quite fit the mold. Mom was an active homemaker, and
Dad was working as a CPA. My parents had met at Wright-Patterson Air
Force Base, ten miles north of Dayton, where my mother had an office job
and my father was a lieutenant in the air force.

I grew up in a neighborhood of typical middle-class homes, in a modest three-bedroom ranch on a small lake, with my three sisters: Cindy, the oldest by twenty-one months; Judy, three years younger than I; and Barb, another three years behind her. I was an underachiever in school, but got through the public school system reasonably well. I don't think I would have been classified as a nerd, but I was on the nerd cusp—not good at sports and a member of the drama club. Oddly enough, while in the drama club, I performed in a play with Angela Bassett—that's right, the actress. She was a year behind me at Boca Ciega High School, and a very sweet girl. If that wasn't accomplishment enough, I also captained our High-Q team, which participated in a local TV quiz bowl. Thirty-two teams competed in single-elimination matches over the school year. We won that year—Go, Pirates! Okay, maybe I was a full-on nerd.

In 1975 I graduated from high school in the respectable upper middle of my class and enrolled at Saint Petersburg Junior College. I started studying philosophy and logic and found it intriguing. I even made some money tutoring in those subjects. For my junior year, I transferred to the University of Florida in Gainesville and graduated with a B.A. in Philosophy in 1978. My father, the accountant, was always nagging me to take business classes, but I wouldn't hear of it. I didn't like numbers. I liked rational argument and thoughtful discourse. I wanted to be an intellectual. As it turned out, I was the only one in my family who did not go into some aspect of accounting.

I finished my undergraduate degree in three years, going to school summers and taking tests for college credit without classes. I didn't know I was allowed to have fun in college. My father never told me that he had been anything less than studious when he was an undergraduate. It was only later, too late for me to follow in his footsteps, that I found out he had quite enjoyed the college life, drank his share, and played poker for spending money. I don't know why I was in such a rush to complete school, but I kept up the breakneck pace at the University of Florida Law School, completing my J.D. degree in two and a half years. I was even fast-tracking my personal life. Halfway through law school, I married my high school friend and college sweetheart, Amy Brotman. We went on to have two wonderful sons, Adam and Jonathan. Sadly, the marriage didn't last and we split up after eight years.

Right out of law school, I was hired by the State Attorney's Office in

Orlando and assigned to the area from which many successful prosecutors have been launched—the traffic division. My buddy Ted Culhan and I shared an office in an old building that used to house the Federal District Court. We were a block from the main office, so we were relatively unsupervised. We weren't above a good-natured prank or two. Our favorite was waiting until someone was on the phone, and then taping the receiver to his head. I did do serious work, too; I had a chance to prosecute some drunk driving cases, and I actually got my first taste of scientific evidence when I was doing hearings on the admissibility of Breathalyzer machines.

After eleven months, I moved to a misdemeanor branch, which was out in the western part of the county. Seven months after that I transferred to the felony prosecution division. My father had been somewhat relieved when I went to law school, but he absolutely loved it when I became a prosecutor. My parents were living two hours away, but even then, they would occasionally make the trip to Orlando to watch me in trial.

In 1983 I prosecuted my first murder case—and won. Two years later, I tried my first death penalty case. The victim was a businessman with a wife and children who took "business trips" to a local gay resort called the Parliament House. On one visit he hooked up with the wrong young man. When they got back to the hotel room, the young man slit his throat and robbed him. The jury convicted the defendant and then recommended the death penalty, which the judge imposed. Before the state could execute him, he hung himself in his prison cell.

Then in 1987 came the case in which I'd become the first prosecutor to introduce DNA evidence. That continued a string of successful homicide prosecutions for me, and in 1990 I created the homicide division of the State Attorney's Office. I was married to my second wife, Joy, and we had two children, Rebecca and Alex, before she and I parted ways.

It was around that time that Court TV, the twenty-four-hour trial channel on cable TV, came into existence. The channel broadcast some of my cases, and my father loved it. He would watch me from his desk at work. Once, in the late nineties, a trial of mine was moved to Pinellas County, my parents' neck of the woods, and my father came almost every day to watch it. Those years in homicide were the most enjoyable of my professional career. For starters, no other cases present the challenges that homicide cases present. But I was also damned good at them.

EVEN THOUGH LINDA WANTED ME on the Casey Anthony case, it was not, strictly speaking, up to her. Linda had gotten the case after Casey was arrested and charged with child neglect, lying to investigators, and interfering with a criminal investigation. Now that it was looking more like homicide, State Attorney Lawson Lamar had the option of turning the case over to the homicide division, headed by Robin Wilkinson, or leaving it with Linda.

That afternoon at the Daily News Café, I told Linda I wanted to be on the Anthony case, but I was all too aware of the politics that surrounded my name. I was nearing the end of my career with the State Attorney's Office, so I didn't need a career boost. I was twenty-eight years into a pension that would allow me to retire at thirty years, and for a while now, that retirement had been my plan. As I explained to her over a burger and fries, I would understand if the pressure made her pick Robin over me. No hard feelings. She could always count on my support and expertise, even if I weren't on the case with her.

But Linda was unequivocal: she needed a bulldog and she was going to ask Lawson to have me officially appointed to the team.

In the end, my arrival on the case turned out to be easier than Linda or I had anticipated. Lawson was very proud of my reputation in the DNA evidence field. He also had great respect for me as a trial attorney, as my prosecution record spoke for itself, one of the best in the state of Florida. A few days later, Linda came to my office.

"I've talked to Lawson," she said. "He wants you to be involved in the case, and so do I."

She handed me the telephone number of Dr. Arpad Vass, the forensic anthropologist, and within an hour I was phoning the distinguished scholar in Tennessee to talk odor and decomposition.

CHAPTER TWO

TWENTY-FOUR HOURS

Once on the team, I got myself up to speed by unearthing the specifics of the case to date. The whole thing had been put into motion by a 911 call that was made on July 15, 2008, by Casey's mother, Cynthia ("Cindy") Anthony. She had made the call to the Orlando police department from her car, saying that she wanted to have her daughter, Casey, who was beside her in the passenger seat, arrested for stealing her 1998 Pontiac Sunfire and withdrawing money from her bank account without authorization.

Because these thefts were all in the family and Cindy already had her car back, the 911 call had the trappings of a family fight taken too far. I dug around to determine exactly when Casey had taken her mom's car without permission and learned that Casey and her daughter, Caylee, had pulled away from the Anthony house in the white two-door Pontiac on June 16, a month before the 911 call. At the time, Casey had informed her parents that she and Caylee would be spending the night at the home of Caylee's nanny and that they would be returning in a day or two. During the ensuing thirty-one days, Casey's phone calls provided various excuses why she and Caylee could not return home, including a twelve-day stay in Jacksonville, Florida, with a male friend, but not to worry, she and Caylee were doing fine.

On July 13, however, Cindy's husband, George, had found a notice stuck on their front door stating that a certified letter was waiting at the post office. The Anthonys rarely used that door, so the notice had been there for days without anyone seeing it. When they went to retrieve the letter, the contents informed them that their Pontiac Sunfire had been towed to Johnson's Wrecker Service off Narcoossee Road. The car had been found abandoned in the parking lot of a business located at the intersection of East Colonial Drive and Goldenrod Road. It had been in the impound lot since June 30.

Cindy and George drove to the towing yard to retrieve their Pontiac. By this point, Cindy was frantic. She had been under the impression that Casey and Caylee were in Jacksonville, yet the car was in Orlando. In the fine print, I read that she snapped at the tow yard supervisor, and George had to instruct her to wait in his car while he claimed their vehicle. As he approached the Pontiac, he became aware of an unmistakable smell emanating from the trunk. Having worked as a law enforcement officer, George thought he recognized the odor as that of a decomposing body.

By his own admission, he whispered, "Please God, don't let this be Casey or Caylee," as he raised the trunk. Relieved to find only a bag of trash, along with some flies and maggots, he watched the tow yard manager toss the bag into a nearby Dumpster. He drove the Pontiac home, while Cindy returned in the other family car. The smell was so strong and unpleasant that he had to open all the windows and the skylight to get the car the seven miles to their house.

Once George had the car back at the residence, Cindy inspected it and found a piece of paper in a bag on the front seat with the cell phone number of Casey's friend Amy Huizenga. Cindy dialed Amy and reached her at the Florida Mall, Central Florida's largest mall, with more than 260 stores. Amy told her that Casey had been staying at the home of her boyfriend, Anthony, who went by the name Tony Lazzaro, a guy Casey had met on the Internet. A twenty-one-year-old transplant from Long Island,

New York, Lazzaro wanted to be a club promoter and was currently working at the Fusian Ultra Lounge, a sushi bar by day and a club by night.

Cindy picked up Amy at the mall, and the two drove together to Tony's
apartment. Amy did the knocking, and when Casey answered, Cindy surprised her by popping out from around the corner, ordered Casey into
the car, and demanded to be taken to Caylee. Finding Casey's responses
regarding the little girl's whereabouts grossly unsatisfactory, Cindy dropped
Amy back home and started for a satellite office of the Southeast Community Police on Pershing Avenue. However, the satellite office had closed at
5 P.M., three hours earlier. Without another clear option, Cindy called 911.

CINDY ANTHONY: Hi. I drove to the police department here on
    Pershing, but you guys are closed. I need to bring someone in
    to the police department. Can you tell me the closest one I can
    come into?
DISPATCHER: What are you trying to accomplish by bringing 'em to
    the station?
CINDY ANTHONY: I have a twenty-two-year-old person that has
    grand theft sitting in my auto with me.
DISPATCHER: So, the twenty-two-year-old person stole something?
CINDY ANTHONY: Yes.
DISPATCHER: Is this a relative?
CINDY ANTHONY: Yes.
DISPATCHER: Where did they steal it from?
CINDY ANTHONY: My car and also money.
DISPATCHER: Okay, is this your son?
CINDY ANTHONY: Daughter.
DISPATCHER: So your daughter stole money from your car?
CINDY ANTHONY: No, my car was stolen, we've retrieved it today, we
    found out where it was at, retrieved it, I've got that and I've got an
    affidavit from my banking account. I want to bring her in, I want
    to press charges.

Reading the transcript of this first 911 call after knowing so much about the case, I was impressed by the omission of significant details, like the trunk odor and the amount of time that had elapsed before Cindy reported the "grand theft auto." To me, Cindy's call presented like an annoyed mother hell-bent on consequences for her unruly daughter. Since Cindy was in the car with the person she was accusing, the dispatcher tried to establish in what jurisdiction the alleged crimes had occurred. Cindy explained that the car had been taken from her home, and provided an address on Hopespring Drive in southeast Orlando.

The dispatcher told Cindy that she needed the Orange County Sheriff's Office, and he patched her through. During the transfer, the 911 recording machine picked up bits of a conversation between Cindy and her passenger:

CINDY ANTHONY: . . . 'cause my next thing . . . we'll be down to child . . . and we'll have a court order to get her. If that's the way you wanna play, we'll do it.

Casey's voice was heard in the background, but it was unclear exactly what she said.

CINDY ANTHONY: . . . No, I am not giving you another day. I have given you a month!

The operator at the Orange County Sheriff's Office instructed Cindy to go home and call back from there. Deputies would be dispatched once the call was made. There seemed to be no urgency to any of it, since no "suspect" was at large. Cindy did as instructed, only this time when she called, the crime she was reporting seemed to have mushroomed into something bigger than a car "borrowed" without permission. I noticed that Cindy was finally mentioning her granddaughter.

CINDY ANTHONY: I have someone here who I need to be arrested in my home.

911 OPERATOR: They are there right now?

CINDY ANTHONY: And I have a possible missing child. I have a
    three-year-old who has been missing for a month. [Though
    Cindy said Caylee was three in this phone call, Caylee was still
    technically two. Her third birthday was to be in early August.]
911 OPERATOR: A three-year-old? Have you reported that?
CINDY ANTHONY: I'm trying to do that now.

I sensed that Cindy was bringing Caylee into the conversation not so
much to alert the operator to a dire, potentially tragic situation, but more to
let Casey know she meant business. She wanted to see her granddaughter,
even if that meant she had to call the police about something else. After
Cindy had informed the operator of Caylee's name and status, she went
on to repeat her primary accusations—Casey had stolen her car and her
money—and asked the police to send someone to the house. Two hours
passed before a third call was urgently placed from the Anthony home. This
time, Cindy was hysterical.

CINDY ANTHONY: I called a little bit ago to the deputy sheriff's and
    I've found out that my granddaughter has been taken—she has
    been missing for a month. Her mother has finally admitted that
    she had been missing.
911 OPERATOR: What is the address you are calling from?
CINDY ANTHONY: We are talking about a three-year-old little girl.
    My daughter finally admitted that the babysitter stole her. I need
    to find her.
911 OPERATOR: Your daughter admitted that the baby is where?
CINDY ANTHONY: She said she took her a month ago and my
    daughter has been looking for her. I told you my daughter has
    been missing for a month and I just found her today. But I can't
    find my granddaughter. She just admitted to me that she's been
    trying to find her by herself. There is something wrong. I found
    my daughter's car today and it smells like there's been a dead body
    in the damn car!
911 OPERATOR: OK, what is the three-year-old's name?

CINDY ANTHONY: Caylee, C-A-Y-L-E-E, Anthony.

911 OPERATOR: How long has she been missing for?

CINDY ANTHONY: I have not seen her since June 7.

The call became inaudible when Cindy started addressing her daughter in the background, but the operator coaxed her back to the phone.

911 OPERATOR: Can you calm down for me for just a minute? I need to know what is going on. Is your daughter there? Can I speak with her? Do you mind if I speak with her?

Casey took the phone. Her voice was casual, almost uninterested. When I heard her one word, "Hello?" starting low and then rising quietly, as if "*hello*" were a question, I was stunned. She was the polar opposite of frantic and was clearly on the line against her own volition. She calmly and deliberately answered the operator's questions as if she were letting someone know about a missed manicure appointment. There was no sense of panic, just a hint of fear and a dash of annoyance.

CASEY ANTHONY: Hello?

911 OPERATOR: Hi. Can you tell me what's going on a little bit?

CASEY ANTHONY: My daughter has been missing for the last thirty-one days.

911 OPERATOR: And, you know who has her?

CASEY ANTHONY: I know who has her. I tried to contact her and I actually received a phone call today from a number that is no longer in service. I did get to speak to my daughter for about a minute.

911 OPERATOR: Did you guys report a vehicle stolen?

CASEY ANTHONY: Yes, my mom did.

911 OPERATOR: OK, so there has been a vehicle stolen too?

CASEY ANTHONY: No. This is my vehicle.

911 OPERATOR: What vehicle was stolen?

CASEY ANTHONY: It's a 1998 Pontiac Sunfire.

911 OPERATOR: We have deputies on the way to you for that, but now your three-year-old is missing—Caylee Anthony?

CASEY ANTHONY: Yes.

911 OPERATOR: You lost her a month ago?

CASEY ANTHONY: Thirty-one days.

911 OPERATOR: Who has her? Do you have a name?

CASEY ANTHONY: Her name is Zenaida Fernandez Gonzalez.

911 OPERATOR: Who is that, the babysitter?

CASEY ANTHONY: She's been my nanny for about a year and a half or two years.

911 OPERATOR: Why are you calling now? Why didn't you call thirty-one days ago?

CASEY ANTHONY: I've been looking for her and have gone through other resources to try to find her—which is stupid.

Just then a sheriff's deputy arrived at the Anthony home, and the 911 call came to an end. The three 911 calls amounted to only a few minutes of audiotape and transcript, but there was a lot to find suspicious in them. Most obviously there was Casey's calmness: most parents would be in hysterics if their child was missing. I have six children (I remarried again in 2005, and my wife, Rita, and I have two adopted children, David and Emma), and I cannot imagine one of them going missing for five minutes, let alone thirty-one days. I once lost track of my son Jon on a crowded beach one summer afternoon. I was diligently watching him, and he disappeared from one second to the next. I was panicked beyond words; every horror story I had ever heard and then some was taking residence in my head. Within minutes he was escorted back to us, but those few moments of paralyzing panic are eternally etched in my memory.

As a prosecutor and a parent, I was left incredulous by Casey's reaction—even by her explanation that Caylee was with a babysitter. How was it even possible for a loving, caring parent to take that long to report a missing child? Helping herself to her mother's money and credit cards may be acts of a young person angry at an authority figure, especially when it's a family matter and the young person lives at home with easy access to the monies and wheels she covets. But to me, accusing someone of kidnapping a baby a month ago, without any sense of urgency or emotion, seemed completely incomprehensible. Casey had much to answer for. Of course, as investigators quickly found out, her answers had some serious problems.

CHAPTER THREE

WHERE IS CAYLEE MARIE?

One weekend shortly after Linda put me on the case, I got into my 2002 Sebring convertible and went on the eleven-mile ride to the Anthonys' part of town. I'd been catching up on the case, talking to the people involved, and reading the various reports that had been filed, but I thought it would be helpful to get a view from the ground, of the house where so much of the initial action in the case had taken place.

The Anthonys lived in Chickasaw Park, a pleasant neighborhood of well-kept ranch houses and manicured lawns southeast of downtown Orlando. Their ranch was prettier than any other on Hopespring Drive—meticulous, well-orchestrated landscaping with lots of cacti, red elephant ear, and a towering palm tree to the left of the front door. The walkway had a brick border lined with solar-powered lights, the front yard nary a weed. The grass was well watered and evenly mowed. The house was board and batten siding, painted a soft shell pink. The front door matched in color but in a deeper tone, and a welcoming plaque of flowers and a blue butterfly hung beneath its arched window. I couldn't see the aboveground pool and toolshed. They were tucked behind the house in a backyard protected by a wooden stockade fence.

I had heard that the Anthony family was well liked by neighbors on the block. They were charter residents of the subdivision. They'd moved into the just-built four-bedroom, two-bath, L-shaped ranch when Casey was only three. It was a quiet, family-oriented community then, as it is now. Whereas George had once helped Casey ride her tricycle, more recently he had often been seen helping his little granddaughter, Caylee, ride hers. He had even assembled a playhouse in a corner of the backyard for her, with its own landscaped border, tiny mailbox, and meticulously installed pavers under the playhouse so that she would never have to play on a dirt floor.

There had never been any trouble at the house, even when Casey and her older brother, Lee, were at the height of their teenage years. The Anthonys seemed the definition of blissful suburbia, especially with the addition of the angelic, bright-eyed baby girl. I could only imagine what the neighbors must have thought when that first squad car showed up at their curb, lights flashing, shortly before 10 P.M. on July 15, 2008.

ACCORDING TO THE POLICE REPORTS from that night, Corporal Rendon Fletcher was the first officer to go up the home's cement walkway. His knock was answered by Cindy Anthony, and he was surprised to find her sobbing and distraught. Based on the 911 calls, Fletcher had thought he was responding to a stolen vehicle report, but from the moment he walked through the door, Cindy didn't say a thing about the car. She looked like a wreck. Her short blondish hair was as combed as it could be at that hour, but she was pale, her blue eyes bloodshot and swollen.

In between sobs, Cindy explained to the officer that she had just learned that her two-year-old granddaughter, Caylee, had been missing for thirty-one days. Choking out the words, Cindy said that her daughter, Casey, had dropped Caylee with her babysitter a month earlier and had not seen the little girl since. As Cindy told it, for the past few weeks whenever she'd called Casey, Casey had said that she and Caylee were vacationing in Jacksonville. But Cindy had dreaded that something was wrong when her requests to speak with Caylee were met with excuses every time. Cindy then went on to tell Fletcher about retrieving the Pontiac at the tow yard and confronting Casey at her boyfriend's apartment. What seemed odd to me was that Cindy failed to mention to the officer the sickening smell emanating from the Pontiac's trunk, which she had described with horror in her 911 call, although later on George would share that detail with another detective.

George's demeanor that night was in stark contrast to his wife's. Standing behind her in the living room with his gray hair groomed back, he appeared calm and in control. Investigators later learned that he had been a detective in Ohio and had been involved in a few homicide investigations before the family moved to Orlando in 1986. His stoicism had been learned from years on the job, but he was just as devastated as his wife. Yet, ever the cop, George had already moved into investigation mode. Emotions would get in the way of finding the facts, and finding Caylee was all that mattered at that moment. He had to be the strong one, since clearly Cindy could not.

George agreed with his wife that Casey had been very vague about why they couldn't speak to Caylee. He said the last time he'd seen the child was on June 16 around 1 P.M. He had no idea she was missing until he'd come home, just minutes before Corporal Fletcher arrived, to find his wife crying in the garage. The Pontiac he had picked up at the impound was parked there, where he had left it, but Cindy had found Caylee's favorite doll in the still-buckled car seat, which put her over the edge. She had tried to reach him at work, but he had missed her call. When George had called her back, there was no answer, so he called their son, Lee, who lived about a half mile away and told him to go to the house and check on everybody.

As Corporal Fletcher interviewed Cindy and George Anthony, other police officers began to arrive. Though the precise order was not totally clear, Deputy Adriana Acevedo, Deputy Ryan Eberlin, still in training, and his sergeant, Reginald Hosey, showed up on the scene within minutes of each other. The sergeant instructed his officers to take written statements from everyone at the house. Eberlin began with Lee, interviewing him in the living room. Lee was almost four years older than Casey, tall and stocky, with dark brown hair and bushy eyebrows. He told the deputy that he had his own place now, but he knew his sister had not been around for the last couple of weeks. When his father had directed him to stop by the house to check on his mother and sister, he'd learned for the first time that something was wrong.

Lee had arrived at the house minutes before Cindy and Casey. When they came in, they were in the midst of a heated argument. Casey didn't stop to explain but blew by him, heading straight for her room and leaving him alone with their mother. Despite her rage and frustration, Cindy told Lee everything she knew, including the fact that Caylee was apparently at some unknown location. It was clear to Lee that his mother was not going to be able to get a straight answer from Casey, so he decided to talk to his sister himself.

Lee was often the intermediary between the two hotheaded, obstinate women. Cindy and Casey argued a lot, and Lee was the peacemaker, when possible. He headed for Casey's room, assuming that his sister was simply trying to upset his mother by hiding Caylee somewhere. He didn't actually believe that Caylee was missing in the classic milk carton "Have you seen me?" sense. To Lee, this was a typical Cindy-Casey power play, and Caylee was only a pawn.

Lee was hoping to talk to Casey alone in her room, but Cindy kept slamming in and out, venting her frustration and threatening to call the police. Once he convinced her to stay out, he attempted to talk with Casey, brother to sister. He pleaded with her to tell Cindy where Caylee was. He even offered to go and see her by himself so he could reassure everyone that she was safe. He couldn't fathom why Casey was going to such great lengths to upset their mother. Yet he received the same response that Cindy had: Caylee was with her babysitter, probably asleep, and should not be disturbed.

Cindy continued with her angry outbursts while Lee and Casey talked. During one of her rantings, she informed them that she had called the police and they were on their way. Still, Casey's story stayed calmly consistent.

Lee didn't think the situation warranted the police. As a last-ditch effort, he decided to try role-playing, and he told Casey to imagine he was a police officer.

In the voice of an imaginary cop, he introduced himself and informed Casey that her mother had contacted law enforcement, concerned about the welfare of Caylee. He acted coplike as he explained that the best way to quickly resolve the matter would be for Casey to take him to Caylee so he could see the little girl for himself.

For her part, Casey sat stone-faced, not revealing anything, but giving Lee's logic some consideration. After ten to fifteen seconds of silent reflection, she began to cry.

"You want to know the truth?" she asked him. "I haven't seen my daughter in thirty-one days." Believing that he had finally broken through, Lee leaned in, whispering to keep Cindy from hearing, and questioned Casey more. All she would say was that "she was kidnapped."

Lee was stunned. For all his commitment to resolving the conflict between his sister and his mother, he had never entertained the thought that Caylee was actually in danger. How could his little niece be missing? How could she have been kidnapped, and how could Casey keep that fact a secret?

What Lee didn't realize was that he was witnessing the birth of a lie. Something had made Casey determine that she wasn't going to be able to produce Caylee under any circumstances, and so she made up a story about a kidnapping. In the coming months, we in the prosecutor's office would title this first spontaneous fabrication, sprung from desperation, Casey Anthony 2.0.

WHILE LEE WAS GIVING HIS statement about the events of earlier in the evening, Casey was being interviewed by Corporal Fletcher. She told him that on the Monday after Father's Day, sometime between 9 A.M. and 1 P.M., she took her daughter to the apartment of her current babysitter, Zenaida Fernandez Gonzalez, also known as Zanny. She had been introduced to the woman eighteen months earlier by her friend Jeffrey Hopkins, who had also hired Zanny to babysit his son, Zachary. She said that Zanny was half black and half Puerto Rican, twenty-five years old, and originally from New York. She described her as being five feet seven and 140 pounds, with dark brown curly hair and brown eyes. She even said that her birthday was in September. She gave Zanny's address as the Sawgrass Apartments on South Conway Road in Orlando. There, she said, Zanny and two roommates, Raquel Flora and Jennifer Rosa, shared Apartment 210.

After dropping her daughter off at Zanny's that Monday, Casey said, she had gone to her job at Universal Studios, where, she claimed, she was an event planner. At the end of the day, around 5 P.M., Casey drove straight back to the Sawgrass Apartments to pick up her daughter, but no one was home. She tried Zanny's cell phone number and was surprised to learn that the line was out of service, since it had been working earlier in the day. Casey said that she spent two hours on the steps to the second floor of the building waiting for Caylee and Zanny to return, thinking they were either having car trouble or were just running late. It seemed odd to me that Casey's story now failed to mention the two roommates she had earlier created for Zanny, who should have been home or come home sometime that evening.

As time passed, Casey said, she became increasingly worried, so she spent the next few hours going to familiar places in the area looking for Zanny and Caylee. She started at Jay Blanchard Park, one of Caylee's favorite spots, and moved to other places where she thought Zanny might be. After she gave up, she spent the rest of that evening at Tony's, pacing and worrying. His apartment was, in her words, "one of the few places she felt at home." To me, saying that reconfirmed that things weren't great at her parents' house, and spite and retaliation might be at work.

As Casey recalled her version of the events of the last thirty-one days, she stated that she had lied and stolen from her family and friends during that time, claiming, however, that her actions had been justifiable, desperate as she was to find Caylee. Every day since the toddler's disappearance, she had gone to malls, parks, even banks, any place that she could remember Zenaida taking Caylee. When asked why she had not alerted authorities, she claimed that it was out of fear for her daughter. She had seen movies and reports on TV in which bad outcomes came about when the police were called, and she was hoping to handle it on her own. I wondered why she didn't mention a ransom note, that inevitable terror-laced prop in kidnapping movies.

Her tone contradicted her words of concern. During the ten-minute

College of the Ouachitas

conversation, the young mother was completely unemotional, her answers flat and unembellished. In many instances, the officer had to prod and pry responses from her. Her presentation didn't even hint at the hysteria one would expect of a young mother who had not seen her daughter in a month. Even if she were just hiding Caylee, some emotional tone should have been present. Her demeanor just didn't make sense.

Her composure was not the only suspicious thing; the story itself grew increasingly more preposterous. By this point, Officer Eberlin had taken over for Fletcher, and Casey informed him that Zanny had made contact once during the last four weeks. She was unable to provide the deputy with the exact date or time of the call and said it had been disconnected before anything was said, so the report was not very valuable. Even more shocking, that very morning, Casey said, she had gotten a call from her daughter. Caylee had started to tell her what she had been doing, but Casey had interrupted her and asked her to put an adult on the phone. The child had hung up without telling her how or where she was, and there was no way to call her back. The number was blocked.

As odd as this story sounded, members of law enforcement know that it does no good to call your only witness a liar when you are trying to find a missing little girl. By treating Casey like a victim until the investigation proved otherwise, Eberlin was doing his duty as a police officer and following a procedure that's been proven to uncover the truth. Implausible as Casey's version of events sounded, there was value for the officers in going along with it. Sooner or later, they hoped, Casey would crack and the little girl would be brought home safely. They just had to be patient.

In keeping with this protocol, Eberlin took down all her information in his report. He listed the case as a possible kidnapping of a child, and Zenaida Fernandez Gonzalez as the prime suspect. Ten minutes before midnight, Sergeant Hosey, the supervisor on the scene, instructed Deputy Acevedo and Corporal Fletcher to escort Casey to the Sawgrass Apartments on South Conway Road so she could point out the location where she last saw her daughter with Zenaida. Casey, dressed in a pale blue short-sleeved football hoodie sporting the number "82" and tight blue jeans, was in the back of Acevedo's patrol car, and Fletcher was in his vehicle fol-

College of the Ouachitas

lowing behind. She directed them ten minutes away to an appealing and well-maintained three-hundred-unit apartment community with all the amenities—a swimming pool, tennis courts, and a small private lake with a fountain. Each building had three floors, and the units had small terraces with sliding glass doors that opened on a view in one direction or another. Casey directed the deputy over a speed bump and pointed to the first building on the right, just past the WELCOME sign. She did not get out of the patrol car, but simply indicated a unit on the second floor, saying it was Apartment 210.

Corporal Fletcher walked alone up the stairs to the second floor. He knocked on the door of the apartment, but no one answered. Looking in the window, he saw no furniture or personal belongings anywhere inside. The unit was completely vacant. While Deputy Acevedo took Casey back home about twenty minutes after they arrived, Fletcher remained at the complex to investigate further.

When Casey and Acevedo arrived back at the Anthony house, sheriff's deputies were still taking statements from the other family members. Cindy had not calmed down at all, while George remained grim and quiet, and Lee, confused. Sergeant Hosey had now been at the house for two hours, and in that time he'd witnessed a lot of drama.

There was unmistakable tension between Casey and her mother. Casey was making accusations that Cindy wanted to take Caylee away from her, while Cindy was incredulous and frustrated about her daughter's behavior. Sergeant Hosey was of the opinion that some undercurrent of a custody battle was playing out, so he invited Casey to walk privately with him, out of earshot of Cindy and the rest of the family. He wanted to reassure her, in case she was hiding Caylee, that no one was going to take her daughter from her. In fact, he was hoping that she was hiding Caylee. The other possibilities were awfully dire.

——

CHAPTER FOUR

FOUR LIES

A phone ringing in the middle of the night is never a good sign, but Yuri Melich was used to it.

A detective with the Orange County Sheriff's Office, Melich had been working cases in Orange County for more than ten years. In that time he'd had his share of calls in the hours before dawn. Earlier in his career with the sheriff's office he'd been in the homicide unit, but it wasn't long before he'd been promoted to his current role as a missing persons corporal, a position he'd been in for seven years when his phone rang in the early morning hours of July 16.

Answering the phone, he got the specifics of the situation and where he'd be headed. A two-year-old child was missing. The dispatcher instructed him to report to the Anthony home on Hopespring Drive, where officers were already on the scene. Melich hung up and started getting ready.

Melich has the look of a seasoned lawman, with close-cropped hair and a chiseled face. Though he joined the homicide unit after I left it in 2000, I'd known him for a while, having met him through my occasional work on cases in later years. Melich's wife, Sam, was also a detective in the sheriff's office. It was on the murder of Deputy Michael Callin, the son of an old friend and former homicide detective, that I'd first met Melich. I'd been impressed with his work then and had continued to hear good things since. All in all, he always struck me as the kind of officer who's seen it all and then some—confident without being arrogant, and usually in command of the situation. In the years since I first got involved with the Anthony case, I have continued to marvel at the quirk of fate that just happened to place this experienced homicide detective on this call for a missing persons alert.

When Melich arrived at the house at 4 A.M., he was greeted by Sergeant Hosey, who quickly brought him up to speed. Hosey told him the story of the thirty-one days, the attempts to locate Caylee and Zenaida, and their inability to verify anything that Casey had told them. Before speaking to anyone in the house, Melich took a few moments to read the handwritten statements taken from the four family members.

Once he'd read the statements, Melich sat down with Casey, explaining that they were going to go through her statement together, line by line, and that this process would be recorded. However, before they began, Melich made it clear that this was her chance to be forthcoming with the truth. He showed her the signed four-page document, and proceeded:

"You're saying that everything contained in these statements is true and accurate?" he asked her.

"Yes," replied Casey.

Melich wanted to be certain that Casey knew what was going on before launching into the consequences of lying.

"I want to explain what happens if you make a false report or if there's something about this incident that you're not telling us the truth about."

"Uh-huh."

"I want to make sure I make it perfectly clear that if you want to go ahead and rescind this statement and if you want to tell me a different story about what happened, if you're trying to fabricate a story to kind of make something look a little bit better, now is your time to tell me. Are you telling me that this is the story you want to stick with?"

"That's the truth," Casey said. "It's the story I'm gonna stick with, yes."

It was an odd choice of words. While on the one hand she was simply par-roting back Melich's language, that wording left open the possibility that there were other versions beyond the one she was selecting. It was the story she was "sticking with," but did that make it the truth? Either way, she'd been given the chance to correct a story that already stretched credibility, but instead she'd vigorously insisted that her statement was accurate in every way.

For the next hour, she matter-of-factly took the detective through her version of events, repeating and in some cases elaborating on what she'd said in her initial statement to Corporal Fletcher. When Melich arrived at Zanny, he began to probe a bit deeper.

"So you knew her before you had your child?" Melich asked.

"Well, I met her just before. I was actually pregnant at the time," Casey responded.

"When did she start watching your child?"

"It's been within the last year and a half, two years that she started watching Caylee. I had another friend watch Caylee that I've known since middle school. When she went back to school I was looking for a new nanny. Jeff offered to have Zenaida watch both kids. She agreed, and it kind of went from there."

Detective Melich asked for Jeff's phone number, but Casey claimed it was stored in her personal phone, which she had lost. She said she had reported the phone missing to security at Universal Studios nine days ear-lier. Launching into what proved to be a convoluted explanation, she said that even though she still had the phone's SIM card, which stored her num-bers, she lacked Jeff's specific number because it had been saved on the internal memory of the phone she'd lost. It was a bizarre explanation, one that was technically problematic but also raised questions about why she appeared to be making it harder to get in touch with Jeff Hopkins. But more to the point, she seemed to have an excuse for everything.

Melich turned the conversation back to the nanny. Casey said that Zanny had only lived in the Sawgrass complex for four months, but she described in detail going to get Caylee on the day she went missing:

"I got off of work, left Universal, driving back to pick up Caylee like a normal day. And I show up to the apartment, knock on the door. Nobody answers. So, I called Zenaida's cell phone and it's out of service. Says that the phone is no longer in service. Excuse me! So, I sit down on the steps and wait for a little bit to see if maybe it was just a fluke, if something happened. And time passed. I didn't hear from anyone. No one showed up to the house so I went over to Jay Blanchard Park and checked a couple other places where maybe possibly they would've gone. A couple stores, just regular places that I know Zenaida shops at and she's taken Caylee before. And after about seven o'clock when I still hadn't heard anything I was getting pretty upset, pretty frantic."

Casey said she opted to stay with her boyfriend, Anthony Lazzaro, rather than in her own house. "I went to a neutral place. I didn't really want to come home; I wasn't sure what I'd say about not knowing where Caylee was. Still hoping that I would get a call or, you know, find out that Caylee was coming back so that I could go get her. And I ended up going to my boyfriend Anthony's house, who lives in Sutton Place."

"Did you talk to Anthony about what happened with Caylee?" Melich asked.

"No, I did not," Casey responded.

"Had Anthony ever seen Caylee before?"

"Yes, he has," she announced, with no further explanation. She claimed that that night she went to the Fusian Ultra Lounge and other bars—places Zanny was known to frequent.

Melich was puzzled about why Casey's mother, Cindy, and not Casey had made the 911 call and why it had taken so long for that to happen. "I was naive enough to believe that I could find Caylee myself, which obviously I couldn't," Casey told him. "And I was scared that something would happen to her if I did notify the authorities or got the media involved. Or my parents, which I know would have done the same thing. Just the fear of the unknown, fear of the potential for Caylee getting hurt, of not seeing my daughter again."

According to Casey, she had confided in two people about Caylee's disappearance in the weeks following the event. The two people were Jeff Hopkins and Juliette Lewis. She said that Juliette was a coworker at Universal Studios, but then quickly backpedaled, explaining that the woman was actually a former coworker who had moved away some months earlier. Like Jeff's phone number, Juliette's contact information had also been lost with her phone.

"Is there anything about your story that isn't true?"

"No, sir."

"Did you harm Caylee in any way, or did you leave her somewhere?"

Casey was unequivocal in her reply. "No, sir."

"You're telling me that Zenaida took your child without your permission?"

"She's the last person that I've seen with my daughter," Casey said, without answering the yes or no question.

They were beginning to wind down, and Melich ran down some final questions. He asked Casey about her employment. She said she'd worked at Universal Studios for about four years and added that Zanny had worked there part-time also, as a seasonal employee. Melich then asked Casey if she had any problems with drugs, or if Caylee took any kind of medication. Casey answered both questions in the negative.

DAWN WAS JUST BREAKING AS Melich and Casey set off on an investigative tour of the three last known residences of Zenaida Fernandez Gonzalez. Casey was going to show the detective Zanny's former and most recent apartments, as well as the house of Zanny's mother, where she said the nanny had lived before Sawgrass.

Melich had instructed uniformed officers to follow behind in a marked patrol car in the event they needed to enter someone's house or apartment. Their first stop was a building on North Hillside Drive. Casey pointed to a window on the second floor of the structure, which she identified as the apartment where Zenaida had lived in the early part of 2006. She said the units were all three stories and indicated that the window directly above Zenaida's had belonged to the babysitter's roommate.

Moving on, Casey directed the officers to the Sawgrass apartment complex on South Conway. Casey didn't see anyone she recognized, so they moved on to the Crossings at Conway, a townhouse community on South Conway Road near Michigan Avenue. It was there, Casey said, that Zanny's mother, Gloria, owned a condo, and Zanny had lived with her mother there for a short time. She recalled dropping Caylee there several times between mid-2006 and early 2007.

The detective drove slowly through the streets of the complex as Casey tried to find Gloria's unit. She pointed out three as possibilities. The uniformed officer knocked on all three doors, but none of the tenants knew Zenaida or her mother. Casey apologized for not being able to remember the correct address, saying that she had gone there so often it had been as though she was on autopilot.

Just before 6 A.M., Melich dropped Casey back home.

"I'll call if I need anything," he said as she climbed out of the unmarked vehicle. Before he pulled away, Melich was approached by George Anthony, who related concern that his daughter was holding back information. Both he and his wife were worried that something might have happened to Caylee. George mentioned the putrid smell in the Sunfire's trunk. The detective acknowledged their distress and said he would be in touch.

For the next several hours, Melich set out to confirm Casey's story. He began at the Sawgrass complex, where he met with the manager, Amanda Macklin, and maintenance man, Dave Turner. Neither knew Zenaida, nor did they recognize the photograph of Caylee given to Melich by Cindy Anthony.

Macklin stated that Apartment 210 had been vacant for 142 days, and then ran Zenaida's name through their computer database. Sure enough, they got a hit: a Zenaida Gonzalez who had come to look at an apartment on April 17. She was never a tenant, but she had completed a guest card and left a cell phone number. *One lie.*

Next, Melich looked into the apartment on North Hillside Drive. It had been the first apartment Casey visited with him, the location where she said Zanny had lived with a roommate in early 2006. Not only had no one named Zenaida Gonzalez lived there, but the complex itself was a seniors-only facility. Coincidentally, when the initial responding deputies had searched the Pontiac the night before, they'd found an address writ-

ten on a piece of paper, an address that was right across the street from
the seniors facility. It turned out that that address belonged to Casey's ex-
fiancé, Jesse Grund. So not only was there no way Zanny could have lived
in the building, but there was another connection to the street that offered
a possible hint of where the deception came from. *Two lies.*

As Melich turned this over in his head, it didn't add up. Every clue
that Casey had given them was looking bogus. That alone was disturbing, but when combined with the fact that the police were trying to use
Casey's clues to find her daughter and kidnapper, it didn't make any sense.
The obvious conclusion was that wherever Caylee was, Casey clearly did
not want her found. So either there had not been a kidnapping, or there
was some other reason that Casey was hindering their progress. Was she
afraid? If she was, she certainly didn't act like it. Melich had seen people
lie out of fear before, and they usually weren't as calm about it as Casey had
been. Another possibility was that this was just a continuation of the power
struggle with her mom, and when the right moment arose, Casey would
fess up about Caylee's whereabouts. If that was the case, though, Casey
was taking this incredibly far, and was now using police resources to fight
with Cindy. It was a concerning possibility, but not nearly as concerning as
what actually happened next.

With new questions arriving by the minute, Melich went about trying
to confirm other aspects of Casey's story; only this time he knew he was
dealing with a liar. By 9 A.M. Melich was at Universal Studios, looking for
the friends, Jeff and Juliette, whom Casey claimed to have confided in
about Caylee. More important, he wanted to see if the suspect, Zenaida
Gonzalez, worked there, and if so, to learn more about her. He began with
Universal Studio's security manager, Leonard Turtora, and from Turtora's
office he called Casey, putting her on speakerphone.

Even though he was already at Universal, Melich lied, telling her that
he was about to go to her place of employment and needed to confirm some
contact information before he went there. Deception like this is a common
tactic during an investigation. You never want a witness to know what you
know; otherwise you lose your advantage. The hope is that if you let them
lie to you and catch them in some small part of it, they will crack and aban-

don the lie in its entirety. Most people aren't good at adjusting their lies on the fly, so their only options are to tell the truth or clam up altogether. At least that's how it usually works.

Melich asked for her work number, direct extension, and boss's name. She provided a number, an extension, and the name Tom Manley, who she said was her direct supervisor. After hanging up with Casey, Melich tried the extension she had provided, but it wasn't a valid number. The name "Manley" did not exist in the company's database, and Zenaida Gonzalez, who Casey claimed worked at the park on a part-time, seasonal basis, was also not in the system. A man named Jeffrey Hopkins had worked for Universal, but according to their records, he had been fired in May of 2002. Turtora could find no record of a Juliette Lewis, past or present.

And then there was Casey herself. There was an entry for Casey Anthony, but she was not an event planner, and even more surprising, she was not a current employee. Apparently she had worked at the park selling photos at a souvenir shop but had been fired on April 24, 2006. Yet more than two years later, she was still claiming that she worked there. *Three lies.*

Stunned, Melich leaned back in his chair. Over the course of a few short hours, her entire story had unraveled. Even though she'd sworn up and down that the version of events she'd given was completely true, his preliminary investigation had revealed just about every aspect to be a lie. And not only was she lying to the police, this woman had been playing everyone around her, including her parents and brother, for the last year at least. If not even those closest to her knew her reality, was there anything about her that was true? Did she really want to find her daughter, or was that the biggest lie of all?

After ten minutes, he called Casey back and asked her to come to Universal, saying he'd send officers to bring her and would meet her there himself. Melich also asked her to bring her Universal ID card, but Casey said she had misplaced it. Still, she agreed to meet him at the theme park, and a few short minutes later Sergeant John Allen and Detective Appling Wells picked her up in an unmarked car.

The scene at the security gate was almost comical. Sergeant Allen and Detective Wells followed Casey's directions to the Universal employee parking lot and kept pace as she walked directly to the employee gate. There, they were met by Melich, Turtora, and the security guard working the gate. Everybody except the guard knew that Casey was not an employee there.

Casey approached the security guard and informed him that she had forgotten her ID card. He took her name and ran it through the computer. When he informed her that they had no record of her, she persisted, stating emphatically that she worked there. The guard requested the name of her supervisor, which she dutifully provided. He ran that name and again was unable to find it in the computer.

The three cops and Tutora watched the scene unfold, each intrigued to see how and when Casey would relent. She had completely committed to a lie that had no chance of being true—she knew it, and they knew it. Even if she made it past the security guard, what then? There was nothing she could show them that would make her an actual employee of Universal Studios. Their experience, not to mention simple logic, told them that sooner or later Casey would have to admit the truth.

As a prosecutor, I've spent a lot of time around people who aren't telling the truth and have gotten caught. I've seen good liars and I've seen bad liars, but regardless of whether they're good or bad at it, most people, when confronted with such an obvious lie, simply give in. Yet it was clear, even then, that there was something different about Casey. She was completely unwavering. She insisted to the security guard that she worked there, and she refused to accept his answer that neither she nor the supervisor she'd conjured up was in the system. She was adamant that what she said was true. If she wasn't admitting to the lie now, when would she?

When this scene had gone on for long enough and everyone's patience was becoming exhausted, Turtora presented his identification and instructed the guard to allow her to enter under his supervision. But even though she was beyond the gate, that did not make it any easier for her. The cops looked at her and at each other, their eyes speaking the question that no one would say aloud: "Now what?"

To their surprise, Casey strode confidently through the maze of office buildings that housed the business side of Universal Studios. She took a left at the first building, walked to the end of the roadway, and took them left again. At the next intersection, they crossed to the opposite side of the street through a parking lot, passed the first of two connected buildings, and entered the door of the second. Turtora knew that the building did not contain the event planning division, where Casey claimed she worked.

By this point, the cops' curiosity had morphed into incredulity. As they went through doors and turned corners, each of them silently tried to figure out how far she was going to take this. Somehow, the charade that should have ended back at the security gate was still going on, and no one, perhaps not even Casey, could predict when or how it would stop. What kind of person would do this—and to what end? It was no longer a mystery whether she was lying; the real mystery was why.

Just as confident as she had been when she left the security gate, she led them halfway down the building's main hall, and then she stopped suddenly. Shoving her hands in her back pockets, she turned to them, flashed her cutest shy-girl grin, and said the words they'd been waiting to hear ever since she'd arrived: "Okay, I don't really work here." *Four lies.*

No one was shocked by the revelation itself. Indeed, more than anything they were confused by why she'd chosen that moment to fess up. Only in retrospect would the answer become clear: she'd backed herself into a corner. She'd reached the end of the hall, and with literally nowhere else to take the lie, she gave up on it. It was the same thing that had happened with Lee the night before, shifting her story just before the police arrived, from Caylee being with the babysitter to Caylee being kidnapped. It was the second time in as many days, and it would not be the last. It was a pattern that we would become all too familiar with over the next three years.

CHAPTER FIVE

———

CAUGHT

Turtora found Detective Melich a room inside the Universal offices with nothing in it but a white plastic couch and armchair, and Turtora said the investigators could use it for speaking to Casey. Melich wanted to get to her while she was vulnerable, before she had time to think. Whether because of her guilt over being caught in a lie or her fear of arrest because of the lie, experience told him that her defenses should be lowered, and this was probably his best opportunity yet to get at the truth. There was no way she would be able to maintain her story once such a large part of it had given way beneath her; they'd have Caylee back home by the end of the day.

Casey and Melich sat on the couch, and the two detectives perched on either arm of the chair. The ensuing conversation was taped.

"I know and you know that everything you've told us up to now has been a lie. Correct?" Melich began.

"Not everything I told you."

"Okay, uh, pretty much everything, including where Caylee is right now."

"That I still . . . I don't know where she is."

"Sure you do."

"I absolutely do not know where she is."

Detective Melich asked Casey about Caylee's father. She told him that he had died in a car accident. When Melich asked if she had proof, she said she had an obituary from the newspaper in her bedroom.

"Let me explain something," the detective continued. "Together, combined experience in this room, we have thirty years of doing this. Both myself and Sergeant Allen worked in the homicide division for several years. We've dealt with several hundred people and conducted thousands of interviews, the three of us. . . . I can tell for certainty that right now, looking at you, I know that everything you've told me is a lie, including the fact that your child was last seen about a month ago and you don't know where she is. I'm confident you know where she is. We have to get past that. We can sit here and go back and forth with 'I don't,' 'I do,' 'I don't,' 'I do.' It's pretty obvious that you know where she is."

If Casey was surprised by his words, her face didn't show it. Collected as ever, she allowed the detective to continue.

"Now, my question to you is this: We need to find Caylee. I understand that right now Caylee may not be in very good shape, you understand what I'm saying? She may not be the way you and your family last saw her. We need to understand right now, from you, where Caylee is. This has gone so far downhill and become such a mess that we need to end it. It's very simple. We just need to end it."

"I agree with you, but I have no clue where she is," Casey replied.

"Sure you do."

"If I knew in any sense where she was, this wouldn't have happened at all. It wouldn't have happened whatsoever."

The fact that she was still sticking to the same story, even after being caught in a lie, was frustrating. Changing course, Melich decided to show his hand a bit. Maybe if he showed her that more of her stories were lies, the dominoes would all fall.

"Listen, this stuff about Zanny the caretaker, the nanny, is not the truth, because I went to the apartment complex and no person that's ever lived there went by that name. The apartment's been vacant since March, that same apartment. Now, the apartment you pointed out to me, the two-story apartment, that's an old folks' home. It's right across the street from your ex-boyfriend's house, who you never mentioned. And you said you wrote the address down because it was across the street, that's a lie, because I've already talked to him, and we've already been by the house, and, you know, we've looked at everything we could look at over there."

"Um-hmm."

"Everything you've told us is a lie."

And yet, when she was confronted with these facts, they seemed to do little to sway her. Shifting directions once again, Melich tried to give her an out and allow her to admit to something, something that would help her save face and paint herself in a sympathetic light. He was essentially inviting her to tell him that if Caylee was dead, it was an accident.

"I've never met you before, and I could look at you as a person who's scared, who's concerned, and who's kind of afraid of what's going to happen because of something bad that's happened before. Or we can look at you as cold, callous, and a monster who doesn't care, who's just trying to get away with something bad that's happened and is trying to cover it up."

Casey sat closemouthed as she listened to the detective before saying, "I'm scared that . . . I don't know where my daughter is. I would not have put my entire family—"

Sergeant Allen interrupted. "Whoa, whoa . . . I want to ask you something."

"Yes, sir."

"Like he said," Allen continued, "you seem like a pretty bright person. You're willing, right. You're here to try to help, right?"

"Oh, absolutely."

"Your whole reason of talking to us is to try to help. Right?"

"Um-hmm."

"No one's forcing you to talk to us, right?"

"No."

"You want us, you're here because you called, and you want us to help find your daughter, right?" Sergeant Allen asked.

"Um-hmm."

"Now, let me ask you something. I want you to put yourself in my shoes for a minute, okay."

"Um-hmm."

"Since you've talked to him this morning," Allen said, motioning to Detective Melich, "in an attempt to try to find your daughter, you've given him bad addresses, okay?"

"Okay."

"You drove me all the way out here, we walk from the gate back here, all the way to your office, right?"

"Mmm."

"Okay, to an office that you don't have. We got all the way into the building, into the hallway out here, before you finally say, 'Well, I don't really have an office here.' Prior to that, we were walking to your office, right?"

Casey nodded in the affirmative.

"Okay, does any of this make any sense to you?"

"I understand how all that sounds. I—"

Sergeant Allen grew stern. "No, no, no. Here's the problem with that, here's the problem with that, okay? Um, you can carry the weight of this around for a long time. It's not going to get any easier, okay? What he's trying to tell you right now, I'm going to tell you, you know, in the amount of time I've done this, almost thirty years, I've learned this: People make mistakes. Everybody makes mistakes. All the three of us, we have all made mistakes in our lives. We've done some things that we're not proud of, okay? But there comes a point in time when you own up to it, you say you're sorry, you try to get past it, or you lie about it and you bury it, and it just never, ever, ever, ever, EVER, EVER goes away, that's it. Okay?"

Allen went on to emphasize the contradictions in Casey's story. She said she was afraid of calling the police, but once they were there, she lied to them. She said she wanted the police to help, but she fed them more lies. In short, she didn't seem like someone who cared about finding her daughter.

"Now, you know," Allen continued, "by hiding this, by burying this, you are not going to get yourself to a better place. What you're going to do is make everybody else around you suffer, and at some point, this thing is going to come out. It *always* does. It always comes out. Now your best bet is to try to put this thing behind you as quickly as you can. Go to your parents and tell them, you know, some horrible accident, whatever happened, get it out in the open now, instead of letting them worry and worry and worry, okay?. How old are you?"

"Twenty-two," Casey answered.

"At some point, you are going to want to mend things with your family. You let this drag out for another three days, another week, another two weeks, and you make us solve this some other way, and we'll solve it, we always do. There's no point in coming forward and saying, 'Oh my God, this is what really happened,' once we've already figured it out."

In retrospect, this entire scene is astounding. To those of us who have experience with this kind of questioning, at least one of the tactics used by the officers should have gotten through. I have seen countless sessions like this one unfold, and as the evidence mounts, those who have never been through a police interrogation will usually leap at the opportunity to justify their conduct by adopting an explanation that's less morally repugnant than the facts would suggest. Whether because of guilt, fear, self-interest, or all of the above, sooner or later the truth comes out. However, it seemed that no appeal—not to Caylee's safety, not to the damaging impact this was having on her family—could stir a reaction in Casey. She remained unmoved by Sergeant Allen's invitation to explain that what happened to Caylee was an accident and spare her family the pain of not knowing.

Allen moved on to a different tactic, appealing to Casey's sense of guilt and responsibility over the lies themselves. On a normal person this might have worked. But Casey was far from normal.

"Have you ever had anybody do anything wrong to you?" Sergeant Allen asked. "Have you ever had anybody hurt you in any way?"

"Of course."

"Let me ask you a question. . . . When someone's hurt you in the past, and they come to you and say, 'I'm sorry from the bottom of my heart. I'm really sorry for what happened,' do you forgive them?"

Casey said she would.

"What about if somebody who does something to you and then lies and lies and lies and lies. Do you forgive them?"

"It's a lot harder to," Casey replied.

"A lot harder to? Tell me the last time someone hurt you over and over and let you suffer for a long time and then you caught them. Well, once you caught them, that apology doesn't mean a thing, right?"

Allen let her think about that for a minute before he went on.

"There's nothing you're going to tell any of the three of us that's going to surprise us, okay? I've had to sit down with mothers who rolled over on their babies accidentally. I've had to sit down with mothers whose kid had drowned in a swimming pool. . . . I've had mothers whose boyfriends have beaten their kids to death, who felt horrible about what happened.

"And I've had to help them try to explain it to their families, okay? And then I've also had to deal with people who have done horrible, unspeakable things to children, and have lied about it and lied about it and lied about it. And I'll bet you that somewhere in there I've probably dealt with somebody who maybe made a mistake but continued to lie about it, and maybe they weren't such a bad person, but maybe the whole world didn't see it that way. Maybe their family didn't see it that way because they kept lying about it."

And then, for the first time, Casey gave an answer that wasn't either an "uh-hmm" or a lie. She said her mother was having a horrible time with the news.

"My mom," she began, "told me flat out yesterday that she will never be able to forgive me, and I even told her, I am never going to be able to forgive myself. Every single day I have been beating myself up about this. I've been running in circles, it's all I can do at this point. I learned the biggest lesson from all this. I made the greatest mistake that I ever could have made as a parent."

It appeared that she was getting more comfortable, but as with everything they'd heard that day, there was a question about honesty. Casey was either opening up with real emotions for the first time in the interview or aping the emotions that she felt the officers expected of someone in her position. Regardless, nothing the officers said convinced Casey to talk or explain where Caylee was. One of the things that struck Detective Melich was that at no time during any of his discussions with Casey did she show any obvious emotions about the loss of her child. She did not cry or give any indication that she was legitimately worried about her child's safety. In fact, in his official report he noted that Casey remained "stoic and monotone during a majority of our contacts."

They were trying to get her to confess to what had really happened to Caylee, but she remained emphatic about her original story. Her words were just as resolute as they had been earlier in the morning when she was trying to convince the guard at the security gate that she worked there. It was the same determination, the same steadfast belief she'd displayed then, only this time she was attempting to persuade them that Zanny had taken Caylee. But she didn't realize how little the words of a liar are worth. The detectives weren't biting.

"I think you have been in here a long time," Sergeant Allen said, rising from the chair. "I appreciate you talking to us."

One thing that is clear from the tape of this encounter is the sense of relief in Casey's voice when she realized the interview with the detectives was drawing to a close. She was convinced that the officers were on board with her story, and that her biggest failure was not reporting Caylee missing earlier. The fact that she then went on to apologize for giving them the runaround was almost comical. As was the fact that she said she was available to help in any way.

"I just wish I honestly had more things to help with," she added. "We've talked about going through my computer, maybe trying to find past conversations through instant messenger or through e-mails, something. I'll offer up my computer in a heartbeat, just like with my phone logs and anything else, anything that can possibly help. That's why we set up websites and have been making phone calls and trying to get ahold of people.

"I had such a limited number of people that I was actually trusting that could help at this point, thinking maybe they had some insight. I didn't want to involve a bunch of people who maybe didn't know the situation. The mistake was not calling you guys right off the bat. I understand all of that. It's the biggest slap in the face to have done that to myself. The worst part is what I've done to my daughter by allowing her to still be with someone else."

Sergeant Allen agreed. "By failing to notify somebody, you put your daughter in greater risk." He said he was going to return to headquarters and try to track Zenaida down, first by putting her name in the department's database.

Detective Melich asked Casey to accompany him back to the Central Operations Building to work on missing child fliers. There, Melich and Casey walked into the glassed entrance, past the reception area and a store selling T-shirts, patches, and other law-enforcement-related items. While Casey stayed in the division's waiting room with Sergeant Wells, Melich went to talk to Sergeant Allen.

Their conversation didn't last long. Melich believed that Casey had committed the crime of child abuse in leaving Caylee for so long without reporting her missing. Even if the story she'd told had been true, her failure to do anything to find her child would have constituted child abuse. While Caylee's actual fate was unknown, no matter what had happened to her, Casey was, at the very least, guilty of neglect. She had lied to law enforcement about dropping Caylee at a nanny's house, about alerting two friends that Caylee had been kidnapped, and about having recently spoken to her daughter. Clearly, leaving her out of jail was not going to get them any closer to finding Caylee. They discussed a concern that, if left on her own, Casey would take her own life, like Melinda Duckett, another Central Florida mother whose toddler had gone missing. After the disappearance, Melinda taped a segment on *Nancy Grace* to help get clues to bring her two-year-old son home. She committed suicide after Nancy pointed out inconsistencies in her story and exposed her embarrassing past as a porn star.

No one wanted that to happen to Casey, so Melich did the logical thing. He decided to arrest Casey Anthony then and there.

CHAPTER SIX

KIDNAPPED OR
MURDERED?

From the beginning, there was something about this case that drew
people to it, something in the story that simply struck a nerve. While
I've always understood that fascination, what astounded me was how
quickly Caylee's disappearance affected people. It was literally overnight.
As early as the morning after Casey's arrest, I remember that Caylee was
the topic of the day at the Orange County State Attorney's Office—just as
she would be almost every day for the next three years.

When I arrived for work on the morning of Thursday, July 17, everybody
was commenting on what might have happened to two-year-old Caylee.
The story her mother was telling was so far-fetched that any theory we
came up with could be entertained. Most of us thought that perhaps Casey
had placed the child somewhere to spite her mother. Clearly those close to
Casey felt the same way; members of the Anthony family were already on
television asking for the public's help in bringing little Caylee home.

That morning, Casey Anthony appeared before a judge of the Ninth
Judicial Circuit Court of Florida for the first time. The purpose of the pro-

ceeding is to ensure that arrestees know their rights and why they are in custody. The judge's role is to review the evidence to ensure that it's sufficiently strong to establish probable cause that a crime has been committed. A defendant's first appearance is fairly routine, and he appears by video link from the jail three miles away, which was what Casey did that morning.

Appearing by video, Casey was accompanied by her newly acquired counsel, Jose Baez, and his associate, Jose Garcia. Casey, who was shorter in stature than either man, stood silently behind the podium looking pale and tired. Few sleep well on their first night in jail. Casey's cell mate had recommended Baez, who was a thirty-nine-year-old lawyer from Kissimmee, Florida, and whatever arrangements Casey had made to pay him were unknown, since it appeared that she had so little money that she had been stealing from others. Prior to Baez's arrival that day, I had never heard of him.

On that first day, Casey's appearance was brief. In a hearing lasting less than one minute, the judge determined that Casey should initially be held without bond, so she was returned to protective custody at the Orange County Jail, and the search for her daughter continued without her.

Seeing as how Casey had done more to hinder the search than help it, searching without her didn't seem like it would be a problem. Indeed, on July 16 following her arrest, Casey had three phone conversations—all of which were attempts not to provide new information about Caylee, but to get Tony's phone number. Taken together they offered a fascinating look at where her thoughts were as her daughter was missing with presumably the entire Orlando area looking for her.

The initial call had been to Cindy Anthony and, like all jailhouse phone calls, it was recorded by the police. Strangely, Casey did not begin the call by expressing concern over her missing daughter, but by referring to the fact that she'd been on TV. From there she proceeded to have a conversation with her mother that overflowed with hostility and put the frustrations of the previous month on display yet again.

CASEY ANTHONY: You don't know what my involvement is in stuff?
CINDY ANTHONY: Casey.

CASEY ANTHONY: Mom!

CINDY ANTHONY: What?

CASEY ANTHONY: No!

CINDY ANTHONY: I don't know what your involvement is sweetheart. You keep, you're not telling me where she's at.

CASEY ANTHONY: Because I don't fucking know where she's at. Are you kidding me?

CINDY ANTHONY: Casey, don't waste your call screaming and hollering at me.

CASEY ANTHONY: Waste my call sitting in, oh, the, the jail?

CINDY ANTHONY: Well whose fault is it you're sitting in the jail? Are you blaming me that you're sitting in the jail?

CASEY ANTHONY: Not my fault.

CINDY ANTHONY: Blame yourself for telling lies. What do you mean it's not your fault? What do you mean it's not your fault, sweetheart? If you'd have told them the truth and not lied about everything they wouldn't . . .

CASEY ANTHONY: Do me a favor, just tell me what Tony's number is. I don't want to talk to you right now. Forget it.

Cindy passed the phone to Lee. Once again the conversation was an attempt to try and get Tony's phone number, and once again, Casey's family member seemed incredulous that at a time like this, Casey was trying to get Tony's number rather than strategizing a way to find her daughter. The anger that Casey displayed with her mother carried over to her brother, as she appeared adversarial because her family seemed to care more about Caylee than they did about the fact that she was in jail.

LEE ANTHONY: Hey?

CASEY ANTHONY: Hey, can you give me Tony's number.

LEE ANTHONY: I, huh, I can do that. I don't know what real good it's going to do you at this point.

CASEY ANTHONY: Well, I'd like to talk to him anyway.

LEE ANTHONY: Okay.

CASEY ANTHONY: Because I called to talk to my mother and it's, it's a fucking waste. Oh, by the way, I don't want any of you coming up here when I have my, my first hearing for bond and everything else. Like don't even fucking waste your times coming up here.

LEE ANTHONY: You know you're having a real tough, you're making it real tough for anybody to want to try to, even assist you with giving you somebody's phone number.

CASEY ANTHONY: See, that's just it. Every single thing . . .

LEE ANTHONY: You're not even letting me finish. Like . . .

CASEY ANTHONY: Well, well that's because . . .

LEE ANTHONY: . . . I really . . .

CASEY ANTHONY: Just go ahead.

LEE ANTHONY: You're asking me, first you're asking me for Tony's phone number so you can call him and then you immediately want to start cussing towards me and saying don't even worry about coming up here for all this stuff and trying to cut us out. What . . .

CASEY ANTHONY: I'm not trying to cut anybody out.

LEE ANTHONY: I'm not going around and around with you. You know, that, that's pretty pointless. Uh, I'm not going to go through, you're not going to put everybody else through the same stuff that you've been putting the police and everybody else through the last twenty-four hours, and the stuff you've been putting Mom through for the last four or five weeks. I'm done with that. So, you can tell me what's going on. Kristina would love to talk to you because she thinks that you will tell her what's going on. Frankly, we're going to find out something, whatever's going on, it's going to be found out. So why not do it now and save yourself . . .

CASEY ANTHONY: There's nothing . . .

LEE ANTHONY: . . . some issues.

CASEY ANTHONY: . . . to find out. There's absolutely nothing to find out. Not even what I told the detectives.

LEE ANTHONY: Well, you know, everything that you're telling them is a lie.

CASEY ANTHONY: I have no clue where Caylee is. If I knew where Caylee was do you think any of this would be happening? No.

Finding Lee as much of a "waste" as Cindy, Casey next spoke to her friend Kristina Chester, who was at the house with Cindy and Lee. Casey hoped Kristina would finally give her Tony's phone number. Once more, Casey ran into difficulty. All Casey wanted was Tony's phone number, but all everyone else wanted was to find Caylee.

KRISTINA CHESTER: I said does Tony have anything to do with Caylee.

CASEY ANTHONY: No, Tony had nothing to do with Caylee.

KRISTINA CHESTER: Oh, so why, why do you want to talk to him?

CASEY ANTHONY: Because . . .

KRISTINA CHESTER: You probably don't want to tell me.

CASEY ANTHONY: . . . he's my boyfriend and I want to actually try to sit and talk to him because I didn't get a chance to talk to him earlier because I got arrested on a fucking whim today. Because they're blaming me for stuff that I never would do. That I didn't do.

KRISTINA CHESTER: Okay. Well, I'm on nobody's, I'm on your side. You know that, right?

CASEY ANTHONY: Oh, uh, sweetie, I know that. I just want to talk to Tony and get a little bit of . . .

KRISTINA CHESTER: But . . .

CASEY ANTHONY: . . . of, of . . .

KRISTINA CHESTER: . . . Casey, you have to tell me if you know anything about Caylee.

CASEY ANTHONY: Sweetheart, if I . . .

KRISTINA CHESTER: If anything happens to Caylee, Casey, I'll die [crying]. You understand I'll die if anything happens to . . .

CASEY ANTHONY: Oh, well . . .

KRISTINA CHESTER: . . . that baby [continuing to cry]

CASEY ANTHONY: Oh, my God. Calling you guys, a waste. A huge waste. Honey, I love you. You know I would not let anything happen to my daughter. If I knew where she was this wouldn't be going on.

It was a striking series of phone calls. As each of her three conversations led her back to Caylee, all she did was try to get to Tony. Even as everyone worried about her daughter, she seemed more preoccupied with trying to sustain her fledgling relationship. Her sense of priorities was baffling, and in the end, this only added to the portrait of her as callous and uncaring about her missing daughter.

AT THAT POINT THE CRITICAL focus of the investigation was on determining just how much of Casey's story was a lie. The detectives' hope was that if they could find a hint of truth somewhere, that hint might lead them to Caylee.

Ever since Casey had named Zenaida Fernandez Gonzalez, aka Zanny the Nanny, as the person she had last seen with Caylee, Detective Melich had been trying to locate her. While Casey's wild-goose chase the previous day had yielded nothing of real substance, there was one promising lead on Zanny: the guest card with the name "Zenaida Gonzalez" and a phone number on it that Melich had been given by the manager at the Sawgrass Apartments. Melich had called the number and reached a woman going by the name of Zenaida who lived in Kissimmee, about thirty minutes south of Orlando. She said she was forty-two, had six children, and drove a car with New York license plates. She was friendly and cooperative. However, she denied knowing Casey or Caylee Anthony or having ever been employed as a babysitter.

Zenaida agreed to give a sworn statement to an investigator, and on July 17, Missing Persons Investigator Awilda McBryde and Investigator Kari Roderick visited her at her home. She was shown photos of Casey and Caylee and denied knowing either. Likewise, Casey was unable to identify this Zenaida from a packet of photos shown to her.

How and why Zenaida Gonzalez came into Casey's crosshairs has never been determined. There was speculation that Casey somehow got hold of

Zenaida's guest card at the Sawgrass Apartments and from there came up with the fact that she was from New York by her license plate, or perhaps it was someone from her past and the real Zenaida was just a coincidence.

While Melich still couldn't be sure that Zanny was a complete fabrication, Casey's story had gone from implausible to impossible. But as he'd learned at Universal Studios, he was dealing with a woman who was willing to follow her lies to the bitter end. If he was going to get her to admit the truth about Zanny, it would take more than he currently had.

In the meantime, he tried to learn a bit more about the person they were dealing with. Casey had no criminal record, and prior to the 911 call two days earlier, she had apparently been an upstanding citizen. And yet there was something unsettling about how easy it had been for her to lie to him and the other police officers. Her determination at the security gate, her confident walk through Universal Studios—it all seemed so comfortable to her. Lies are like muscles: it takes practice to make them strong. Casey Anthony had clearly been giving hers a lot of exercise.

As news of Casey's arrest spread, Melich began receiving additional information that fleshed out this portrait of Casey Anthony as a liar. Calls came in to headquarters from close friends of Casey's, claiming she was a "habitual liar" who had been known to steal from them in the past. One such call was from Amy Huizenga, who'd been one of Casey's best friends up until a few days earlier. It had been Amy who'd helped Cindy collect Casey at Tony's apartment prior to her first 911 call. Amy told Melich how Casey had recently driven her and her roommate, Ricardo Morales, to the airport, an apparently thoughtful gesture, as the two roommates were headed to Puerto Rico.

Ricardo had once been Casey's boyfriend. They had met in January at a birthday party for Ricardo, and went out for five months. On at least one occasion, Casey and Caylee had spent the night at Ricardo's place, three in a bed, Casey in the middle. Casey and Ricardo broke up in June, but they remained friends. But shortly after Casey dropped them off at the airport, she'd started forging checks from Amy's account. It had been only a few days since Amy had returned home to Florida and discovered the fraud, but already she had discovered seven hundred dollars missing from her account.

Meanwhile, Casey's boyfriend, Tony Lazzaro, also shed light on Casey's fabrications. He called the police the afternoon she was arrested, telling Melich that he'd met Casey on Facebook in May, and they'd been dating since early June. Even though Casey had basically been living with him since June 16, she had never mentioned that Caylee was missing or in any type of danger. He claimed that he first learned of the toddler's disappearance from sheriff's deputies who had shown up at his apartment on the morning of July 16. The last time he'd seen Caylee had been when he invited Casey and Caylee to swim in the pool at his apartment complex on June 2. Casey had never introduced him to a babysitter named Zenaida Fernandez Gonzalez, nor did he know where Zenaida lived. And yet during the time Casey had been living with him, she'd told him on multiple occasions that Caylee was with the nanny, either at Disneyworld, Universal Studios, or the beach.

When authorities obtained Casey's cell phone records, they found that Tony had exchanged text messages with Casey shortly before her arrest. Casey seemed to expect more consolation from him than he was interested in providing. The texts showed Tony's understandable anger both that Casey had been lying to him for a month, but also that Casey wasn't saying where Caylee was. Like Cindy Anthony, he too had been deceived:

TONY: Where is Caylee?
CASEY: I honestly don't know.
TONY: I don't know . . . are you serious?
TONY: When did you find out?
CASEY: been filling out reports all night and driving around with multiple officers looking at old apartments I had taken her to.
  I am the worst fucking person in the entire world. I don't know what I'll do if something happens to her.
CASEY: Too long let's just leave it at that.
TONY: Y wouldn't you tell me of all people? I was UR boyfriend that cares about you and UR daughter. Doesn't make sense to me.
  Why would you lie to me thinking she was fine and with your nanny?

CASEY: I lied to everyone what was I supposed to say I trust my daughter with some psycho how does that look?

TONY: I don't know what to say . . . I just hope your daughter is OK and I'm going to do whatever i can to help your family and the cops.

CASEY: I was put in handcuffs for almost ten minutes and sat in the back of a cop car the best thing and the most important person in my life is missing and god only knows if I'm ever going to see her again.

CASEY: I am the dumbest person and the worst mother I honestly hate myself.

CASEY: The most important thing is getting Caylee back I truly hope that you can forgive me granted I will never be able to forgive myself nor will my family.

TONY: Who is this Zanny nanny person?

CASEY: Someone I had meet thru a personal friend almost four years ago she used to be my buddy Jeff's nanny before she became mine.

CASEY: I'm scared.

TONY: Are you home?

CASEY: Yeah almost twelve hours of stuff finally getting a shower I feel like hell.

TONY: Where did you dropoff Caylee last time you saw her?

CASEY: At her apartment at the bottom of the stairs

TONY: Specifically where?

CASEY: Sawgrass Apartments

CASEY: Have told and showed the police the apartment

CASEY: told them and drove out there with two different officers I just got back from the second drive.

CASEY: If they don't find her guess who gets blamed and spends an eternity in jail.

TONY: Yea no shit, this is serious why would U say something sooner about this? To anyone?

TONY: Oh and why are you texting me and not calling?

CASEY: I talked to two people that have been directly connected to Zannie how can I sit there and be so blind and stupid it's all my fault.

CASEY: I was scared to admit it I was scared something was going to happen to my baby.

The deeper Melich dug into Casey's past, the more other stories arose. Casey's former fiancé, Jesse Grund, also reached out to the police. He and Casey had met three years earlier, when they were both nineteen. She'd been a seasonal worker at Universal Studios, where he was a security guard. They had dated for a while and he had strong feelings for her. Then Jesse had moved to Tampa for a time and they drifted apart. When he received a call from Casey that she was pregnant and that he was going to be a dad, they rekindled the relationship. They were engaged at the time Caylee was born. After she was born, a paternity test determined that Caylee was not his child, but by that time he was hooked on Caylee's adorable smile and agreed to raise her as his own.

However, Jesse noted a change in Casey after Caylee was born. The sweet young woman he'd fallen hard for had turned selfish and untrustworthy. He'd ended the relationship, but they maintained a friendship. Supporting Amy's characterization, Jesse also said that Casey had been a frequent liar during the time he'd known her. When they were engaged, she had stolen $250 from him with every excuse in the book why she couldn't pay him back. He told Melich about a phone call he'd received from Casey on June 25, when she'd called him in an attempt to cheer him up over a recent job loss. She said that if he wanted to get together, she was free that weekend because Caylee and her nanny had gone to the beach.

AS MELICH WAS COMING TO understand just how unreliable and suspect Casey was, a different part of the investigation was taking place at the Forensics Garage on Colonial Drive, part of the Orange County Sheriff's Central Operations Building. The facility housed the department's administrative offices, investigative units, and a state-of-the-art forensics section where the Pontiac that Casey had been driving when Caylee went missing was being examined.

George had given the police permission to process the vehicle, so they didn't need a search warrant to proceed. The car had been brought into the garage by Johnson's Wrecker Service, the same tow company that had removed it from the Amscot check-cashing lot on June 30. Crime Scene Investigator Gerardo Bloise was there to receive the car, along with a black plastic bag containing items that Cindy had removed from the car when it was at the house.

Bloise inventoried the contents: a doll, a backpack, a child's toothbrush, a black leather bag, various papers, a dinner knife, a blue plastic crate, and plastic clothes hangers. The contents of a white plastic garbage bag were also inventoried. When George had picked up the car, the bag was in the car's trunk, and the tow yard manager had removed it and hurled it into the Dumpster exactly as he had found it. Police had gone back to the Johnson's Wrecker Service yard, and the bag had been recovered in its entirety from a Dumpster there. Inside the bag were a can of Copenhagen chewing tobacco; an empty bottle of Arm & Hammer laundry detergent; aluminum foil; part of a plastic hanger; a big pile of paper products; empty Sprite, Cherry Cola, Dr Pepper, Pepsi, and Mountain Dew soda cans; an empty Milwaukee's Best Light beer can; one hairpin; three plastic tie wraps; an empty Oscar Meyer plastic container; several dryer sheets; empty containers of Crystal Light; a cut-up pizza box; a receipt from the Fusian Ultra Lounge; a document from Full Sail University; an empty plastic bottle of Coke; a Crystal Light plastic bottle containing brown liquid; a cherry Coke carton; and a cardboard Velveeta container, among other things. There were maggots crawling on a plastic dinner tray.

Next, Bloise moved on to the car itself, photographing the exterior of the Pontiac, which was clean but not remarkably so. He then opened the sealed driver's-side door and was immediately blasted by a smell he described as the "odor of decomposition," quite startling in light of the physically well-maintained vehicle. The interior was tidy and vacuumed, although a few personal items were found on the seats. The right rear passenger seat had a car seat buckled in. The left rear passenger seat contained two pairs of black women's shoes. On the front passenger seat were a brown belt, sunglasses, and a black case containing CDs.

Bad as the smell in the car was, the absolute worst of the odor was in the trunk. A dryer sheet found inside was not disguising the stench. The truck had been vacuumed but still had some type of dirt residue. Noting a stain on the right side of the trunk, Bloise cut two pieces from the D-shaped particleboard spare tire cover, surfaced with the same carpet as the trunk. He also collected a hair from that area, a hair from the middle area of the trunk liner, four hairs from the left side of the trunk area, and another from the directional light wire of the vehicle.

With a smell as potent as this, it was decided that a K-9 unit should be brought in, and so Detective Jason Forgey and his cadaver dog, Gerus, came for an inspection. Law enforcement has long recognized the superior olfactory abilities of canines, and they use different dogs for different purposes. Some are trained to separate the subtle differences between the body odors of individual humans and track those scents through the air. Others are trained to detect the presence of certain drugs or the chemical components of explosives. Still others are trained to detect the distinct odor of a decomposing human body: Gerus was such a dog. Normally Human Remains Detection Canines, or cadaver dogs as they are commonly referred to, are called in to find human remains; this call was a little different.

After circling the car just once, Gerus started showing interest by sniffing aggressively at it. Forgey opened the car door, and Gerus tried to get into the trunk from the backseat. Gerus then exited the car and ran another pass around it and alerted on the trunk for a second time. When the trunk was opened, Gerus tried to climb in, indicating to Forgey that the source of the odor was in the trunk.

The K-9 team then went to the Anthony residence on Hopespring Drive to continue working. George had discovered a newly dug shallow hole near the shed, five inches deep and about twelve inches long, that concerned him. Gerus didn't care about that, but showed special interest in the playground and playhouse areas. A second K-9 unit was brought in from neighboring Osceola County to confirm Gerus's findings. The second cadaver dog was interested in three areas of the backyard, the same ones

Gerus had alerted us to, plus the ground near the patio porch. Investigators checked all three locations for human remains but found nothing.

The house next door to the Anthonys' on' the left was 4929 Hopespring Drive. It belonged to Brian Burner, and was where investigators headed next. They had been made aware of a potential piece of evidence there. The owner had a shovel in his garage that Casey Anthony had borrowed on June 17, the day after Caylee was last seen alive. Burner said that Casey had told him she wanted dig up some bamboo in her yard, although an hour later, when she returned the shovel, it did not appear to have been used much, if at all.

WITH MELICH SIFTING THROUGH CASEY'S lies and the crime scene investigators taking apart the car, the case began to take shape. For most of the next week, investigators continued to piece together what they knew and the story of how Casey had spent the thirty-one days that she did not report Caylee missing. Meanwhile, everyone in Orlando seemed to be on the hunt for little Caylee. Nothing brings a community together like a missing child, and though confidence still seemed high that they would be able to find her, the results from the cadaver dogs were concerning.

The investigation had a bit of a split personality. On the one hand the sheriff's office was aggressively following every possible lead in an attempt to find Caylee alive, but at the same time they were investigating what was coming to look like a homicide. While the Anthonys were eager to do whatever they could to assist in the missing child investigation, they were less thrilled when the investigation turned to murder and their daughter's possible involvement in it.

Such was the state of affairs for Casey's bond hearing on July 22. Jose Baez was in court representing Casey before Judge Stan Strickland, while Linda was on the other side representing the state of Florida. I had worked with Judge Strickland in 2001 as the lead prosecutor assigned to his division, and during that time I'd found him very easy to work with. He was one of those judges who encouraged lawyers to work out cases rather than take them to trial; we all liked him, but he didn't exactly strike fear into the hearts of attorneys who appeared before him. On the bench, he was pleasant and usually made the correct ruling, but he didn't have much experience with big cases or with capital homicides. To my recollection, he had handled only one other high-profile case before Casey stepped into his courtroom.

At the hearing, Detective Melich and canine handler Jason Forgey were called to testify about their findings. Melich explained the circumstances that had led law enforcement to be called to the Anthony home on July 15, 2008, the tale Casey had woven that night, the trip to Universal Studios, the lies she told, and the attempts made thus far to confirm any of the details Casey had given. Forgey testified as to the background and qualifications of Gerus, his examination of the car, and the significance of Gerus's alerts on the trunk and in the backyard.

Cindy, George, and Lee all took the stand to testify about Casey's life history. They all testified that she was a good mother to Caylee. If she couldn't post bond, they would do it for her. Cindy broke down in tears when she saw her daughter for the first time since her arrest. During her testimony, Cindy defended her daughter: "I know Casey as a person. I know what she is as a mother. I know there is only one or two reasons why Casey would be withholding something about Caylee, and I believe it's something someone is holding over her and threatening her in some way."

These words were a surprising turnaround for a woman who less than ten days earlier had seemed ready to have her daughter declared an unfit mother. In truth, it was during this time that Cindy Anthony seemed the most ambivalent in her feelings about Casey's behavior. There had certainly been enough to justify her original feelings. As Cindy had alluded to in her 911 call, Casey had been stealing from her parents for months in amounts totaling several thousand dollars, but more recently they'd learned that she'd been stealing from Cindy's mother as well. The theft was uncovered before Casey had left with Caylee. Combine this with Casey's lies over the thirty-one days, and Cindy's anger on July 15 was understandable. That resentment had probably spilled over into that 911 phone call. A couple of days after Casey's arrest, however, Cindy was far more protective and defensive of Casey's actions. She had changed course. No longer did she suspect that Casey had been involved in something nefarious. Instead, she justified Casey's not coming forward. According to Cindy, Casey's behavior made sense.

"No one can imagine why you wouldn't go to the police. Well, I can imagine a reason," Cindy Anthony later said to the press. She said that Casey's lack of emotion and odd, conflicting stories only supported the idea that Casey was doing everything she could to protect Caylee and her family from danger. It was a strained logic that neither the court nor the media seemed eager to embrace.

The difficulty for Linda at the hearing was that since Casey was only arrested for child abuse, she was entitled to bond. Under Florida law, generally only persons charged with offenses punishable by life imprisonment or death can be held without bond, and while this was trending toward becoming a murder case, it wasn't there yet. Linda argued that Casey's knowledge that this might someday be a murder charge gave her a reason to flee, and thus argued for an extremely high bond.

At the end of the three-hour hearing, Judge Strickland set bond at $500,000 on the felony child neglect count. He also ordered that Casey be placed on home confinement with electronic monitoring, be evaluated by two psychiatrists, Jeffrey Danzinger and Allen Burns, and that she surrender her passport upon her release from jail. Casey's attorney called the half-million-dollar bond "outrageous," saying it was more than the Anthony family could afford. That afternoon, Casey was returned to the Orange County Jail, where she remained. No one had $500,000.

CHAPTER SEVEN

JAILHOUSE
CONVERSATIONS

I n the days following Casey's arrest, the split personality that the Anthonys had displayed at the bond hearing continued. They wanted to believe Casey, as she held the only clues to finding Caylee, but no one—not George, Cindy, or Lee—seemed convinced that she could be trusted.

Between Casey's lies and the groundless theories sprouting up around Orlando, the only certain thing about the case was that it was exploding in the media. From the local papers to the national news, everyone, it seemed, had taken up the cause of finding Caylee. It put additional strain on Cindy and George, and as the fervor built around them, made it harder and harder for them to deal with the twenty-four-hour news circus outside their front door. The strange disappearance of Caylee had become a story around the country, and as Caylee's most public and determined advocates, Cindy and George became the face of the campaign to find her—a role that, understandably, neither of them took to well. Every few days it seemed as if they floated a new possibility about where Caylee was, which would send the media into a frenzy, but they never offered any possibilities of real substance. In truth, they were as clueless as the rest of us. Casey wasn't giving them much to go on either.

But their difficulties in managing the media did little to discourage their search for their granddaughter. Cindy, more than anyone, was desperate to believe that Caylee was alive, and she thought Casey was only lying and holding back to protect Caylee's life. Having my own six children, some about Casey's age, I no doubt have engaged in my share of denial. But to hypothetically put myself in Cindy's shoes, to determine how many fabrications I would believe in such an unbelievably horrific scenario, is absolutely impossible for me.

Still, in spite of all the evidence that Casey was lying, Cindy continued to believe her. When Cindy would speak to law enforcement about the events of the month before her 911 calls and leads in finding Caylee, she was unreceptive to either the possibility of Caylee being dead or her daughter having any role in the matter.

George, however, was a different story. Early on, he was willing to speak more frankly with law enforcement about the possibility of Casey's involvement. On July 24, he reached out to investigators and asked for a meeting outside the presence of his wife. He agreed to come to police headquarters and sit down with Corporal Melich and Sergeant Allen. Their ensuing conversation was surreptitiously recorded.

"Well, I need to set the record straight between you guys and me," George began. "You guys are doing what you can. I know that. Deep in my heart and my gut and my brain, I know it. I know how you guys, at least I have a rough idea of how everything's put together. Granted, it's been years since I've done my stuff, but I know the basic techniques . . . are still there. I understand all that good stuff.

"Where this is leading I don't want to think about it. I don't want to think about that, but I had bad vibes the very first day when I got that car," George said, referring to the day he retrieved the Pontiac from the tow yard. "I can be straight with you guys and I hope it stays in the confines of us three. I don't want to believe that I have raised someone, brought someone into this world that [sic] could do something to another person. I don't want to believe that. And if it happens, all I can do is ask that you guys can please call me, so I can prepare my wife, because it's going to kill her."

George acknowledged that if they had lost their granddaughter, they had also lost their daughter. "But I guess the reason why I'm here today is I, I'm just having a hard time grasping what my wife is doing to you guys and I apologize." Shifting direction, George then admitted that he had issues with Casey's defense attorney Jose Baez.

"I don't like this freaking attorney that she has. I can tell you that right now from personal experience, I don't like the guy." According to George, Casey had told him that she supposedly had at least $1,400 of Baez's $5,000 retainer. The fact that there was money changing hands, along with the fact that she'd only heard about Baez because of a fellow inmate, both seemed to make George all the more skeptical.

"We did not contact this man," George explained, speaking for himself and his wife. "When he came to our, called us, we thought he was a court-appointed attorney. Because my daughter does not, I don't think she has any money. If she does . . . Well, besides stealing from me, my wife . . . other people . . ."

Changing the subject away from Baez, Melich reminded George of the smell in the Pontiac he had mentioned during their first conversation at Anthony house after Cindy had called 911. "Do you remember what you told me?"

"I believe that there's something dead back there," George replied without hesitation. "And I hate to say the word human. I hate to say that . . . I've been around that. I mean the law enforcement stuff that I did, we caught people out in the woods, in a house, in a car. So I know what it smells like. It's a smell that you never get rid of.

"When I first went there to pick up that vehicle, I got within three feet of it I could smell something. You look up and you say, please don't let this be. Please don't let this be. Because I'm thinking of my daughter and my granddaughter first. I glance in the car on the passenger side, I see [Caylee's] seat's there and I see some other stuff around in it. And as I walk around to the driver's side and put the key in it, I said, 'Please don't let this be what I think it is.'

"The wrecker, I don't know what the gentleman's name [is]. I still don't know. But he and I opened up the door and he said, 'Whoa, does that stink.' I sat in the car for a second. I opened up the passenger door because I was trying to vent that thing.

"You know and I smell and I'm like, 'Oh, God.' I tried to start the car for a second and I said, 'No, George, if there's something wrong. You got to find out now. You can't take it away.' I told the guy, I said, 'Will you please walk around to the back of this car and look inside this with me?' As I walked around, I don't believe I said to him, you know, aloud, and I think I whispered out to myself, 'Please don't let this be my Caylee.' That's what I thought. That's what my heart was saying. I opened it up and that's when I seen that bag. I did see a stain. I think it's right about where the spare tire was at."

"The guy said, 'Sir, I'll take care of it. I'll get rid of it.' But the smell never went away. When I drove around I told my wife, I said, 'This car stinks so bad I can't, I don't know how I can drive it home.' It's raining outside. Oh, well, I have the windows down in the car probably about this much," he explained, gesturing about halfway. "I couldn't freaking breathe. The air conditioning and stuff . . ."

Melich asked if Cindy had noticed the smell.

"Oh, after we pulled inside the garage she said, her exact words were, 'Jesus Christ, what died?' That's exactly what she said. But then she said it in a way, she says, 'George, it was the pizza, right?' And I said, 'Yeah, it was the pizza.' And I let it go at that, but I'm sitting here, as the grandfather, as the father, as George Anthony, and as a guy who smelled the smell before years ago, and you just never forget it. I even stuck my nose down on it and I'm concerned."

Melich let that thought sink in before continuing, "Do you think the reason your daughter doesn't want to tell us what happened is for fear of what her mom might do? Might say I told you so, or something along that? Do you think that it would be so disappointing to mom and that's why [Casey's] taking this to the bitter end?"

"Now, my daughter lives on the edge. You know that from all the lies. All the contradictions. And like my daughter takes things as far as she can take them. And then she piles on some other stuff. This is going to sound really crazy at the point, but my wife and I still believe that Casey still resents my wife [from] the day that our granddaughter was born."

George next described the tension between Cindy and Casey. "A lot of times they've gotten into it because of Casey not being where she's supposed to have been. The lying about working . . ."

George told the investigators that when it came to Casey, he had played the role of detective himself. A while back, he'd suspected she was lying about a supposed job at a local Sports Authority, so he had gone to the store and confronted the manager. He asked if Casey worked there, and was told she did not.

Bringing the conversation back to Caylee, Sergeant Allen asked George if he thought that his daughter "believes that nobody would forgive her if something happened, if some accident happened, some bad thing?"

"I'm not able to answer." George responded. "I'm going to have to think about that . . ." It seemed at this point that George wasn't sure about many things about his daughter. He brought up the money she'd stolen, catching her in lies. There was a whole backstory of Casey's lies that the investigators were just learning. Before long Allen steered him back to the search for Caylee.

"Well, you understand we keep looking for Zenaida but if she doesn't exist, we're going to continue looking in the wrong places. And you know what? It isn't the manpower. It isn't our time. It's that if we continue with all these resources. If we focus all these resources in the wrong area . . ."

"She gets further and further away," George completed Allen's thought. "And that's if she's still with us."

When asked what he thought may have happened, George mentioned that Cindy had found the side gate open and the pool ladder up, meaning it straddled the pool, allowing someone access to the water. It was up sometime around the time Caylee was last seen. He wasn't sure of the date. In his notes, Melich pointed out that when at Universal Studios with Casey on July 16, Cindy had called him mentioning this same incident and the fact that she thought it odd. Both George and Cindy say they keep the side gate closed and the pool ladder down, meaning the ladder was closed up and away from the pool.

The investigators asked George if he wanted to listen to the 911 calls made by Cindy. The media had made a public records request for them earlier that day, and it appeared likely the judge was going to agree to their release. George said he wanted to hear them and he wanted his son, Lee, to also be present. George didn't want Lee to know he was speaking with the investigators, so Melich called and asked if he wanted to come listen to the tapes. Lee agreed. While waiting for Lee to arrive, George began feeling nauseous and officers took him outside for some fresh air. Once outside, George began shaking and vomiting, but refused medical attention, saying it was his nerves. When Lee arrived, George went to the bathroom and Lee listened to the 911 tapes. After that, Lee drove his father home.

AFTER CASEY'S BAIL HAD BEEN set, the judge had ordered her to meet with two psychiatrists for evaluation. On July 24, Casey had an interview with the second of those psychiatrists, and the initial reports from both doctors stated that she was perfectly normal, that there was no indication of any mental illness. Casey reported that she had never had any mental health treatment and that she did not have a drug or alcohol problem. She also stated unequivocally that she had never been physically or sexually abused. The only item of note was an observation made by one of the psychiatrists, Dr. Jeffrey Danziger, who reported that Casey was "unusually happy considering her circumstances."

Casey's brother, Lee, was the first to visit Casey in jail. This was the first of the so-called jailhouse conversations. The policy of the local jail is that all visits are on video and are subject to monitoring and recording, but they are not recorded as a matter of course. Casey's visits were by video link, with Casey communicating remotely with her visitors, who remained in a separate location nearby. Because Casey was being held in protective custody, she was not permitted to have contact visits, not even with her closest family members.

The conversations were extraordinary in capturing the family dynamic. When I reviewed them, I was impressed by everyone's initial cooperation, George and Cindy assuring Casey that they would follow any clue she could give them, and Lee methodically evaluating people they should trust or suspect. In the early visits, no one in her family accused Casey of having a hand in her daughter's disappearance, even as evidence mounted that she was lying. They seemed to be walking on eggshells in her presence, trying to get valuable information without provoking her anger or frustration. By mid-August, all that would change dramatically, and these cordial family dialogues would devolve into something else entirely. But even their video-taped unraveling offered clues to the family's inner workings.

Approaching the situation in an organized and professional manner, Lee read from a set of notes, and even though he was greeted by his sister with a giggle, he remained composed for the entire visit. He told her how the jail mail system worked: that everything she wrote would be read, nothing was private. He also explained that her conversations with her attorney, Jose Baez, were protected and that the lawyer was not obligated to pass along anything she said. Lee thought that Baez was interfering with Casey's ability to communicate with the police by telling her that she should always speak through him.

It appeared that Lee, and perhaps George, saw Baez's commitment to advocating for Casey as hampering the investigation into Caylee's disappearance. While Baez may have been doing his job as her defense attorney, that job also seemed to be at odds with finding Caylee. And Lee, like his parents, believed that Caylee should be everyone's number one priority.

Lee listed his own priorities as he had written them down: (1) Caylee; (2) Casey; (3) Mom; (4) Dad; (5) Me. "I don't give a shit about the cops or Baez," he said.

Casey laughed and agreed with her brother, assuring him that her priorities were identical to his. "I will stay here as long as I have to," she announced. "My only concern is Caylee."

Lee was clearly there to get answers, and he had a long list of questions for his sister. He wanted to be sure Casey understood that she could tell him anything, and even had a plan for secret communications, suggesting that she give him a hand signal if he asked her a question she objected to.

The first thing Lee wanted to know was which of Casey's friends he could trust. Casey identified Amy Huizenga as trustworthy but said that her roommate, Ricardo Morales, wouldn't know anything. She was cagey about Tony Lazzaro, and pointed a finger of suspicion at her ex-fiancé, Jesse, even suggesting that he be brought to the attention of the police. When Lee asked her for more information about where Caylee might be, Casey was vague about places to search, saying that she had already given her mother her best ideas.

Still, Lee seemed to take every word she said seriously. He listened, even as she talked in circles and hinted that she had information without actually providing anything of use.

In her first jailhouse conversation with her parents, Casey appeared relaxed, happy, pleased to see her mother and father—even giggly during the first minutes of their visit. She casually asked her father about the white T-shirt he was wearing, which had HELP FIND CAYLEE lithographed above a huge butterfly, with Caylee's photograph in one of the wings. George and Cindy told her how the entire country was looking for their little angel; her disappearance was even the subject of a cover story in *People* magazine.

The conversation quickly turned serious when Cindy began questioning Casey about a photograph that Cindy claimed was taken in Zanny's apartment. "You know the pictures of Caylee in Zanny's apartment?" she began. "Is Zanny's apartment the one with the drums?" Cindy knew that it was not.

Casey responded without so much as a hesitation. "She had a drum set, yes."

"The one in the picture?"

Casey appeared to answer, but evaded the real issue of the question. "I think there are even other pictures," Casey replied. "I told Lee to look through everything."

"Okay, is that Zanny's apartment?" Cindy asked again. She paused before completing the rest of her question: "Because I know whose apartment it is." By saying that she knew whose apartment it really was, the protective mother was giving Casey an out before she was too deep into her lie. "Is that Zanny's apartment?"

"That exact apartment? No, that is Ricardo's apartment," Casey replied, taking advantage of the opening her mother had given her. "It's set up a lot like Zanny's apartment."

To me, this conversation revealed a lot about the relationship between these two women and demonstrated the conflict that existed in Cindy. It seemed apparent to me that Cindy brought up the photograph with the intent of trapping Casey in a lie. Yet at the last moment she could not bring herself to spring the trap and instead gave her daughter room to squirm out of the lie. Cindy's ambivalence was palpable. Suddenly it was clear why Cindy had been so easy to lie to for thirty-one days: that was the way she wanted it, classic codependency.

Casey took the drum thread and ran with it, following up on Zanny's being a drum hobbyist with more biographical information about her supposed babysitter. According to Casey, Zanny had roots in North Carolina, New York, and Miami. Casey even provided the name and age of Zanny's mother.

"Did Lee tell you how much the reward is to find Caylee?" Cindy asked.

Casey said no, he hadn't.

"It's over . . . I think it's two hundred twenty-five thousand dollars."

"Jesus Christ, that's half my bond," Casey gasped.

"Well, a lot of people want that little girl found," her mother replied.

Cindy asked if Casey wanted to talk to George, who was sitting slightly behind her. Casey smiled and giggled affirmatively. George Anthony took the phone from his wife and addressed his daughter. "Hello, gorgeous. How are you doing?"

"I look like hell," Casey replied.

"Well, you know something, you really need to keep your spirits high through all of this," her father told her.

Casey cried as her father told her he just wanted to give her a big "Papa Joe hug," and that his only concern was getting Caylee back. George had had the phone for only a minute when Cindy grabbed it back. Teary-eyed, Casey gave her mother a message to communicate to Caylee through the media: "Mommy loves you very much. You are the most important thing in the world to me. Be brave.

"I truly love and miss that little girl and you guys," she continued in between sobs.

Cindy handed the phone back to her husband. "Casey, what can I do?" George asked.

"Keep in front of the media and focus on Caylee."

I found George's overall demeanor to be both indulgent and supportive. He was just this big sympathetic marshmallow that Casey seemed incredibly comfortable with. From the differences between Casey's exchanges with Cindy and George, you could imagine that Cindy was the one who punished the kids when they were growing up and George was the one they ran to for comfort. There was a sense in these discussions that George was afraid to question Casey aggressively, that if he did she would simply shut down and cut off all communications. Keeping the lines open appeared to be his primary focus, so he didn't ask his daughter the hard questions.

What he did do was suggest that she reach out to law enforcement for help. Casey discounted the idea, complaining that the investigators had misconstrued and twisted her words and had not bothered following up on the leads she had given them.

Once Cindy had the phone back, Casey jumped from one topic to the next. First, she lamented about her disappointment with Tony, who had not come to visit her in jail and was not responding to Jose Baez's requests for an interview. Her ex-fiancé, Jesse Grund, was also on her bad side, as she expressed her opinion that he couldn't be trusted and she wanted him nowhere near the family. Casey closed the visit by providing her mother with an abundantly detailed description of Zanny's car—right down to the color, model, and location of the car seat—and claiming that Zanny had a complete set of clothes for Caylee, including shoes.

Later that same afternoon, George and Cindy returned to the jail for a second visit with their daughter. This time George took the phone first. The cop in him was coming out, and he was angling toward the kidnapping theory, asking Casey if she had taken something from someone who might hold Caylee as collateral.

"No!" Casey replied emphatically.

George next alluded to the money she had taken from her mother and her best friend, Amy. But Casey defended her actions, insisting that she had stolen from Amy only in "times of desperations."

"What does that mean?" George asked.

Casey dodged the question, claiming that she would communicate to them secretly.

George wanted to know if there was anything he personally could do for Casey. "If I could get you out of here today, I would, but we have to get Caylee back," he said. "I miss her."

"I miss her, too," Casey replied, tearing up.

"I want to take your pain away from you. You know you can tell me anything?"

"I know that, Dad."

"I miss you, sweetie."

Casey again started to cry. "I know that and I miss you, too."

"I wish I could have been a better dad . . . a better grandpa, you know?" George said with sadness.

"You've been a great dad, and you've been the best grandfather. . . . Don't for a second think otherwise. You and Mom have been the best grandparents. . . . Caylee has been so lucky to have both of you."

George choked back tears as he told his daughter how much he missed her and Caylee, and how hard it was to see all their belongings around the house. He told his daughter the Anthony family was like a hand, and he was the thumb. He appeared heartened when Casey agreed to communicate with the FBI.

On July 28, Lee returned to the jail. Without using names, he asked if any of the three people she had communicated with by phone or text on the day Caylee went missing could be involved in her disappearance. Casey left that open as a possibility. She told Lee that she had been doing her own search for Caylee during the daytime, but not at night.

During the visit, Lee asked Casey about her new MySpace password, Timer 55. On June 16, she had used her computer to change the password to her account, a move that had been discovered by the police computer forensics lab. She would later tell Lee that the password had something to do with Caylee. We in the prosecutor's office did some calendar arithmetic and discovered that the number of days between June 16, when Cindy last saw Caylee, and August 9, Caylee's third birthday, was fifty-five. That, combined with the word *Timer,* led us to conclude that fifty-five was the number of days Casey thought she could hold Cindy at bay, knowing that on Caylee's birthday, Cindy would be unstoppable.

The two discussed the tremendous outpouring of support for Caylee. Lee asked if she had a message she wanted to communicate to the people holding Caylee. "I know with every ounce of my gut we will be with her again," she dictated. "You know how much I love you and how much I appreciate this every day." Casey then repeated her father's message to her brother: "Our family is like a hand," she said, telling her brother she loved him.

"I love you, too," Lee replied, tears welling. "I know we are going to find Caylee."

That morning, Jose Baez made a motion to keep the visits between Casey and her family private. One reason he cited was that "the release of any visitation video-conferencing could impede the investigation, chill the public's willingness to report any leads, and compromise the integrity of the Defendant's right to a fair trial." This was the beginning of a trend by the defense to attempt to control the media message. They would routinely appear before the cameras to give opinions or leak information favorable to Casey, and then complain when unfavorable information was released.

Rather than simply being something on which the judge could rule, however, this was an issue dictated by Florida law. The public and the media are afforded the right of access to a broad range of records maintained by government agencies. The law was clear that the jail was obligated to release the recording; the motion had no chance of being granted.

The following day, the motion was denied.

ON JULY 30, GEORGE AND Cindy visited again. This time both parents were wearing Caylee T-shirts. Casey was once again happy and relaxed. George took the receiver and told Casey how much he loved and missed her, and she said, "Ditto" back to him.

George discussed the outpouring of support for Caylee. After about two minutes, Cindy took over the visit. She discussed Caylee's picture on the cover of *People* magazine.

"God, I just want to go home," Casey blurted out. "Every day I wake up just hoping and praying that I just get to go home. I just want to be with you guys, I just want to help find her."

The situation was much the same a few days later, on August 3, when George came to see his daughter alone. Casey arrived looking more jubilant than usual. She smiled when she saw her dad. She seemed much more comfortable with her father now that her mother was not with him.

"Hi," she chirped.

"Hey, good morning, beautiful. How are you?" George looked equally happy as he went on about how all the extended family was missing her. "Hopefully you can get that energy just from my voice."

George talked about Caylee's third birthday coming up in a week. He wanted the little girl back to have a big party for her.

"I want to be out so that I can be there," Casey sighed.

"Your little girl, my granddaughter, has captivated the world." George recounted the calls he had received from people as far away as Washington State.

"All I want is Caylee home, but I want to be there when she comes home," Casey said, breaking into tears. She listened as her father, his voice cracking, described going outside every evening to talk to Caylee. "The moon, the stars, and the sky, sweetheart. Mommy loves you, Jo Jo and CC love you, Uncle E loves you," he told her. "I wish there was more I could do. I would give my life right now for you and for her. This is destroying your mother. She hurts so much." Casey seemed nonchalant.

George again tried to apologize for not being a better father and for not listening more. "You were a great dad and grandpa, and Caylee was lucky," Casey responded with apparent sincerity.

George told Casey to forget about Baez; he'd arrange the meeting with the FBI. Casey agreed, but started manipulating the terms of her talking to law enforcement. She wanted to get out of jail more than anything, so she made it seem as if she could speak more freely if she were bonded out and at home. As George explained, financially they just couldn't do it. He wept frequently during the visit, and begged for anything Casey could do to help get Caylee back.

Casey ended the conversation by repeating her desire to be home when Caylee finally returned. George agreed, saying he wanted to do all the things he used to do with Caylee before she went missing.

• • •

THE LAST RECORDED JAILHOUSE VISIT between Casey and her parents took place on August 14. Her brother Lee had already visited earlier in the day. Cindy was already crying when Casey entered the visitation area that day. After a month of searching for her granddaughter, Cindy was pale and drawn, exhausted and emotionally distraught. She had been the one to say it smelled "like a dead body in the damn car"; she had called 911 to turn her daughter in; she was holding on to both the hope and the fear that Caylee was being held hostage.

Meanwhile, Casey, who had yet to give anyone a useful piece of information, sat smiling widely as usual, in stark contrast to her disheveled mother. Casey, George, and Cindy had been together only a few minutes when Cindy blurted out her biggest fear. "Someone just said that Caylee was dead this morning. She drowned in the pool. That's the newest story out there."

Casey barely reacted, shaking her head from side to side as one would upon hearing something that sounds utterly ridiculous. "Surprise, surprise," was her sarcastic reply.

"We need something to go on," said Cindy plaintively, her tone indicating she'd reached the end of her rope.

Casey responded in kind, snapping back, "Mom, I don't have anything! I'm sorry. I've been here a month, a month today. Do you understand how I feel? I mean, do you really understand how I feel in this?"

The loving air that had marked their first meeting was disintegrating under the weight of Casey's tone. Whatever emotional closeness remained was further decimated as Casey began to discuss a plan in the works that would permit her a private contact visit with one member of her family. She attempted to explain to Cindy that she had chosen to see her father and hoped that her feelings would not be hurt.

George quickly took the phone, hoping to diffuse the blow to his wife. He changed the subject and explained to his daughter that she was the boss, and not Jose Baez, when it came to decisions. He wanted her to know that whoever she spoke to was *her* choice. It seemed clear, though unspoken, that George saw Jose's concern for protecting Casey's legal rights and shielding her from possible prosecution as an impediment to finding

Caylee. He apparently wanted Casey to bypass Jose and speak directly to the police.

"The police are not helping us," Casey moaned. She complained that the cops hadn't even given her twenty-four hours to help find Caylee. She also pointed out that Jose was focused on *her* and Caylee and the family was focused simply on Caylee. While she would mouth a concern for Caylee, statements like this, combined with her actions, showed that the most important thing to Casey was Casey.

As George returned the phone to Cindy, his daughter grew angry, clenching her fists and taking on an aggravated tone: "No one is letting me talk. I am not in control. Everybody wants to know things, but I have nothing to tell."

George tried to reassure her, telling her that she was in charge, but his words only infuriated her further. Casey accused her father of suggesting that she had the power to give the police more information about Caylee's whereabouts.

"There is nothing more I can do till I am home, and even then I don't know what I can do from that point. But I can, at least, do something other than sit on my butt." Considering that Casey had supposedly been looking for Caylee for a month on her own and had yet to give anything useful to investigators or her parents, it was strange that she seemed to believe that the only way she could help was if she was free. Watching the tapes, it seems clear that this was just another example of Casey trying to move the story forward without providing anything new. Casey meant to give her parents more of an incentive to get her out of jail and, at the same time, lower their expectations of her actually giving them anything more to help find Caylee.

In her anger, Casey briefly showed her hand, announcing that her focus had to be on her own case, but she quickly corrected herself, saying that her focus was on Caylee. She insisted that she had told the police everything.

"I am getting truly angry about all this," she fumed. She complained that she had no one to comfort her. "What's keeping me here is you're not helping me to help myself."

Cindy responded by telling her daughter that she and George did not have the financial means to get her out. By now Cindy was bent over with her head lying on the counter, obviously in great emotional pain. But Casey was not fazed by her parents' anguish and persisted with her rant.

"This is the most angry I have been since this started," she retorted. "People expect me, having been in jail for a month, to be able to give helpful information."

George chimed in, encouraging his daughter to speak to law enforcement and to go around Jose. He suggested that she send a letter to the sheriff requesting a personal contact visit. But Casey seemed to be ignoring any and all suggestions as she focused on herself and her own misery. "Everything is out of my control," she whined.

By now, Cindy was all but collapsed on her husband's shoulder. She didn't bother to lift her head as Casey once again bemoaned her powerlessness. "I wish there was something I could do to make things easier on the family. I am just as much a victim as the rest of you."

The Anthony family didn't know it, but Corporal Melich had been watching their visit from an adjoining room. Casey became frustrated with her mother for dominating the conversation. When Casey was talking to George, he mentioned that she could write a letter to the Orange County Sheriff's Office and request to speak to someone in law enforcement. Casey had made earlier indications to her parents that she was willing to do so, but had never officially asked to speak with anyone in there.

So Melich was surprised when later that day he received word that Casey had sent a note to Sheriff Kevin Beary. She wanted to speak privately with someone—not to law enforcement, but to her dad. The note said, "Is there any way that I can have a meeting set up with my father George Anthony? I would in every way appreciate it. I know it is an unusual request, but it is important nonetheless."

The investigators were encouraged, thinking George would be able to convince her to share clues that she hadn't revealed before. They arranged to pick up George and bring him to the jail.

The conversation in the police car, which was surreptitiously recorded by law enforcement, captured George confirming that the meeting with his daughter had not been the idea of law enforcement, that police were not asking him to feed his daughter specific questions, and that he was not acting as an agent of the state. George told the officers he hoped this opportunity would help bring "closure" and some answers.

The group arrived at the jail at 7:30 that evening. They found Casey meeting with an attorney named Adam Gabriel, who at the time was associated with Jose Baez's office. He was trying to convince her not to speak with anyone. The officers told Gabriel they were just escorting George Anthony to the jail at Casey's request. If she wished to speak to George privately, they would facilitate that. They also told the attorney that he was allowed to sit in on the conversation if Casey wanted him to. Ultimately, it was Casey's decision whether she wished to see her father and on what terms.

After waiting for ninety minutes, the investigators learned that Casey had changed her mind. She no longer wished to speak with her father, and George was returned home.

This was the last of the jailhouse visits. The family was sick and tired of having their private time with Casey all over everyone's evening news. All four of them—George, Cindy, Lee, and Casey—decided that future communication would be through Jose Baez only. With that decision, the hope of either the family or the police getting any new information from Casey all but vanished, forcing everyone to hope that some truth about Caylee's whereabouts could be extracted from Casey's earlier statements.

CHAPTER EIGHT

THIRTY-ONE DAYS

While Casey's family tried and failed to get new information from Casey in person following her arrest, the police continued to try and track down the leads she'd given them in any way they could.

In the weeks before Linda asked me to join the case, investigators had started piecing together a timeline of Casey's actions beginning when she and Caylee left Hopespring Drive with their backpacks, on June 16, until thirty days later, when Cindy Anthony called the police, on July 15. (Casey called this period of time "thirty-one days" from her own recollection, so there's a discrepancy with the actual number of days. Despite being incorrect, that number "thirty-one" became part of the case's vocabulary, so we will refer to this time period of June 16 to July 15 as thirty-one days.) Not surprisingly, Casey's version and witnesses' stories did not add up. Deciphering fact from fiction and cross-referencing phone records with statements from the people involved, the investigators began the painstaking job of establishing a real day-by-day account of events. Casey's deliberate deceptions had led them to believe they were almost certainly dealing with a homicide, although they still didn't know the how, why, when, or where.

Caylee had last been seen on a Monday, June 16, 2008. Initially, on Cindy's 911 phone call and for a few days after, there had been some honest confusion about that date, with Casey and Cindy saying that it was June 9 when she was last seen. Finally it was determined that Cindy had taken the toddler to visit her grandfather, Caylee's great-grandfather, at an assisted-living facility on Father's Day, Sunday, June 15. The following day, Cindy had left for work before Caylee was awake, but George and Casey each claimed to have seen Caylee alive for the final time.

On that Monday, June 16, George saw Casey and Caylee leaving the house at around 12:50 in the afternoon. She told her dad as they were on their way out that she was going to work and Caylee was going to the nanny's. Casey was wearing dressy charcoal-gray pinstriped slacks and a beige blouse, while Caylee was dressed in a blue jean skirt, pink top, white tennis shoes, and white-rimmed sunglasses, her brown hair pulled back in a ponytail. Both Casey and Caylee were wearing backpacks; Caylee's was white and decorated with little monkeys. As Casey explained to her father, she and Caylee would be spending the night at the nanny's house, and she had already told Cindy. Shortly afterward, at around 2 P.M., George left for his job as a security guard. Later on, Casey told her mother the same story about spending the night at Zanny's; however, cell phone records showed that Casey was still in the vicinity of the Anthony home until 4 P.M. Whether or not she returned there after George left that afternoon has never been established.

By 7 P.M. that evening, Casey was in the area around the home of her boyfriend, Tony Lazzaro, and at 7:45 P.M., Casey and Tony were captured on video at a Blockbuster renting a movie, strolling with their arms around each other. There was no sign of Caylee on the camera footage. When Tony later recalled that evening, he said that the two watched a video, went to bed, and—wink-wink—didn't leave the bedroom until late the next day. According to Tony, he did not see Caylee that day. In fact, he hadn't seen the little girl since June 2, which was when she had come to his complex to swim in the pool.

The next thing the phone records confirmed was that Casey left Tony's place around 2 P.M. the following day, Tuesday, June 17, and drove back home. This was supported by a neighbor, Brian Burner, who saw the Pontiac Casey had been driving parked at the Anthony's house and backed into the garage. At that point George would have just left or would just be leaving the house for work, and Cindy, a nurse, was working until five. No one knows what Casey did there that afternoon.

What we do know is that Casey called Cindy later that day to tell her mom that she and Caylee were going to spend another night at Zanny's, even though cell phone records indicated that she was already back at Tony's when the call was made. Cindy wasn't the only recipient of a lie from Casey on June 17. Casey also sent a text message to her best friend and confidante, Amy Huizenga, saying that she couldn't wait to get Amy moved into the Anthony family home. Casey had previously told her friend that her parents were moving out and giving the house to her, and that Amy was welcome after that occurred.

All of that, it turned out, was a lie; Casey's parents had no such plans to vacate the house.

At 12:30 the next afternoon, June 18, Casey called her parents' house from Tony's. The length of the call indicated that no one answered the phone, leading investigators to speculate that Casey was calling to confirm that the house was empty. An hour later, the same neighbor noticed Casey's Pontiac again backed into the garage. Sometime between 1:30 P.M. and 2:30 P.M., Casey borrowed the neighbor's shovel, saying that she needed it to dig up some bamboo in her backyard. Less than an hour later she returned the shovel, but it did not appear to have been used. After she was done at her parent's house, Casey went back to Tony's, where she spent her third consecutive night, once again confirmed by phone records.

That evening Casey began spinning bigger and more elaborate lies. She called Cindy to tell her that she had to attend a work-related conference at Busch Gardens Theme Park in Tampa. Since Casey had been leading her parents to believe that she was an event planner at Universal Studios for some time, the trip made sense to them. As Casey explained it, she was taking Zanny, Zanny's friend Juliette Lewis, Juliette's daughter, Annabelle, and Caylee to Tampa with her. Annabelle was Caylee's age, and would therefore be a perfect playmate for her. She told her mother that the group would be there until Friday, June 20.

Putting aside the scene with the detectives at Universal Studios, it was clear from these early stories alone that Casey was a skilled, habitual liar. Whatever her audience, she would pad the lie with elements that would appeal to that person. In telling Cindy that Caylee would have a playmate in Tampa, she knew her mother would be much more amenable to the idea. In adding Juliette, she would eliminate questions about why Zanny would want to travel all the way to Tampa. As I would come to see, most of Casey's lies were packed with these kinds of specific details, which made her stories more believable but also demonstrated that she was always plotting them with her audience in mind.

Any con man will tell you that the true skill in crafting a great lie is finding what the mark wants to believe and giving it to him. Her fabrications centered on promoting herself as a responsible working mother, dedicated to both her job and Caylee. Whether the lie involved adding another day of work to her job, or making Zanny the Mary Poppins of Orlando, one lie seemed to flow effortlessly into the next. Casey could explain a discrepancy in a series of lies with a small, convincing tweak that would satisfy the most doubtful audience.

Since her mother had been falling for the Zanny lie for over a year, Casey knew that Cindy would follow along in this instance, too, so she made Zanny a crucial part of the story. Zanny seemed like such a too-good-to-be-true, warm, generous babysitter that anyone who would complain about her had to be nasty, no good, jealous, and selfish. At the same time, what mother wouldn't want to see her daughter advancing at work? At Cindy's removed distance, her daughter appeared so vital to the company that her employer was paying to send her out of town to a conference. It was enough to make a mother proud or, in this case, keep her from getting suspicious.

While Cindy believed that Casey was in Tampa, phone records indicated that Casey spent the next day, Thursday, June 19, in Tony's neighborhood, where the two of them hunted for an apartment. At the time, Tony had been sharing an apartment with a bunch of roommates, and he wanted to get his own place. By 9:20 P.M., they were back at Tony's. Throughout this time, whenever Tony asked about Caylee, Casey lied to him. As far as Tony knew, Caylee was either home with Cindy and George or with the babysitter.

In their discussions with the police, the friends in Casey's gang said that she was enjoying her stay at Tony's. She was the model housemother to Tony and his roommates, cooking all the meals, cleaning, doing laundry, and sleeping with Tony, while telling different people different stories about where Caylee was if the question arose. When Casey called her mother that night, she continued her lie, telling Cindy that she and Caylee were still at the conference at Busch Gardens. Even though Casey was lying constantly to her mom, she was also checking in with Cindy every day like clockwork so as not to arouse suspicion.

The night of Friday, June 20, was originally the night when Casey had told her mother she would return home with Caylee, but instead, Casey was partying with many of her friends at Fusian, the club where Tony worked. Fridays at the club were geared toward college kids, and Tony was trying to do business as a club promoter, getting people in the door through social media and using "shot girls" to sell booze. That Friday night, Fusian hosted a "hot body" contest, and Casey spent the evening showing off her body and managing the shot girls. Photos of the event show Casey in pure delight, wearing a short blue dress and high black boots, grinding and dancing with others on the dance floor.

Needless to say, this was not the story she'd given Cindy. In Casey's nightly phone call to Cindy, Casey was all work, explaining that she was still in Tampa because her conference had gone an extra day, but it would be over on Saturday. That same night, however, Casey told a friend, Maria Kissh, that Caylee and the nanny were at the beach. And all the while she continued to shack up with Tony.

By Sunday, June 22, her story for Cindy changed again. This time Casey said they were staying another night at Busch Gardens because she had been so busy with work that none of them had even gone to the amusement park to enjoy the rides. Of course, as Casey told Cindy, that hadn't stopped Caylee and Annabelle from having a great time.

The next day, Casey was at Tony's until 1:41 P.M., when she left in the Pontiac. She soon called him to say that she had run out of gas and asked him to come get her. Rather than buy gas, she directed him to the Anthony home, where Tony broke the lock on her father's shed so that Casey could take two red portable gas cans. They took the gas cans back to her car, poured their contents into the tank, started the car, and drove back to Tony's in their separate vehicles.

Casey's call to Cindy that night contained bad news: on the way back from Tampa, she had been in a car accident. Zanny was hurt and had been taken to the hospital. She, Caylee, Juliette, and Annabelle would stay in Tampa so Casey could tend to Zanny in the hospital.

In reality, a week had passed since anyone had laid eyes on little Caylee Marie Anthony.

ON THE MORNING OF TUESDAY, June 24, George Anthony had been planning to mow his lawn when he discovered the broken lock on his shed and two missing gas cans. Casey had stolen his gas cans before, and though he suspected her in this instance as well, he called the police because he didn't know for sure. He reported two stolen gas cans holding fifty dollars' worth of gas, and fifty dollars in damages from the broken lock.

That afternoon, Casey returned to the house to find George still at home. It was the first time either of her parents had seen her in more than a week, and her reaction made it look as though she had not been expecting him to be there. According to George, his daughter rushed past him to her bedroom, claiming that she needed to retrieve some insurance papers because of the accident.

As I was reading this account from George to the police, I was amazed how effortlessly Casey was able to adjust her lie to accommodate the situation. In an instant, she had built on her original lie in a way that was both plausible and fitting. Her mental agility was incredibly impressive. Nevertheless, George's suspicions were far from allayed.

Still suspecting that Casey had stolen the gas cans, George pretended to need something from the trunk of the Pontiac. As he was heading for the car, Casey beat him to it, grabbed the two containers from the trunk, shouted, "Here are your fucking gas cans!" shoved them at his chest, and drove off. Because of the way she was standing, he didn't get a good look inside the Pontiac's trunk, and at that point had no reason to try.

Records showed that not twenty minutes had gone by when Casey started calling her mother. She called five times with medical updates on Zanny, telling Cindy that there were complications with Zanny's injuries and the nanny would have to stay in the hospital for a few more days. She also told her mother about going home to get the insurance papers, making sure to repeat the story she had told her father.

The deceptions seemed to move fluidly from one day to the next, evolving and compounding each other. On Wednesday, June 25, Casey called Amy. During the conversation, she mentioned a smell in her car, which she said was the result of her running over a squirrel. Casey again spent the day at Tony's, but told Cindy in her nightly contact that they were still in Tampa. The next day, Casey told her mother that Zanny had been released from the hospital, but it was so late that they would spend one more night in the Tampa area. In reality, she was again at Tony's.

Phone records from the following day, Friday, June 27, indicated that Casey traveled from Tony's apartment to the vicinity of the Anthony house. At 11:30 A.M., she texted Amy about the smell in her car, saying that a dead animal was "plastered to the frame." Seventeen minutes later, she called Tony to pick her up at the Amscot check cashing store at the intersection of East Colonial and Goldenrod in Orlando, because she had run out of gas again. When Tony got there, he offered to put gas in the car, but Casey said her father would take care of it. Even though two gas stations were immediately adjacent to the Amscot store, they left the Pontiac in the parking lot next to a Dumpster and went back to Tony's. As it was a Friday night, they again spent the evening partying at Fusian.

That weekend, Casey's nightly calls to Cindy took her lies in a strikingly new direction. Knowing that she had reached the end of the story with Zanny, her story now contained the deception that Casey was back in town but wouldn't be home because she was staying at Universal's Hard Rock Hotel with a friend. The version she gave her mom was that her friend, Jeff Hopkins from Jacksonville, was visiting. He had a son, Zack, the same age as Caylee, and he had invited Casey and Caylee to stay with them at the hotel. In Casey's telling, Jeff was wealthy and had a trust fund. Furthermore, he was a single dad, his wife having passed away, and he was interested in her. This story resonated in part because Cindy had heard the name Jeff Hopkins before. A year or so earlier, Casey had told Cindy that Jeff was the person who had introduced her to Zanny. Building on that older lie had made Jeff seem like a recurring, and therefore more plausible, character.

Yet for all that her mother seemed to be taking Casey at her word, some of the lies were beginning to crumble. By Sunday, the Pontiac had been at the Amscot parking lot for two days. Casey had told Tony that her father was going to pick it up, so Tony didn't think too much about it. In the meantime, however, the owner of the lot had taken note of the abandoned vehicle. The next day the car was towed, putting into motion the events that would lead to Cindy's 911 phone call.

Of all the lies that Casey had been telling, I found myself most drawn to her decision to abandon the car. If ever something was bound to reveal her bizarre behavior, it was the car. Nothing seemed to add up about it. This move demonstrated such an apparent lack of planning, such an absence of consideration for the consequences, that it seemed like a spur-of-the-moment decision. Was that the case with all these lies? Was she really just making them up as she went along, elaborating on older lies and dusting them off to suit her ends? Did she have a long-term strategy? Abandoning the car at the Amscot lot was playing with fire. And yet she had enough forethought to park the car next to a Dumpster, an act that could have been designed to hide the odor that George Anthony would discover a few days later. One possibility was that she was hoping to leave it there to air out without drawing attention. That way she could return to it in the future, gas it up, and drive away. Hopefully by then the smell would be gone. The fact that George missed the notice of a certified letter on his door certainly was a lucky break for Casey, since her next big lie a few days later—that she and Caylee were headed for Jacksonville—depended on her car not being discovered in Orlando.

The day the Pontiac was being towed from the parking lot, Monday, June 30, was a busy one for Casey. She went shopping with Amy, then drove Tony to the airport in his Jeep for a flight he was taking home to

New York. She was supposed to return the vehicle to his apartment, but she continued to use it while he was gone. With Tony away, she started staying with Amy and Amy's roommate, Ricardo Morales, who was an old boyfriend of Casey's. As Casey transitioned from Tony's place to Amy's, her lies transitioned as well. Cindy was informed that Jeff Hopkins wanted Casey and the gang to stay at the hotel until July 3. No one had seen Caylee for two weeks.

Shortly thereafter, Casey stopped calling her mother nightly, which in turn only frustrated Cindy more. For weeks, Cindy had been planning on taking a vacation around the Fourth of July holiday and hoping to spend time with Caylee. As Cindy's vacation began, Caylee was nowhere to be found. Though Cindy was desperately trying to reach her daughter, Casey continually ignored her calls. When Casey finally replied to a text from her mother, she said that Caylee was at Universal Studios with Jennifer Rosa, Zanny's roommate.

On Wednesday, July 2, Casey made an appointment to get a tattoo the next day. She ate lunch at Buffalo Wild Wings, shopped, and went out clubbing in the evening. She decided to spend the night at Amy and Ricardo's. When Amy asked where Caylee was, Casey said she was with the nanny. By midnight, Cindy was becoming frustrated and infuriated. She called Casey eight times in the twenty-four minutes between 12:13 A.M. and 12:37 A.M., but nobody answered.

In an odd twist of fate, Casey coincidentally ran into Jeff Hopkins that night at Waterford Lake Alehouse in Orlando. As investigators later learned from Jeff, he and Casey had been acquaintances in middle school and high school, but since then the two hadn't remained in contact. At the Alehouse, they'd exchanged phone numbers, but except for an e-mail blast about a gathering at Fusian Ultra Lounge, Jeff hadn't heard from her again. Not only were they not in contact, but Jeff, it turned out, had no children, no trust fund, no dead wife, didn't live in Jacksonville, wasn't interested in her, had never meet Caylee Anthony, and couldn't provide any information about Caylee's supposed babysitter, Zenaida.

On Thursday, July 3, Casey got her tattoo, the words *"Bella Vita,"* Italian for "beautiful life," inked on her left shoulder. The tattoo artist told the police that the wording was popular among other younger customers he'd seen, as it was an expression of the desire to live the good life. Her choice had made sense to him. Since she seemed happy when he met her, he assumed she was living a *bella vita*. She made an appointment to return for another tattoo and even told the tattoo artist about her daughter, who was with her nanny, saying she would bring her along the next time.

Meanwhile, Cindy's anger was growing. She was on a singular mission to see her granddaughter, trying Casey's phone seven times that night and the next morning, without getting an answer. Eventually, Casey took a call and told her mother that Caylee was at Universal Studios, enjoying a day of fun at an event designed for the children of employees. Casey would have loved to invite Cindy, but unfortunately it was for employees only. Cindy drove there anyway, and called Casey from the parking lot, assuming that Caylee and Casey would have to come out sooner or later. Casey had been giving her the runaround about where she was for too long, and Cindy didn't trust her anymore. Before Casey had left with Caylee in June, Cindy and she had been arguing about Casey's lifestyle. Now Cindy felt she finally had Casey cornered.

Or so she thought. When Casey answered her mother's call and learned that she was in the Universal parking lot, she realized she was trapped, and altered the story again—this time putting enough physical distance in the lie so that her mother couldn't stake her out. Telling Cindy there had been a change of plans, Casey explained that Jeff Hopkins had invited her and Caylee to go to Jacksonville with him and his son. They were already en route.

After Casey hung up, George tried to call her, but he got no answer. Completely frustrated, Cindy recruited Lee to look for his sister at the clubs downtown. First, he attempted to locate Casey through the places mentioned on MySpace postings by friends. He went to one spot, but missed her by minutes. She had gotten word that he was coming and left before he arrived. He tried calling her cell phone, but she didn't answer. He then enlisted his girlfriend to call, thinking Casey would pick up for her. They spoke briefly before the girlfriend passed the phone to Lee. Casey was nasty to her brother, blew him off, and hung up.

When Cindy heard this, she had her son create a MySpace page for her so that she could post a lengthy paragraph about hurt and betrayal for Casey to discover. Her subject line was "My Caylee is missing," and she posted her mood as "distraught." The seventeen-line entry was filled with sadness and anger: "What does the mother get for giving her daughter all of these chances? A broken heart. . . ." Cindy ended her indirect message to Casey with thoughts about Caylee. "Who is now watching out for the little angel?"

CASEY SPENT THE FOURTH OF July holiday shopping and celebrating. When she finally responded to Cindy's MySpace post, Casey told her mother to leave her alone. Elaborating further on her lie about Jeff Hopkins, Casey claimed that she was trying to pursue a long-term relationship with him. She told Cindy to accept that she was now an adult and that she and Caylee would someday move out for good. Apparently, Casey's response had the desired effect. Cindy agreed to give her daughter some space.

On Saturday, July 5, Tony returned from New York. Casey met him at the airport, and they picked up where they left off, with Casey playing housemother for Tony and his mates. That day, Casey told her mother that her car was being fixed in Jacksonville, that she and Caylee were staying with Jeff Hopkins's mother, Jules, and that they would be returning to Orlando on July 12.

Looking at all this together, I couldn't help but wonder what Casey had planned for her end game. Since mid-June, her lies had taken so many different shapes that it was hard to believe they had gone on for so long. She seemed to move deftly from one deception to another, and yet couldn't see that it was all going to fall apart. While it didn't seem as if she had any way out, one thought that occurred to me was that, on some level, the Jeff Hopkins story was meant to be the end of it all, the culmination of the lie. Perhaps a sudden elopement with the wealthy young friend who was also the perfect family man—"Mom, it just happened so suddenly, sure I would have loved to have you and Dad there, but it was just so perfect"—followed by the impetuous honeymoon abroad—"Jeff is such a wonderful man, he insisted we bring the kids." It's hard to say what she was setting the narrative up for, but as her lies seemed only to be building in size and scope, it wasn't hard to imagine her creating some kind of an escape scenario. It was easy for me to see that Casey's explanation to her mother was her setup for the long-term solution, that Casey was maneuvering to set it up that she and Caylee had moved out for good. If only my talent for fiction were one-tenth of hers, I could have seen it, the ultimate storybook ending. But all I, or any of us on the prosecution, could do was speculate.

Surely, though, something was going to force her hand, whether it was the demands from Cindy, the interference from George, the discovery of the Pontiac, or simply fate. Until then, her lies would simply get bolder and more reckless, generating a momentum that could lead only to a dead end.

On July 8, Casey drove Amy and Ricardo to the airport in Amy's car. Amy and Ricardo were headed to Puerto Rico. Somehow Casey also got hold of Amy's wallet and checkbook, and within an hour of dropping off her friends at the airport, she was at Target, where she enjoyed a two-hour shopping spree. At 9:48 A.M., surveillance cameras captured her entering the store, where she shopped until 11:55 A.M., at which point she took her purchases to the checkout counter. She paid the $111.01 for the purchases with one of Amy's checks.

Casey continued to forge checks on Amy's account for the next five days, knowing that her friend was out of the country. During that time, she made two more visits to Target and a trip to a Winn-Dixie grocery store. Her purchases during this time included the light blue hoodie she was wearing when she was arrested, lingerie, oversize white sunglasses, toilet paper, cherries, orange juice, and a six-pack of Bud Light. At no time did she buy anything for her toddler, and Caylee is not seen on any of the stores' video surveillance tapes.

Stealing from Amy seemed a natural progression for Casey. After all, Cindy and George had discovered the forgeries and thefts from their accounts, not to mention the more recent discovery that Casey was stealing from her grandmother as well. As a result, all the family accounts were under a watchful eye, so those avenues were now closed. Once Tony was out of town, Casey needed money again. Amy was so trusting it was like she was asking to be taken advantage of. If Casey was caught, she'd probably just plead desperation and promise to pay her back. After all, it had worked with Cindy, surely it would work again. Live for today, and deal with the consequences when and if they arise. In her experience, she could talk her way out of anything.

As it turned out, though, the law wasn't far behind her. On Sunday, July

13, George Anthony found the notice of a certified letter from Johnson's Wrecker Service stuck in his front door, which marked the end for Casey and the beginning of the mystery about Caylee. Having no idea what the notice was about, and scheduled to start a new job on Monday, George decided that the earliest he could make it to the post office was Tuesday, July 15. Casey, meanwhile, was still staying at Tony's, though she told Cindy that she and Caylee had been invited at the last minute to Jeff Hopkins's mom's wedding ceremony in Jacksonville.

On the afternoon of July 15, Casey cashed a forged check for $250, written to her, by her, on Amy's account. She then drove to the airport in Amy's car to pick up her two friends, back from vacation. During the ride to Amy's, Casey said that she had spoken to her daughter earlier that day. It was a lie that capped off nearly a month of lies, but it was all about to come to an abrupt end, as George and Cindy barreled toward the tow yard.

In my years as a prosecutor, I have seen my share of liars—but never one quite like this. If it was just the lies to her mother, we might be able to understand that. After all, kids lie to their parents from time to time, mostly because they're young and immature. Still, if that was all it was—simply a lie taken to an irrational extreme—you'd expect to find Caylee stashed away with some friend, happy and healthy, while Casey laughed to herself about how she'd showed Cindy who the real boss was in the relationship.

But these thirty-one days were about more than just a series of lies. These days were about the adoption of a completely new lifestyle. A lifestyle that had no room for Cindy or George. A lifestyle that had no room for actual responsibilities. A lifestyle that had no room for Caylee.

Kidnapping seemed increasingly implausible. On August 15, the sheriff said as much when he announced that they had yet to turn up any credible evidence in support of the kidnapping theory. While they had not ruled out kidnapping, there was less and less for them to go on, with all of Casey's "leads" proving to be lies.

With that said, none of this alone made it a murder. Yet it was looking more and more as if the case would have to be resolved with science. We had plenty of clues and evidence, but there were also many holes, holes that only forensics could help fill. It was now up to the scientific experts to help uncover the truth.

PART II

CHAPTER NINE

——

DEALING IN FORENSICS

After getting word from Linda that I was on the case, my first call was to Arpad Vass, a forensic anthropologist at the Oak Ridge National Laboratory in Tennessee, where many of the country's scientific breakthroughs occur. Vass, an expert in the odor of decomposition, was in the process of developing a standard for decomposition odor analysis, or DOA. This standard was being designed to help identify the more than four hundred chemical compounds that emanate from a decaying human body. I needed to know if he thought his new technology could be of help in determining whether the odor in the Pontiac was undeniably that of human decomposition.

Prior to my conversation with Dr. Vass, I reviewed some of his published writing so that I wouldn't sound like a complete moron when we spoke. His work is based on the principle that all odors are simply combinations of different chemical compounds released into the air through chemical and/or biological reactions. Some of those compounds are detectable by human beings, and we perceive them as smells. My mom's spaghetti, the odor of which is instantly recognizable to me, is simply a group of chemical compounds in a certain concentration that my brain has learned to interpret, recall, and react to. Similarly (and I hope Mom forgives my use of her delicious spaghetti in this analogy), the odor given off by a human body during decomposition—which, if you have ever experienced it, is instantly recognizable—is also simply a combination of chemical compounds.

The challenge of the work is that our brains can't distinguish individual compounds in the odors themselves. The goal of Vass's work is to determine which compounds are most common. Once those compounds can be determined, a device can be developed to detect them in the air, in much the same way machines at the airport examine our luggage for the presence of compounds found in explosives. It was the first part of his research, the isolation of the common compounds, that had potential application to this case.

When I reached Dr. Vass at his office, he was happy to talk science, but he did not warm to the idea of testifying. It was out of his comfort zone. He had testified only once before, sixteen years earlier, in a case based on the chemical analysis of soil near a body, called postmortem interval testing. I recall him repeatedly telling me that the thought of testifying was not making him feel "warm and fuzzy." I liked him from the beginning.

Dr. Vass was an unapologetic science geek. He pursued scientific investigation for the pure fascination of it, loved solving scientific problems, and discussed them with an addictive passion. Speaking with a slight affect, a disarming quality that made him accessible, he seemed to me very atypical of a forensics expert. I have dealt with forensic experts for decades, good ones and bad ones, honest ones and dishonest ones. Regardless of their reliability, one thing that these experts usually have in common is that they're applying the research of other experts to forensics problems. Rarely had I worked with a forensics expert like Dr. Vass, a man who had actually invented the process of which he spoke. True scientific innovation is rare in professional expert witnesses.

In order to reassure him that I was up to the task of shepherding him through this process, I talked to him about my prosecution of the first DNA case, the Tommy Lee Andrews trial. In a sense, my use of DNA started with an NBC news story about a man named Colin Pitchfork in England.

Two girls from two small towns in the county of Leicestershire had been raped and murdered in a similar fashion. Investigators employed a new technology developed by British geneticist Alec Jeffreys to track the killer down. They used DNA fingerprinting to screen the men in one of the small towns in particular. The idea was that someone's blood held a unique DNA that, when matched to the blood at the crime scene, could determine the killer beyond a reasonable doubt. All the men in the village were asked to submit blood samples. Colin Pitchfork paid someone two hundred pounds to donate on his behalf. Eventually, his stand-in gave him up, and his DNA proved to be the match the authorities had been looking for.

For obvious reasons, I thought the Pitchfork case could be very applicable to my work as a prosecutor. At that point in my career, I had been involved in cases where the traditional study of human fluids—blood typing and protein antigen typing—was occasionally being used, but the ability of science to characterize specific blood or semen stains from a crime was very, very limited. If you were able to get a number that limited the possibilities to 10 percent of the population, you were ecstatic. That was about as much information as blood was going to give you. After hearing about the case in England, I thought it was clear that there was a lot more we could learn from blood. But though this technology would obviously be of use in the United States, there was no lab in the United States that did it, so I just filed it away as an interesting bit of trivia.

A year or so later, in 1987, I was flipping through a newspaper put out by the Florida Bar Association when I came across an advertisement that caught my attention. The ad featured a picture of a baby with a caption that read: "He is wearing his father's genes." The ad was for a lab in New York that was doing paternity testing. I remembered the Pitchfork story in England and wondered if this was the same science, even though used in this case to determine paternity. I contacted someone at the lab in New York to find out if it was the same kind of work Jeffreys was doing. I asked the lab's director if they did criminal cases, and he told me they were just starting to do forensics testing.

At the time I didn't have any rape cases, but I went to Tim Berry, one of the state's sex crimes prosecutors, and asked if he had any cases with semen that could be tested. Indeed he did—Tommy Lee Andrews. Andrews had been charged in six cases of rape, but the witness IDs were not great in any of them. Andrews would break into the home of a young woman, put a pillow over her face, rape her, and rob her. At least one of the women had picked him out of a photo lineup from having seen him the moment before he grabbed her, but the light had not been very good. The other victims had not seen him.

We had six samples from six cases, along with a sample from the defendant. The lab in New York was able to get results in two of the six, and matched them to the defendant. We added the names of the lab personnel who had done the testing to the witness list. Nobody else in the United States had ever used this kind of evidence in a case, but even so, I don't think we fully realized how earth-shattering this DNA evidence would be for prosecutors and defense attorneys alike. The bottom line was that we thought it was cool, and we were excited to be the ones giving it a shot.

We decided to get an expert not affiliated with the lab to testify, choosing David Housman, a molecular biologist and a professor at MIT, to explain the science behind what we'd done. Fortunately for us, the judge who happened to be assigned to the Andrews case, Judge Rom Powell, had experience in judging trials that hinged upon cutting-edge forensic evidence. He had been the first to rule on a case that was used a new science called voice print identification. We had a Frye hearing, which is a specialized process to determine whether a new scientific tool is based on generally accepted, established scientific principles.

"Frye hearing" comes from a 1923 case in which a fellow by the name of James Alphonso Frye was being tried for a murder in Washington, D.C. His lawyer wanted to present to the jury evidence from an expert who claimed that the truth could be determined by looking at changes in the blood pressure of an individual during an interview, an early version of the lie detector. The trial judge ruled that the evidence was not admissible, and the appeals court agreed. Those decisions contained a single sentence that to this day determines the admissibility of scientific evidence in Florida and most jurisdictions in the United States: "the thing from which the deduction is made must be sufficiently established to have gained general acceptance in the particular field in which it belongs."

The precise meaning of that sentence has been the subject of fierce debate over the last ninety years, and you could write an extremely boring book exploring all of its nuances. Simply put, it means this: the court will admit new science only if it has a firm foundation in established science.

In the Andrews case, the Frye hearing to determine the admissibility of our DNA evidence was ruled in our favor. After we successfully argued the Frye hearing, Tim Berry and I tried the case; I presented almost all the evidence and made the closing arguments. The jury found Andrews guilty of rape and other charges.

The process used for that DNA analysis was very primitive, and about four or five years later a much better process was developed that could get far more accurate results using much smaller amounts of DNA. The probability numbers back then for whether the DNA actually came from a particular individual were one in a hundred thousand. With today's technology, the results are closer to one in a quadrillion, which would include just about every human being who had ever lived. In 2004, Andrews asked to be retested, claiming that the DNA results in 1988 were inconclusive. The state complied with his request, and a subsequent DNA test was still a match. Tommy Lee Andrew is serving a combined sentence of sixty-six years for the two rapes.

IT'S BEEN ACCEPTED FOR A long time that all scientific advancement comes from those with vision standing on the shoulders of those who came before them. It's simply a matter of taking something that already exists and using it in a new way. The full-on nerd part of my personality finds this fascinating.

The more Dr. Vass and I shared information about our backgrounds and interests, the more I was able to convince him that this was a case that demanded his testimony as an expert witness. We talked about every aspect of his work—what inspired him, what techniques he borrowed from other disciplines, and how he came to his conclusions. We discussed the

process of publication in scientific journals and the responses of his colleagues in the field. In the short time that I'd been researching odor for this
case, one of the difficulties I'd found was that there were very few people
who worked in this field. However, I was lucky to have one of the few pio-
neers on my side.

Reassuring as that was, there were still drawbacks. Dr. Vass's field of
study, odor mortis, or the smell of death, was more complex than DNA, and
I knew from that first phone call that the forensics would be difficult. The
main challenges in trying to collect a forensic sample of an odor are three-
fold. First, how do you capture the odor in a pristine form? The moment
you expose a sample of air to room air, the concentration of the compounds
that make up the odor are diluted. Second, further complicating the process is that once the ambient air mixes with the odor, how do you know
that the compounds you find come from the sample and not the ambient
air? Third, you need to establish that the compounds you find are being
released from something that is still there and not an odor left behind by
something that has been removed.

To help answer some of these questions about sample odor collection
from the Pontiac, the crime scene supervisor for the Orange County Sheriff's Office, Mike Vincent, went to Dr. Michael Sigman, a former colleague
of Dr. Vass at Oak Ridge. Sigman was with the National Center for Forensic Science at the University of Central Florida. The first attempt to collect
the odor sounded simple enough: open the trunk just enough to insert a
small hose and, using a large syringe, pull out a volume of air and then
expel it into a bag. But that method failed to collect a sufficient sample of
air to get any reliable result.

Next, Dr. Sigman used the best technology available to him, placing
small synthetic fibers, known by the acronym SPMI, into the trunk for a
period of time. The fibers act as adhesives to compounds in the air, capturing those compounds immediately surrounding the fibers. The difficulty
with this method is that it can sample only the very small volume of air that
happens to pass over the fibers. Since the air in the trunk couldn't circulate,
the sampling of the air was just too limited to determine the existence of
compounds in very small quantities. The test did nothing to tell us what the
odor was emanating from.

Finally, Dr. Vass suggested that we cut a small sample from the stained carpet itself, seal it in a small metal can, and mail it to the Oak Ridge Lab to be tested by him. He took the carpet sample and placed it in a special bag made of a plastic designed not to react with the substances placed in it. Vass then heated the carpet to the approximate temperature that would have existed in the trunk, removed a sample of the air, and cooled it to concentrate the sample. After the cooling was complete, he ran it through a gas chromatograph/mass spectrometer, a device commonly used by scientists to break a substance into its underlying compounds. The results of all this demonstrated that the odor coming off that stain was consistent with what his research had detected coming off a decomposing human body. Equally important was that it did not match the research on decomposing animal remains.

Another smell that needed analysis was that of pizza. Ever since Casey's arrest, there had been comments by the defense and the Anthonys in the media attributing the smell in the trunk to that of a rotting pizza. An empty pizza box had been found in the garbage bag that had been removed from the trunk while the car was at the tow yard, although there were only crumbs of pizza left. Vass wanted to know if that was possible, so he took a pizza out of his freezer and let it rot in his backyard for a week, then tested the odor. The two smells didn't match.

Vass offered to test another possibility that had received speculation in the media: that the odor was from a road-killed squirrel stuck to the car's undercarriage. This is what Casey had alleged in a couple of her texts to Amy Huizenger during the thirty-one days that Caylee was missing. I told him that testing a squirrel would be great, but I didn't want him running out and killing any innocent squirrels. He laughed and expressed confidence that in rural Tennessee he'd be able to find some roadkill to test, which he did. The dead squirrel didn't match the odor from the car either.

In addition to the pure science he had applied to the problem, he had another tool at his disposal: his nose. Having studied odors as much as he had, he was uniquely qualified to identify them and the differences between them. The first time he opened the paint can containing the carpet sample, he told me he jumped back two feet, the smell was so unmistakable and strong. He was certain it was the smell of death.

His testing of the carpet fibers revealed fatty acids and inorganic elements in concentrations consistent with human decomposition. In addition, he tested a suspicious greasy substance on a paper towel that had also
been in the garbage bag from the trunk. He found that the substance on
the paper towel was chemically identical to another by-product of decomposition called adipocere, or "grave wax." None of these findings alone was
an irrefutable sign of the presence of a dead body, but the combination of
them all was starting to paint a clearer forensic picture.

Of Vass's findings, there was one more piece of particular interest that
was also perhaps the most disturbing. The results of his tests identified a
high level of chloroform in the specimen of carpet from the Pontiac's trunk.
The levels were so high, in fact, that chloroform was the most prevalent
compound discovered. Dr. Vass explained to me: while chloroform might be
produced by human decomposition, it would be in extremely small amounts.
The amounts revealed in his test were thousands of time greater than he
had ever seen from a decomposing body. In his opinion, the chloroform had
another source, although he could not establish it. This discovery of chloroform in the trunk was later confirmed in testing performed by the FBI.

The presence of chloroform in the trunk sample was a surprise to all
of us. Chloroform had been known to be used as an anesthetizer to knock
victims out, and it wasn't something you could get at the local drugstore.
Since it wasn't a commonly abused product, Detective Melich thought it
might be worth a shot to check the Anthonys' computers to see if anyone
had tried to buy it online.

Detective Sandra Cawn, an experienced computer forensics investigator with the Orange County Sheriff's Office, had already been mining the
Anthonys' computers for any leads that might help us learn the whereabouts of Zanny. Melich asked if she could also check for searches involving the word "chloroform." Detective Cawn first searched the hard drive of
the laptop that Casey had been using at Tony's and found nothing. She then
turned her attention to the desktop computer used at the Anthony home.

Her initial inspection of the active files came up empty. She then
looked at the unallocated space of the hard drive. As it was explained to
us, when you permanently delete something from your computer, that digital information gets transferred to another space on the hard drive, where

it can then be overwritten with new information. This computer version of limbo is called "unallocated space." Even though we think the file is erased from our computer, in fact it may still be there. Over time, all or portions of the information will be truly erased, as new information takes its place. Until that happens, though, a computer forensics investigator armed with the right software can mine that data.

When Detective Cawn examined this part of the Anthony family's home computer, she found repeated references to the word "chloroform," but that was as far as her software and her experience could take her. She turned to her boss, mentor, and teacher, Sergeant Kevin Stenger, and using more sophisticated software—even some that was still in development—Stenger was able to determine that on two afternoons in March someone had performed searches for information about chloroform. In one of the searches, someone had actually typed in the query "how to make chloroform."

Given the dates listed on the chloroform searches, Detective Melich wanted to be sure who had access to the computer those afternoons. He thought Cindy and George had probably been out of the house, and subpoenaed their work records to see if they were at their places of employment at the time the searches on chloroform were being done. Cindy's work records showed she was working both those days at those times. George's work records showed he was not actively employed that month, but worked a ten-hour day on one of the afternoons the searches had been done.

Finding chloroform in the trunk and in the search history of the computer added a new layer of suspicion to the case. These, along with the results from Dr. Vass's odor tests, point toward foul play of some kind.

Useful as all this was, it wouldn't do us much good if we couldn't convince the court to accept the science behind it. In other words, the time would come when we would have to establish the admissibility of Dr. Vass's work and the opinions derived from it. When the time came for the Frye hearing, it would be my job to convince the court that this new science of Dr. Vass's had a firm foundation in established science. After all, that was why I'd been brought on the case in the first place.

· · ·

INTRIGUING AS THE POSSIBILITIES WERE with the odor, they were only one part of the forensic evidence in our possession. My second forensic project was the hair collected from the trunk of the Pontiac. We wanted to establish that it was Caylee's hair, but more specifically, we wanted to determine whether the hair had come from someone living or dead.

The person I called was Karen Lowe, a senior analyst in the Trace Analysis Unit of the FBI Crime Laboratory Division in Quantico, Virginia. Lowe was a scientist with eleven years' experience at the lab. I read her report on the examination of the hair found in the trunk, and our conversation about her findings was professional and to the point, as you would expect. In her examination of the hairs, she discovered that one of them, a nine-inch light brown hair, had an unusual dark band at a particular point near the root. She explained to me that, while science has yet to understand precisely why this banding occurs, it has only been found in hairs taken from decomposing bodies. The banding was first documented in the scientific literature in the late 1980s and has been documented in numerous studies since. She noted that she had personally seen it hundreds of times in case work while examining hair known to have been taken from dead bodies, but that this was the first time she had seen it in a scene sample where the body had not been found. In the conservative fashion typical of FBI reports, she could only describe the banding as "apparent decomposition," but with the explanations she was able to give me, I felt we had a bombshell.

The next issue was proving that it was Caylee's hair. Lowe had examined the hair under a microscope and compared it with hair taken from a brush that the Anthonys said was Caylee's. Hair comparisons aren't like fingerprints; no expert can ever say with certainty that two hairs have come from the same person. By looking at the microscopic features of a hair, however, a scientist can eliminate some possibilities. Lowe explained that her comparison revealed that the hair with the banding was similar in length, color, and all other microscopic features to the hair taken from Caylee's brush. She also compared it to samples of Casey's, and she was able to say with confidence that the hair could not have been Casey's, because her hair was colored with dye and too short. We knew that Cindy's hair was dyed, usually blond, and kept short, and Lee's hair was too short as well. In order to be as certain as possible, the hairs were passed on to the DNA section of the lab.

Now, because DNA can only be extracted from a living cell, ordinary DNA testing doesn't work on a hair. Because the only living part of a hair is the root, decomposition makes the chances of successful regular DNA testing of hair slim to none. However, there is another kind of DNA test that can work on hair, a test that examines the DNA found in the hair's mitochondria. The DNA in the mitochondria is much heartier than ordinary DNA, and therefore it exists even in the dead cells of hair. The downside of mitochondrial DNA (mtDNA) is that it is passed on only from mother to child; there is no contribution from the father. Your mtDNA is identical to that of all your brothers and sisters, your mother, all of her siblings, your grandmother, and all of her siblings. In other words, if there is an unbroken maternal connection, then the mtDNA is a match.

The results of the mitochondrial DNA tests were a match. This match, combined with the fact that we'd already microscopically eliminated Casey, Cindy, and Lee by length and color, made me pretty confident that the hair with the "death band," as the media would come to call it, was Caylee's. With Dr. Vass's findings and the other evidence of the smell, it seemed a sad but inescapable conclusion that Caylee was dead.

Still, the challenges to all these forensics would be many. The Frye hearings would be a monster. No doubt the defense would be digging up opposing experts, who were often attracted to big cases for the notoriety it would bring them. There would be requests for examinations of the same samples, logistics surrounding transporting those samples—not to mention depositions, travel, and more time for me spent away from home. And then, assuming we made it past the Frye hearings, there was the difficulty of presenting this cutting-edge science in such a way that the jury might actually understand it.

It was going to be a busy couple of years.

CHAPTER TEN

TRACKING DOWN LEADS

The forensics may have been coming together, but we still couldn't treat this solely as a homicide. Throughout August and into the early fall, the police continued to chase after leads connected to both a possible kidnapping and a possible murder, while interviewing everyone with a link to Casey and of course trying, without success, to get more information from Casey herself.

At the Anthony home, the public was going nuts, with news trucks on their street night and day. Any time Cindy or George left the house, protesters would scream hateful and often ignorant things at them. One woman in front of their house had a child holding up a sign reading WOULD YOU KILL ME? I was disgusted by some of the things they were doing. I'd been around big trials before, but this was something else altogether.

Part of this display seemed rooted in the way the media's coverage focused on the anger at Casey. From the beginning, cable TV's Nancy Grace was the primary person pushing this case, featuring it nightly on her Headline News (HLN) *Nancy Grace* show. The situation was further enflamed by Jose Baez's decision to appear on the show himself. That Casey was not telling the truth was the headline and frustration over her lies was eagerly stoked. Soon a lot of the anger toward Casey was spilling into the front yard of the Anthony house on Hopespring Drive. The media was there to oblige the irate bystanders. Anyone who wanted to be on TV could come to the residence and start ranting.

Inside the house, the Anthonys were trying to hold it together. Cindy did most of the talking, especially after George became incensed at the protesters, even pushing someone off his lawn who called his daughter "trash." Much as the Anthonys frustrated me, I felt for them in this situation. At the end of the day their granddaughter was missing and their daughter was accused of child abuse with the possibility of more on the way. Going through this situation was hard enough, but doing it in front of hostile protesters—well, no one deserves that.

The media frenzy became a magnet for anyone looking for a bit of limelight. With the public uniquely fixated on the case and a general sense of desperation in the search for credible information about Caylee, anyone craving a bit of media attention could grab the spotlight for a day. To that end, one of the more bizarre events of the circus surrounding those early days was Jose Baez's decision to involve Leonard Padilla in the case. Padilla, a cowboy-hat-wearing publicity hound and "bounty hunter" from Sacramento, California, rode into the case with the purpose of arranging for Casey's $500,000 bond.

Padilla offered to arrange the bond for the avowed purpose of getting her out and making her reveal Caylee's true whereabouts. It always perplexed us why Jose would have allowed this character within one hundred feet of his client. Padilla's condition for this largesse was that Casey would live at the Anthony home under the watchful eye of his associates. Casey accepted, and on August 20, Padilla's brother, a bondsman, posted the $500,000 bond and she was released from jail to home confinement.

Needless to say, Padilla was no more successful than the police had been in getting any useful information out of Casey. Casey was rearrested on August 29, charged with check fraud and theft related to the $110 purchase she had made at Target on her friend Amy Huizenga's checking account. However, she was immediately released after being bonded out by Padilla for a second time. Strangely enough, the following day he gave up trying to get anything out of her, revoked her bond, and delivered her back to jail.

The whole episode was an unproductive distraction, one that made me question just how well thought out the defense's approach was. This choice seemed so reckless, so unhelpful. Perhaps the greatest irony of involving Padilla was that it made Casey seem more guilty. Ever since her arrest, she'd been saying to her parents, the police—anyone who would listen—that if only she were released, then she could help find Caylee. So what happened when she finally got released? All that happened was that more people—Padilla's cohorts—related their personal experiences in the Anthony home to whoever would listen, adding to the general opinion that Casey was doing nothing to help find her daughter. The lack of progress upon her release demonstrated just how self-serving she really was. Not only did it make her look worse, it made the defense look as if they didn't know what was in the best interests of their client. Jose Baez's lack of experience was showing.

Making matters worse, Jose's decision to include Padilla saddled us with him for the duration of the case. Like some freeloading distant cousin, once he moved in, you couldn't get rid of him. He kept hanging around, hoping to be the one to break the case and keeping his mug in the news. He caused a stir with a media-hyped search of a small river in the area, calling a press conference when something was found, which he declared was a bag containing human remains. Turned out to be nothing. Of all the opportunistic clowns I came across in this case, he was the most offensive to me.

Not even a week after Casey was reincarcerated, an anonymous person stepped in and posted her bail. We knew who the bail bondsman was, a local guy, but we never learned who had put up the collateral for her release. There was a lot of guesswork, but nothing conclusive.

Because Casey's release hadn't resulted in turning up anything new, the authorities began to search for Caylee's body in different ways. Tim Miller of the nonprofit organization Texas EquuSearch brought in his team of mounted search and recovery volunteers, and they actively searched central Florida, focusing on the area near the Anthony home. They looked in the overgrown, uninhabited areas on Suburban Drive, a street that first intersected with Hopespring Drive and eventually dead-ended a short distance away at an elementary school. Curtains of air potato vines made visibility from the road into the swamps behind virtually impossible. Not only that, but the swamps were filled with water and poisonous snakes at that time of year, and dozens of EquuSearchers were warned to stay out of areas with potentially dangerous water hazards.

Other leads came from different sources. On August 11, a meter reader for Orange County named Roy Kronk called 911 from his home to say he had been working in the Chickasaw Oaks neighborhood and, after reading all the meters on Hopespring and Suburban Drives, had entered a few feet into a vacant swampy area to relieve himself. In the swamp, not very far from the road, he saw a partially submerged, suspicious-looking gray vinyl bag with a white object nearby that resembled a human skull. The 911 operator thanked him and said she would pass on the information.

The next day, Kronk called again from his home, repeating everything about the location and his sighting. He further detailed exactly where he saw the bag. Again the operator thanked him for calling and suggested he also pass the information on to the TIPS line, as they were coordinating all kinds of details such as his.

On August 13, he called 911 for the third time. This time he said he was confirming a rendezvous with someone from the Orange County Sheriff's Office. The operator told him that if someone was planning on meeting him, to stay put and the deputy would certainly be there. He said he'd be waiting in his blue four-door Chevy Cavalier, right at the edge of the swamp. When the deputy arrived, Kronk pointed to the area where he had seen the suspicious item.

Kronk later described how the deputy walked toward the waterline, looked around, and then turned to walk back, slipping on the slope while doing so. He recalled that the deputy got to within six feet of the object but never touched or manipulated it. Kronk said he told the deputy he thought he saw a human skull, but the officer started bickering with him about whether the missing child's remains would be skeletal by then. The deputy then accused him of wasting the county's time. Kronk said he felt belittled.

Kronk said a second deputy arrived at the location after the two had already walked out of the swampy area. He told the newly arrived officer what he thought was in the woods but said the second deputy didn't even bother to go into the swamp. Both officers were under the impression that the area had already been cleared by crime scene investigators. Deputy logs reported the suspicious findings as "trash only," writing off the scene as just one of the many false leads that had come their way since mid-July.

AS THE MOSTLY BOGUS STREAM of tips flowed in from personalities big and small who all wanted to help solve the mystery of Caylee's disappearance, investigators did their best to stay focused on the stories that appeared likely to help. As a result, the investigative team continued to interview Casey's friends, especially those who had seen her during the thirty-one days when Caylee was unaccounted for. The team spent most of August through October trying to acquire a clearer picture of Casey, her relationship with Caylee, and her seemingly fraught relationship with Cindy.

Since the beginning, rumors had been circulating about difficulties between Cindy and Casey. After seeing that Cindy's brother, Rick Plesea, had been posting unflattering information about the Anthony family on the Internet, Detective Melich called him to see if he could provide some insight into the case. Rick spoke by phone with Yuri and three FBI agents: Nick Savage, Scott Bolin, and Steve McElyea. The call was put on speakerphone and the conversation was recorded.

It was immediately clear that Rick had a lot he wanted to get off his chest about Casey Anthony. He told the story, already familiar to the police, of how Casey had stolen a lot of money from her mother, and he also mentioned Casey's theft from her grandmother, in which she had apparently forged one of her grandmother's checks for $354 to pay an AT&T cell phone bill. When Shirley Plesea, Casey's grandmother, found out that Casey had done this, Casey claimed she used the money to buy a new work phone for Universal Studios.

"My mom wasn't buying that at all," Rick told the detectives. "She said, 'That's the stupidest thing I ever heard of.' . . . If you knew Casey's propensity to lie, then you would know that was a lie right off. You know she don't work at Universal."

Shifting gears, Rick began to elaborate more on the strained relationship between Casey and Cindy. He said that Cindy had sought the advice of a counselor through work because of the troubles she had been having with Casey, who had been stealing money, lying, and acting irresponsibly.

"The counselor," Rick said to the police, "had told Cindy, 'Just kick them out on the street,' and Cindy wouldn't do that. She goes, 'Uh, what about Caylee?' She says, 'I can't kick my granddaughter out on the street, because Casey would try to take her.' And finally, the counselor said, 'Well, if you need to, file for custody.' "

It was tough advice, but according to Rick, Cindy took it to heart. Through his mom, Shirley, Rick had learned that Cindy indeed threatened to throw Casey "out on the street" if she didn't behave, and even threatened to file for custody of Caylee. When asked about the friction between the two, Rick did not hesitate. "I would describe it as Casey resented Cindy," Rick replied. "She resented Cindy to the point where she could see that Caylee likes Cindy way better than she likes her. And to me, that was normal for a baby to like the grandma, because grandmas always like to spoil kids, you know?"

As Rick explained it, the family had learned for the first time that Caylee was missing on the day Casey got arrested. Cindy had called their mother on July 16 to tell her that the toddler had disappeared, fearing that Shirley might see it on the news. Their mother then e-mailed him with this information. After watching the news and hearing the stories that Casey had been telling investigators, Rick said he had tried to speak with his sister, but Cindy became upset with him for questioning her. "I talked to my sister once on the phone after all this happened, and then I e-mailed her probably six or seven times. And she wouldn't listen to me anymore. I was telling her, I said, 'Cindy you got to wake up. Casey is telling so many lies.' And I said, 'You're right in the center of it. You can't see what's going on. You're in complete denial.' "

To hear Rick tell it, Cindy's denial when it came to Casey was nothing new. Going back a couple of years, Rick informed investigators about
an incident that had occurred at his own wedding on June 4, 2005, which
Cindy, George, and Casey had attended. Until Casey showed up at his door
with her parents that day, he hadn't thought she was coming.

"I looked up and Casey was at the door. And I go, 'Oh, Casey, I didn't
know you were coming.' And when I looked down she had a tight-fitting
top on and her stomach was protruding, all right? And her belly button was
sticking out at least a half inch," he recounted.

"So I invited them all in. And we're all talking because I hadn't seen
them for a long time. And when I got Cindy and George alone I said, 'Cindy,
George, what's up with Casey? You got something to tell me? What's going
on here?' And they go, 'What?'

"And I said, 'She's expecting?' And they looked at me like I was crazy.
I looked over at my wife-to-be, and she just rolled her eyes, you know. And
I said, 'Cindy, she looks like she's pregnant. Come on.' And Cindy goes,
'Oh, no, she's not. She's just putting on weight.' I said, 'Cindy, I've seen a
lot of pregnant girls. I'm not an expert, but man—she looks pregnant.' And
everyone on my wife's side said, 'Who's the pregnant girl?' You know, every
time they would see her, or they saw pictures of our wedding, 'Who's the
pregnant girl?' "

Rick said that his parents, who were also in attendance at the wedding,
agreed with him that Casey looked pregnant. But said that Cindy swore
she wasn't.

"Cindy's a nurse. And I'm going, 'Mom, she's a nurse, for crying out
loud. She can't see it?' And so I said, 'Cindy, come on. You're kidding me?
Now tell me, is Casey pregnant?' And Cindy says, 'Casey told us that she'd
have to have sex first in order to have a baby and that she did not have sex
with anyone.' So I'm thinking, okay, then, if it's not a baby, then it's a tumor,
and she's only got a short time to live, because it's big. Here she was seven
months pregnant, because she had [the baby] on August 9."

His story spoke volumes. This was the same kind of denial that we
witnessed in Cindy whenever we spoke to her. The same denial that we'd
witnessed in the jailhouse conversation between Cindy and Casey when

Cindy had been seemingly incapable of calling her daughter out on the lie about the photograph of Zanny's apartment. The fact that Cindy's denial about Casey had apparently been going on for so long was incredible, but it also made me realize just how hard it would be to get Cindy to see her daughter for what she really was.

As he was winding down, Rick also said something interesting about Casey, something that vindicated what we in the prosecutor's office had been witnessing on our own as we'd sifted through her various lies: "If she sees something or hears something, she will spin it into her own little world to make it work for her, whatever kind of lie it is." It seemed that Casey's amazing talent for lying had been mastered after years of practice. The trouble was, none of this was likely to be admissible in court.

After Rick, Sergeant Allen, Agent Bolin, and Detective Melich went to speak with Cindy's mother, Shirley Plesea, at her residence in Mount Dora, about thirty miles northwest of Orlando. They called her en route and she agreed to speak with them. Their conversation was recorded without her knowledge.

Shirley greeted the officers warmly and invited them inside. It didn't take long for her to confirm that Casey had stolen money from her. The first time had been on Caylee's second birthday, August 9, 2007. Shirley noticed one of her checks missing and found out that Casey had cashed it at a local Publix supermarket for $54. Shirley was mad at her granddaughter, but said she forgave her.

A couple of months later, however, she noticed $354 missing from her bank account. It was this theft that Rick had told the investigators about. Shirley had again confronted Casey, who admitted to the theft but used the excuse about needing a phone for her job at Universal Studios. As in Rick's version of events, Shirley didn't buy Casey's story. Shirley said that she would have pressed charges, but for Caylee's and Cindy's sake she didn't.

When asked if she knew anything about Casey's supposed nanny, she said she had heard the name Zanny for more than a year, although she had never seen, met, or spoken to the woman. She also confirmed that Cindy had acted as if she didn't know that Casey was pregnant at her son Rick's wedding in 2005.

Shirley knew that Casey and Caylee had left the house in mid-June. Initially, her daughter had told her that Casey and Caylee were "going to bond." But the story later changed to their going on a vacation and then to their going to Tampa. Shirley admitted that she thought the stories her daughter was telling her were "a lot of bull on Casey's part." During the month Casey was gone, she said that Cindy would talk to Casey on the phone, but every time she'd ask to speak with Caylee, Casey would say they'd be home "tomorrow." And tomorrow never came.

ON SEPTEMBER 5, DETECTIVE MELICH received a phone call from Richard Grund, the father of Casey's former fiancé, Jesse. Richard agreed to meet with Melich and Sergeant Allen later that day. Although Richard and George Anthony were not really friends, Caylee's disappearance had brought them back into contact. Richard told the detectives that after Caylee was reported missing, he had offered to help the Anthony family in their search efforts. On the second Sunday that the family was holding a vigil for Caylee, Richard called George, but he got voice mail, so he left him a message. "Why aren't you doing what ex-cops do?"

According to Richard, George called him back immediately and said, "Here's my answer to your question as to why I'm not doing what you think I should be doing: because my wife doesn't want me to."

Richard went on to explain to the police that Cindy ruled that household. "Whatever Cindy wants is what Cindy gets," he remarked. Adding to Richard's sense of unease was a recent conversation with Cindy in which she told him, "You know, I could lose both my girls on this one." This was the first time he believed that Cindy knew something was wrong.

He also had some interesting things to add about Casey, Caylee, and the nanny. He explained that while Jesse was engaged to Casey, she had claimed to be working full-time, but she didn't have a babysitter. Richard said that his son decided to give up his only day off from work to watch Caylee on Mondays. Soon other people in his family were watching the child two other days a week.

"So now Caylee's at our house three days out of the week during work," he said. "I think Casey was there at night and on the weekends. I don't have a problem with that because Caylee's a wonderful little girl. But I work out of my house, and this was a severe disruption to me. So I began to press Casey, 'Have you found anybody yet?' And then when she finally said she found someone, it was really odd. Rather than just saying, 'Yeah, I've got that worked out,' she said, 'Yeah, I found this lady, Zenaida Gonzalez, and she watches my friend Jeffrey Hopkins's son, Zachary. And Zachary and Caylee play together, and they love to be together. So this'll work out great.'

"I'm thinking, 'Wow, that's a whole lot more information than I really needed.' And by this point, I picked up that Casey likes to tell stories. We started to all pick up that Casey had a little problem with exaggeration."

A little problem with exaggeration was an understatement. Richard described one instance in which he caught Casey in a lie. He said that when Casey was engaged to his son, she claimed to work at the Sports Authority, so he went to the store and found out that she was not an employee, nor had she ever worked there. Just as George Anthony had done.

Picking up where Rick had left off, Richard also shed some light on the relationship between Casey and her mother, telling the investigators that he'd been struck by the stories in the media claiming that Cindy and Casey were best friends. "I can tell you, and will testify to the fact that Casey sat at our table over those months when Jesse wasn't there to talk to me and repeatedly said, 'I don't want to turn out like my mother. I don't want to be around my mother. I want out of that house.'"

Richard also said that Casey "hated" her father, something about a gambling thing. He said she had even tried to get Jesse to move into a house with her before they got married. "That's how bad she wanted out. . . . She didn't like her mother. Didn't like her father. Now that may have changed in two years, but that was pretty adamant then."

On the subject of Cindy's denial, Richard's portrait was again consistent with what Rick had said. As Richard saw it, Cindy was unable to deal with the realities of Casey's bad behavior. Recalling one instance when Cindy had been bragging about how special Casey was, Richard said that he had felt the need to burst her bubble a bit and told Cindy about the time

Casey owed Jesse $250 and repaid him with a bad check. According to Richard, Cindy's reply was "Well, she only did it once."

At the time, the exchange had been unsettling for Richard, but to see how this same pattern of denial now appeared to be playing out in Caylee's disappearance was downright disturbing. Even more disturbing for Richard was a recent conversation he said he'd had with Leonard Padilla, the bounty hunter who had bonded Casey out of jail and who had been staying at the Anthony home during the time that she was free. According to Richard, Padilla told him that the Anthonys were actively trying to frame Jesse for Caylee's disappearance.

With all the rumors that Padilla's involvement had created, it was hard to know whether to put any stock in this one, but one thing was clear to the investigators after speaking with Richard: they needed to arrange a follow-up conversation with Jesse. On September 9, Detective Melich, Corporal Eric Edwards from the Orange County Sheriff's Office, and Agent Nick Savage from the FBI spoke with Jesse at the FBI office in Maitland. In addition to trying to get a fuller picture of the relationship between Casey and Cindy, they wanted to get more information about a specific conversation Jesse claimed to have had with Lee Anthony on July 31. Lee had apparently told Jesse that he believed a fight between Casey and Cindy had been the reason Casey left home with Caylee on June 16.

"And would you please just explain that incident for me and how you learned of it?" Melich asked Jesse.

"Shortly after my second interview with Orange County, Lee confided in me that the reason that Cindy confided in him, that the reason he thought she felt that Casey ran off was there was a big fight between the two of them, and the fight concerned Casey not being home a lot and not bringing Caylee by. It got into a very heated argument, which turned physical, and Cindy started choking Casey."

"Was there anyone else in the house when this happened?"

"He didn't actually expand upon that. As far as I understood, from what he told me, it was just Cindy and Casey."

Jesse went on to say that Casey and her mother had a strained relationship but that Casey had never told him anything about a physical confrontation with Cindy. "I mean she [Casey] had been recently in a very much kind of a hatred state for her mother, but she had never mentioned anything in regards to being choked by her mom."

While Jesse couldn't elaborate further on the supposed violence, he could speak to other elements of Casey's feelings for her mom and corroborate his father's words in the process. "She's always had a kind of love-hate relationship with Cindy," he said to the police. "I mean . . . if you ask my dad or anybody else, when we were together, when we were engaged, she didn't want to be anything like her mom. She wanted to get out of the house as quick as possible. And then suddenly she wanted to be just like her mom. And then she goes back to hating her mom again. And then she loves her mom and her mom's going to give her the house and everything's great. And then she hates her mom again. I believe it goes all the way back to when Caylee was born.

"When Caylee was born, Casey wasn't the first one to get to hold Caylee. It was Cindy. Casey's even voiced to me in the past that Cindy has actually called herself 'Mommy' to Caylee in front of Casey. . . ."

In the coming weeks, investigators followed up on other hearsay tips, including one from a neighbor on Hopespring Drive. The neighbor, Jean Couty, claimed to have overheard two very loud arguments between Casey and her mother that past May or June. He said both had taken place on a weekend while he was outside doing yard work. The discussions had been heated, with Casey doing all the cursing and her mother staying calm but firm. He said that Casey was acting like a spoiled brat both times. She'd huff and rant, then drive off in her car. Couty said that if he had ever talked to his mother that way, he'd have been slapped. Caylee wasn't present for either of these two arguments, he said. They both took place about one month before police showed up at the house on July 15, but he couldn't pinpoint the time closer than that.

As the search widened, investigators also began speaking with Cindy Anthony's coworkers at her place of employment, Gentiva Health Services, a national home health-care company where Cindy worked as a nursing case manager. Having worked there for many years with no issues, she was extremely well liked by her fellow staff members. Still, the people at Gentiva that Cindy had confided in were able to corroborate much of what Rick, Richard, and Jesse had said. Everyone, it seemed, had the general impression that there were problems at the Anthony home prior to Caylee's disappearance. Cindy had been doing a lot of complaining about Casey, saying she was spending more and more evenings out of the house, away from Caylee. It seemed like it was a classic case of two people at each other on a downward spiral, Cindy mad at Casey, which made Casey not want to be home, which made Cindy even madder at Casey. In all likelihood, Cindy suspected Casey was out partying based on her behavior, and the tension between the two women was leading to fights.

When Melich arrived at Gentiva, he sat with Debbie Polisano, Cindy's direct supervisor. Polisano said that while Cindy was often aggravated about things at home, in late June, she had been more upset than usual. George and Casey were fighting, and it was impacting her relationship with George. Finances seemed to be at the heart of it, but Cindy hadn't elaborated. Not long after, Cindy confided that Casey had using been Caylee as leverage, trying to keep her from her, while at the same time dumping her with her whenever it was convenient. Cindy was very frustrated. Polisano said that it was not uncommon for Casey to bring Caylee to the office once a week and leave her with Cindy, claiming she had to "go to work."

Polisano said that Cindy took the first week of June off, hoping to spend the time with Casey and Caylee. She even had a little trip in mind. It hadn't turned that way. Instead of spending time as a threesome, Casey hadn't been around the whole week and had used Cindy as a babysitter. Casey hadn't even called her mother on her birthday, which was June 5. That month, Polisano said Cindy had mentioned the pool ladder being removed from the pool in the family's backyard. She suspected a neighbor had been using the aboveground pool while Cindy was at work.

Prior to taking her next vacation, the first week of July, Cindy told her coworkers that she hadn't spoken to Caylee in a while, but she relayed the story that Casey had given her about Busch Gardens, the car accident, and Zanny, who Cindy had been mentioning to coworkers for months, though Cindy admitted she'd never met her. Like so many other people, Polisano thought the story Casey was selling her mother was preposterous. She recalled wondering why Cindy was taking it at face value.

Cindy took her vacation as scheduled, but when she came back to work, she told her coworkers that she hadn't seen Caylee. She'd talked to Casey numerous times, but she'd gotten a million excuses why Caylee couldn't come to the phone. Then Polisano recalled on July 15, Cindy took a call from George. Casey's car had been found in Orlando. Debbie told her she should get the car, find out what was going on, locate Casey, and go home. A short time later that day, Cindy returned to work (presumably before she went to find Casey at Tony's house). Cindy said the Pontiac had been found, and there was a "really, really bad smell in the car." Cindy didn't answer when her supervisor asked her if she looked in the trunk.

Polisano told her Cindy needed to go home and contact the police, but Cindy refused, claiming she had too much work. Polisano was so concerned she went to Nilsa Ramos, the area director, who demanded Cindy go home. Later that night, Polisano received a hysterical call from Cindy. She was almost incoherent. "I found Casey and the baby's gone," she screamed. "The baby's missing. We can't find the baby.

"Oh my God, Debbie. If something happened to the baby or if the baby's dead, I don't know what I'm going to do!"

Next, Melich met with Debbie Bennett, a coworker of Cindy's for the previous six years. Cindy had told Bennett that she had been babysitting Caylee a lot recently. Bennett also said Casey often dropped Caylee off at the office at around 5 P.M. on her way to work to be watched by her grandmother. Casey even wore a laminated ID card around her neck, reinforcing the image that she was on her way to a job. In June, Bennett said Cindy told her she hadn't seen her granddaughter in two weeks because Casey said she needed "time and space" away from her and had taken Caylee with her.

Another coworker, Charles Crittenden, also recalled the laminated ID badge that Casey wore when dropping off Caylee. In addition, he remembered a day in the summer of 2005 when Casey came to Gentiva wearing a long coat and looking pregnant. She didn't stop by his desk to say hi, like she usually did, which he found odd. According to Cindy, her daughter wasn't pregnant. Charles couldn't understand how she could not notice the obvious bulge. Once the pregnancy was common knowledge, Cindy told coworkers that Jesse Grund was the baby's father. When that turned out to be wrong, she went along with Casey's story that the father lived in Tennessee.

All this information about the inner workings of the Anthony family was fascinating. Hearing the echoes in each of the witnesses' words and seeing the parallels develop allowed a more defined picture to emerge: the elements of suspicion, the pattern of lies, even the fact that the people immediately around Cindy seemed to be able to see what Cindy herself could not. Suddenly we could see clearly that the dynamic between Casey and Cindy that we'd been witnessing for weeks had in fact been playing out over the course of the last several years. Cindy was in denial about her daughter on a colossal scale.

As much as this explained what we'd been experiencing with Cindy, it was ultimately frustrating as well because we knew that none of it would be admissible in court. I'd been doing this so long that my brain was accustomed to instantly assessing information and sifting out that which would most likely be inadmissible. Under the rules of evidence, the jury wouldn't be allowed to hear witnesses' opinions about the relationship between Casey and Cindy. Furthermore, thirdhand accounts of fights between Casey and Cindy could be presented only if Cindy was willing to admit that they occurred. From all that we'd seen of their interactions and heard from those around Cindy, it was unlikely that she would ever admit the unvarnished truth about Casey. It was a lethally toxic codependent relationship. One person was skilled at lying to others, while the other was skilled at lying to herself.

THROUGHOUT ALL THESE INTERVIEWS AND developments, our office was regularly updated on the investigation during frequent meetings with members of the Orange County Sheriff's Office and the FBI. The FBI had become involved in the case early on when Caylee was reported as missing, and they continued to offer their support as the investigation shifted focus. Usually in attendance at the meeting were FBI agent Nick Savage (which I always thought was a great name for an FBI agent or a superhero) and FBI intelligence analyst Karen Cowan. Karen was our liaison to the lab and coordinated the transfer of evidence between the agencies.

These meetings were usually held in a large conference room at the sheriff's office, and they were particularly helpful for getting me caught up on the parts of the investigation that I was not directly involved with. Detective Melich and Linda were in constant contact individually on every aspect of the investigation, and while Linda would fill me in during my meetings with her on a day-to-day basis, I had my hands full focusing on the forensics. There were many occasions at those meetings when I'd hear the investigators talk about something seemingly explosive, and excitedly I would turn to her and whisper, "Did we know that?" only to hear her response, "Yeah, that's old news." I remember one time in particular dashing into Linda's office when I knew Frank was there. I was all fired up because I'd just learned about the *"Bella Vita"* tattoo, but when I got there, they just laughed at me, since they'd known of it for months. Such was the nature of being the case's resident science nerd, I suppose.

Sometimes our sessions with investigators devolved into a larger discussion of the issues involving Cindy and Jose Baez. Both of them had used the media quite vocally to criticize how the case was being conducted, and the sheriff's office was understandably frustrated with these public attacks. Cindy was constantly in the media, perpetuating a mythical image of Casey as the ideal mother and attacking the police for not chasing down the red herrings she threw their way. Whether it was someone who'd supposedly seen Caylee at the airport or witnessed Caylee in some security footage from a convenience store, Cindy always seemed to have some lead about Caylee's whereabouts that, upon closer inspection, would turn out to lead nowhere. Yet Cindy spoke to the media with such frequency about these "leads" that there was always something she could accuse the sheriff's office of not following through with. Cindy and George had even gone to the FBI in late August, citing frustration with the sheriff's investigators who, they claimed, were focused on pinning a crime on Casey instead of finding Caylee.

All the agencies worked very amicably together and shared any information they had discovered. The FBI knew what the sheriff's office knew: Cindy's hints and tips had been tracked down and ruled out at every turn, wasting precious time and resources on what amounted to a lot of smoke and mirrors. Theories abounded that Cindy knew more than she was saying or that maybe George was involved in hiding the remains, though nothing was ever uncovered to indicate that either of those conjectures was true.

The investigators were equally frustrated with Jose. They perceived his approach to the case as two-faced. In public statements, he would profess a concern for Caylee's safe return and promise Casey's cooperation, only to thwart every attempt authorities made to get useful information from her. He, too, would then criticize the investigators for their failure to act on the leads he was giving them.

In fact, to try and prove this point, the defense even hired an investigator by the name of Dominic Casey to chase down their leads. From the start, this appeared to be another questionable move on the part of the defense. It appeared that he was hired to assist in the search for Caylee. He tried to find all the people Casey said had known Zanny, but none of those people existed. Following in the footsteps of Melich and his team, he went to all the places where Zenaida had supposedly ever gone, but no one at those places had ever heard of her. They checked all the hospitals in Tampa—not just the one where Casey claimed Zenaida had been hospitalized after a car accident—but still no Zenaida. There was another rumor circulating that Zenaida had taken Caylee by plane to Puerto Rico, but that went nowhere, too.

After a few weeks of this, Baez severed his relationship with Dominic Casey, who then went to work for the Anthonys and continued his efforts into the next year, all the while feeding a constant stream of unhelpful information to the sheriff's office on Cindy's behalf. The end result was only more wasted hours of investigative resources for both that agency and the FBI.

The defense was also unhappy with the way information about the case made its way into the media. Under our discovery rules, most of the information we were getting about the case was provided as expeditiously as possible to the defense. Under our public records statute, once any information was provided to the defense, it became part of the public record, and anyone who made a request had a right to see it and copy it. There were people at the sheriff's office who were giving out information to reporters (called "leaks"). Sometimes these revelations seemed intended to rebut claims made by the defense, and sometimes it seemed as if some cop was just trying to get in good with a reporter. These divulgences may not have been authorized by their agency, but they were not illegal. There is no general confidentiality accorded to information obtained in a police investigation, and the information would have been released eventually anyway. At times, I myself learned things from the media that I didn't know yet—about the tattoo, for instance.

The bizarre part of the whole situation was that the defense team was on TV all the time, giving its opinions on whether Caylee was alive or not and commenting about everything else under the sun. The next thing I'd know, they were coming to court and complaining about leaks inside the sheriff's office. Yet no one was putting out more rumors and hogwash than members of Casey's defense team.

In the end, though, none of their actions or their complaining could derail what seemed all but inevitable as September came to a close: we were building a murder case against Casey Anthony. In all of our weekly meetings with Melich, following all of the various leads, both useful and not, we were slowly tracking this case to what felt like an inevitable conclusion: Casey had killed her daughter. We didn't have a body to prove it, but perhaps that too would come with time. Until then we had to focus on what we did have—solid forensics, a well-executed investigation, and a potential defendant who appeared incapable of telling the truth to anyone.

CHAPTER ELEVEN

———

THE GRAND JURY

As October approached, we had a decision to make. Casey stood charged with child abuse and multiple counts of lying to law enforcement, and she was out of jail on bond awaiting her trial. The trial date for those charges was set for mid-November. The original thinking on the child abuse charge was that by not reporting her daughter missing for a month, she had committed child abuse by neglect. The difficulty for prosecutors was that, unlike defense attorneys, we had to actually believe the theory we were arguing to the jury. Defense attorneys have an obligation to argue their clients' version of the facts or any alternate version of the facts that benefit their client. Their subjective belief in the truth of the version must be disregarded unless there is clear evidence that perjury has been committed. Prosecutors, however, can proceed only if they have a good-faith belief that the prosecution is warranted and that the material evidence on which it is based is true. None of us could have looked a jury in the eye and effectively argued a conviction for child abuse when we all believed the child in question had been dead thirty-one days, not just missing.

In addition, there were two other problems to consider, each of which could have a potentially devastating effect on our ability to prosecute Casey if Caylee's body was ever found. The first was that, in Florida, we have what is referred to as a "speedy trial" rule, which states that when a person is arrested, he or she must be charged and tried within 180 days. That right is waived if the defense delays the case or requests more time to prepare, but the prosecution can't count on that. If a case is not taken to trial within the required period, you can't prosecute it even if new evidence is discovered.

So the first concern we had was whether Casey's arrest in July had started the clock running on the murder charges. The tricky part was that the rule states that the defendant has to be tried in that period for any related crimes as well. Would the law consider the child abuse charge and the murder charge as related crimes? As with many things in law, the answer was uncertain. There were good arguments on both sides, but if we choose the wrong course, then some appellate court years from now could decide we were wrong and Casey might walk, even if we found Caylee's body and she was convicted of murder.

The second issue was double jeopardy. The U.S. constitution prohibits someone from being prosecuted twice for the same offense. Whether child abuse and murder would be considered the same offense was again a question without a clear answer and with potentially devastating consequences if we were wrong. We could convict her of child abuse, find Caylee's body, and be forever prohibited from prosecuting her for murder.

While our course of action was open to debate, the one thing we felt certain of was that Casey had had a hand in the death of her daughter. Whether she had deliberately killed her and disposed of her body, which was my personal belief, or had killed her accidentally, maybe with an accidental overdose of chloroform—either way it was first-degree murder. Linda, Frank, and I were comfortable with the evidence we had when it came time to go forward with the murder charges. At this point, the only potential murder weapon that we had was the chloroform. We had lengthy discussions about every possible chloroform scenario—that Casey had chloroformed her daughter on purpose, but only to render her unconscious so that she could party; that she had accidentally administered chloroform

and killed Caylee, still a felony murder; or that she had used the chloroform
to kill her deliberately.

The bottom line: We believed she'd killed her daughter, and we couldn't
wait for a body to be found. We had to go with what we had. Here were the
facts: We had a young mother who left home with her daughter and from
that point on appeared to begin a new life without her. She got a tattoo
expressing her feeling that she was living a beautiful life. She lied repeatedly about her daughter's absence for months and instead of looking for her,
went out partying. When she was called out for her lies, she was uncoopera-
tive and continued to tell more lies. She blamed her daughter's disappearance on a babysitter who did not exist. She was offered the opportunity on
two occasions (first by Sergeant John Allen in the interview at Universal
Studios and later by Cindy Anthony during one of her visits to Casey in
jail) to adopt an "accident" account of what had happened to her daughter,
and she scoffed at it both times. And of course, she was driving a car that
contained a very suspicious odor, along with one of her daughter's hairs and
high levels of chloroform in the trunk.

AS WE SURVEYED ALL OF this evidence, these last pieces were what we
kept coming back to—the physical evidence. The smell in the car, the hair
in the trunk, and the presence of chloroform. The odor and the hair alone
were bad enough, but there was no reason for the chloroform to be present other than to be used on Caylee. When we combined the presence of
chloroform with Casey's bizarre behavior during those thirty-one days, we
couldn't believe that Caylee's death had been an accident. As a prosecutor,
as a parent, as a person, I couldn't see how any mother could act the way
Casey did if the death had truly been accidental. Each of us on the prosecution had kids. I had raised four to adulthood and had two new little ones
at home. Linda had one child of tender years and so did Frank. As we sat
around talking, all of us could relate one story or another about the panic
that arose from even momentary loss of contact with one of our kids. There
was no scenario we could imagine in which a mom could experience the
accidental death of her child and then proceed to drive around with the

dead body in her trunk, watch a movie, and spend the night with her new boyfriend. Those did not seem like the actions of someone whose daughter had died in a freak and tragic accident. They seemed like the actions of someone who wanted her daughter gone. The reason Casey *seemed* so happy after Caylee was gone was that she *was* happy that Caylee was gone.

From the evidence we had collected thus far, our conclusion was that the child had decomposed in the back of her car, and Casey had attempted to bury the body in her backyard with the shovel she borrowed from a neighbor. The story she'd told was clearly false and, in my opinion, showed an unmistakable consciousness of guilt. Whether it was because of this guilt or something else, she had been prevented from actually burying the body in the backyard, so instead she stashed it in a place where we had yet to find it.

All of these arguments were presented to the state attorney, Lawson Lamar. It was up to him to decide whether we would proceed with presenting the facts to the grand jury. If we did so, and they chose to indict Casey, we would then prosecute the best case we could. Allowing Casey to escape responsibility for her actions was not an option. Lawson sought the opinion of all of us, both in law enforcement and in the prosecutor's office. I told him that I was comfortable with the evidence we had and felt he should move ahead and present it to the grand jury. I believe Linda and Frank were of the same opinion.

The grand jury would consist of nineteen jurors chosen from the same jury pool as trial jurors. Whereas trial jurors usually serve only a few days, grand jury members serve six-month terms, hearing evidence in a variety of murder cases one day a month instead of sitting on one specific trial. The difference between a grand jury hearing and a trial is that the grand jury only has to find probable cause that a crime has been committed to hand down an indictment, whereas at trial, the state has to prove the prosecution's case beyond a reasonable doubt. At grand jury, only the prosecution presents evidence, and it is not refuted or challenged by the defense. The common practice is for the prosecutors there to question the witnesses, and, unlike in an actual trial, hearsay is admissible. The grand jurors are free to ask questions as well. When the testimony is completed and the witnesses excused, the grand jurors are invited to question the prosecutors about legal matters. When all questions have been answered, the prosecutors excuse themselves, and the grand jurors deliberate and vote in private. Fifteen of the nineteen jurors must approve the decision to indict.

Usually the witnesses that appear before a grand jury are police officers and medical examiners. In most cases that is enough. The investigating officer can summarize the testimony provided in the sworn statements of other witnesses that he has gathered during the investigation. A detective can summarize a medical examiner's testimony, but State Attorney Lawson always seemed to think that grand jurors wanted to hear directly from the examiner. I personally felt that it was important to use the process of grand jury testimony to lock in witnesses who might later succumb to pressure and change their testimony. After all I'd seen and heard in the last couple of months, I felt that George Anthony might be such a witness.

Over the preceding months, I'd witnessed how conflicted he was by his love for his granddaughter, what the facts said about Casey, and his relationships with his daughter and wife. It was clear to me that Cindy was in complete denial as far as Casey was concerned. I imagined that the pressure on George to adopt Cindy's denial must have been unrelenting, and while he hadn't succumbed to the pressure so far, if Caylee's body were to be found, his will might falter. But it would be much harder for that to happen if we got his testimony locked in during the grand jury hearing.

I arranged a meeting with him through his attorney, Mark NeJame, a few days before his grand jury appearance. I wanted to meet with George in person, but at the last minute the press made it impossible to do so in secret, so we settled for a telephone conference. We discussed his prior statements to the police and what questions he would most likely face in the grand jury room. He seemed cooperative and cordial.

Similarly, there was brief consideration of calling Cindy Anthony to testify, but her state of denial by then seemed so entrenched that Linda, Frank, and I feared the prospect of some great emotional outburst, or worse yet, an outright refusal to testify. There was no need or desire on anyone's part to have a grieving grandmother held in contempt. In the end, we decided it was best to present her testimony through Detective Melich.

ON OCTOBER 14, 2008, A grand jury was convened to hear testimony in the Anthony investigation. The hearing occurred behind closed doors, in the ceremonial courtroom on the twenty-third floor of the Orange County Courthouse in downtown Orlando. The atmosphere was tense, with members of the media, many of whom I had known for years, angling for any bit of news to report. Unlike the defense team, we had a strict "no comment" policy during the pendency of cases, and this case was no different. While the reporters would ask questions, they always respected our polite "no comment," and largely left us alone that day.

The testimony of the witnesses was sealed, as per standard procedure. The media camped outside the courthouse was certainly speculating about the witnesses, making a brouhaha about anybody involved in the case who was coming up the sidewalk. In all, six witnesses entered the grand jury room that day, and what they said in the two-hour proceeding has been kept secret, by law. All the witnesses had been subpoenaed to testify. They were Casey's father, George; Corporal Yuri Melich; canine handler Jason Forgey; FBI hair analyst Karen Lowe; FBI agent Nick Savage; and computer forensics investigator Sandra Cawn. Each witness was called forth separately to testify in private. While I cannot discuss the proceedings in this case, I can tell you that besides the six witnesses, Linda, Frank, and I were all there for the prosecution team. The state attorney was present and, of course, the courtroom reporter. George Anthony was accompanied by his lawyer. Though Casey was invited to testify without immunity, she declined through counsel. There was no judge involved, only the nineteen grand jurors.

The grand jury reached its decision within two hours of the hearing's conclusion, handing down the primary charge of first degree murder and supplementing it with six other charges: aggravated child abuse, aggravated manslaughter of a child, and four counts of providing false information to law enforcement. After getting word of the grand jury's decision, my boss, State Attorney Lawson Lamar, addressed the press. "The investigation contains intricate forensics that are on the cutting edge of science. We are used to complex forensics, and are ready to manage this evidence at trial."

I appreciated the words of confidence and knew I was already doing everything possible to get my experts in order and be prepared for the trial date.

Jose Baez had alerted us that Casey would be spending the day at his
law office in Kissimmee. In order to waste no time taking Casey into custody, Melich was on his way to Baez's office the minute the indictment was
unsealed. Casey was reported to have been cool, polite, and calm when
he arrived to arrest her. This outcome was no surprise; she always seemed
to keep her emotions in check. Melich placed her in handcuffs and transported her to the sheriff's office, where she was read her Miranda rights.
Melich later reported that she declined to speak to anyone without her
attorney present, but her mood was light and she engaged in chitchat with
the officers processing her back into the system. She could have asked the
court to have another bond hearing, but for some reason never made clear
to us, she opted not to. By that evening, she was back at the Orange County
Jail, charged with first-degree murder in the death of her darling two-year-
old daughter, Caylee Marie. Whether she was to face the ultimate penalty
was an issue to be decided on another day.

IN SPITE OF THE GRAND jury indictment, Cindy Anthony was still convinced that Caylee was simply missing, not dead. As such, she spent the
months of October, November, and December going on TV to say that
Caylee was alive and to wonder why the police weren't looking for her. Now
that the indictment was in, our office started preparing for trial. The pretrial date, when you discuss if you are ready for trial, was set for December,
abiding by the 180 days speedy trial statute. We figured the defense would
try to push the case to trial before Caylee's body could be found, thereby
leaving open the argument that she was alive somewhere, so we had to be
prepared for that. Although it would have been a herculean task, we were
up for it. I was primarily dealing with requests from the defense about the
forensic testing. We assumed that the defense would start taking depositions. They wanted the lab documents from Dr. Vass and the FBI. There
was a great deal of litigation about getting the lab information. Many of
the labs were out of state, so technically they didn't have to comply, but

everybody was fairly cooperative. The defense also made other requests, many of which seemed overboard to me, such as when Baez requested all the e-mails between the sheriff's office and Dr. Vass. Technically we were not required to provide these, but in this digital age we had no problem providing it. Baez also wanted law enforcement to compile and copy each and every tip they had received concerning Caylee sightings. We again had no problem with providing that as long as the agency didn't. The sheriff's office had to spend time and effort to put together those tips—numbering about five thousand—and as a result, they had the right to expect reimbursement for the copying costs.

There was one particularly ridiculous hearing where Baez complained that the sheriff's office was not filtering the tips that were being provided to the defense, and he accused them of giving him the worthless ones first—as if anyone had time to sort them that way. When the tips were all collected and Baez was informed that they were ready for pickup, he balked, claiming that Casey didn't have the money to pay for them. We suspected this wasn't true, since there were rumors floating about that Casey had sold videos and photographs of her daughter to *ABC News* for $200,000. But regardless of the money situation, the whole exercise just felt like an unnecessary waste of time, which it almost certainly was.

It wasn't just the defense's requests that appeared outrageous. In general I found their continued presence in the media to be questionable. Baez was on TV all the time, giving his opinions, making statements, all arguably inappropriate under the rules of the Florida Bar. On November 7 I filed a motion to have the court prohibit the defense attorneys from making comments to the media. I thought Baez was potentially tainting the jury pool, which was a concern that Baez himself claimed to have. I even went so far as to extend the gag order request to all parties involved in the case, including the sheriff's office and the Anthony family. Not surprisingly, the motion was opposed by Baez. In the end, he must have been more concerned about continuing his media appearances than about getting the untainted jury pool he said he wanted. Of course the media opposed us on this as well. The motion was denied.

While we were battling Baez on just about every little thing, there was another issue that we had to address internally at the prosecutor's office: whether to seek the death penalty against Casey. Every defendant charged with first degree murder technically faces the possibility of the death penalty, though few actually meet the eligibility requirements in the statute. These requirements are based upon factors about the crime, the victim, and the offender's prior record. Although the statute does not mandate it, most state attorneys try to inform the court as early as possible if their case obviously does not meet any of these criteria. In some cases the determination is clear-cut because none of the criteria is met. In others, though some of the criteria may be met, we know from experience and research that the death penalty will not fly, either because juries never give it under those circumstances or because the courts have decided in similar cases that the facts aren't sufficiently egregious.

We like to have as much information as possible in making such an important decision, so we invited Casey's defense team to provide us with any information they would like us to consider. After some delay they provided us with a document that was largely useless to us since it provided no new information, just a lot of argument. From reading it, we sensed that it was prepared more for the media than for us. We presented the information we had to the state attorney, and from the outset, Linda, Frank, and I knew how it would go. Since we didn't know how Caylee died, we could not in good faith assert that we could meet any of the criteria related to the crime itself. That left us with only a single criterion met by the case: the fact that Caylee was a child in the care of a caregiver. Strong as that piece was, alone it was unlikely to convince a jury or appellate court that death was justified. On December 3, the state attorney made the decision not to seek the death penalty against Casey.

Meanwhile, Baez continued to file motions, including a request to use his laptop in jail, another to inspect the evidence, and another to review the credentials of the cadaver dogs. Some of the motions were fairly standard, such as inspection of evidence, while others seemed to demonstrate an expectation that Casey should be treated differently than other inmates. Special privileges were requested, and generally, unless there was some security concern at the jail, they were granted. At one point the defense requested that she not be required to appear in court when the motions were heard. We objected, and her presence was required. Some people wondered why we objected. Why should we care if she did not want to hear her own attorney's motions? Baez accused us of just wanting to put her on display. In truth, it was not that simple.

While part of me felt that if I had to sit and listen to him blather on, then she should too, the actual reason was more subtle. We in the prosecution are highly conscious of the accusations that defendants typically make against their attorneys after they are convicted. One way of responding to those allegations is to show that the defendant knew what the lawyer was doing and went along with it. Having her present in the courtroom throughout the trial helps with that argument. As the motions poured in, there was one thing consistent in them all. Every motion attacked somebody. Usually it was the police, but occasionally it was our office. Reading Baez's motions left you with the distinct impression that he felt there was a conspiracy against his client and against him. We learned to grow a thick skin and consider the source. Many of the motions alleged facts that were just plain wrong; Mr. Baez didn't always check his facts very carefully before he put pen to paper. On one occasion, I recall, he filed a motion saying that the sheriff's office had withheld evidence from him when he and a defense expert had come to view it. We decided that our response was going to be: "Prove it."

So turning to Baez, Judge Strickland said, "Call your first witness." He stammered and looked surprised, seeming to be caught off guard. He tried to delay by claiming that he hadn't expected to have to present a witness. Luckily for him, Linda had brought the witnesses in for him (she is so helpful, isn't she?), and when he put the witnesses on they testified that the evidence he claimed was withheld was in fact at an out-of-state laboratory being tested. The whole motion fell flat on its face.

The first trial date was set for January 5, 2009, which was within the six-month window. On December 11, 2008, the pretrial hearing was under way in front of Judge Stan Strickland when Baez came before the judge and asked for a continuance in the case, thereby waiving Casey's right to a speedy trial and giving everybody more time to prepare their cases.

For us it was a gift, but not a surprise. In this instance, Baez did the smart thing. When your client's life is in your hands, it's no time to play chicken. He needed time to depose all the witnesses and inspect all the evidence. Up to this point he had done very little of either. Any conviction we might get would be far more secure if he left no stone unturned. We could have gotten the state's case ready to present in time for January, but this extra time would give us opportunities to pursue things in a different way and go at a pace that would be much more conducive to presenting a thorough case. As it turned out, we'd need every second of the extra time.

At that very moment, Roy Kronk, the Orange County meter reader who'd called the police over the summer about a suspicious bag in a swamp, was revisiting that same swamp on Suburban Drive. He noted that the gray laundry bag he'd phoned in to 911 back in August was still there. Now he had no doubt that the white object he had seen next to the bag was a skull. While Judge Strickland was granting Baez's motion for a continuance, Roy Kronk was calling his boss at the utility company, leading to the fourth call alerting the police to something important on Suburban Drive.

CHAPTER TWELVE

FINDING CAYLEE

I was sick and had stayed home from work on a very gray, rainy December 11 when my neighbor Dawn Feeser called to alert me to the latest "breaking news" in the Anthony case. I assumed it was another of the false alarms I'd heard so often, but I turned on the news anyway. I was in disbelief. At 9:38 that morning, the skeletal remains of a child had been found in a swamp just off Suburban Drive near the Anthony home. Someone had called 911 about a suspicious bag and something that might have been a skull in that area. The CSI team had already confirmed that it was a skull—a child's skull.

I immediately dialed Linda to see what she knew. She had spoken to Melich, who confirmed that a body had been found. Melich told Linda that upon being notified of the find, he had requested CSI Gerardo Bloise to proceed to the scene and verify it. Bloise was there when Yuri arrived, as were the medical examiner's investigator, the crime scene photographer, and another detective. By that point, they'd taped off the scene and Suburban Drive had been closed, though it wasn't a much-traveled road to begin with, being frequented only by people going to the elementary school just down the dead-end road.

Beyond that, there was not much more known, but Melich was on the scene and promised to keep us posted. As the morning wore on, the details started coming in. There wasn't much for me to do yet, even if I had been at the office, so I waited by the phone for updates throughout the morning and afternoon. Roy Kronk had gone back to the Chickasaw neighborhood to read the meters and said he just happened to return to the same spot he'd gone to before to relieve himself again. Once there, he saw the bag, tried to pick it up with the stick he used to open meter boxes, and a skull rolled out. He did not initially tell the deputies that morning that he had called 911 about that same location three separate times back in August. After his discovery, he went back to his utility truck where his partner, Alan Robinson, was waiting. Once there, he called his supervisor, Alex Roberts, who notified the dispatcher, who placed the call to 911.

Roberts said that when he arrived, Kronk was leaning against his truck, smoking a cigarette, and Robinson was sitting in the truck but didn't want to get out. Only Kronk had gone into the swamp, and he was excited when he told Roberts that the reward for information leading to Caylee's discovery would be his. "Alex, I just hit the lottery."

THE REMAINS HAD CLEARLY BEEN in that location a long time. It would have been very difficult to get into the swamp, let alone see something in there, underwater, in very dark conditions. There was a little gap in the air potato curtain, and ironically, there was a discarded yellow sign with black lettering for a day care center just at that opening. But that was the only access point to the woods. You could have walked five feet to the left or right and never seen it, but once the vines and overhanging vegetation were pulled back, the whole gruesome picture became disturbingly clear.

The skull and one of the leg bones were close to the bag. The skull was just behind a log, not quite under it. When Kronk had taken the first officer to show him, they actually walked past it and had to come back. The skull had a hair mat around it, the majority of the hair having fallen to the back of the skull. From above looking down, the hair looked like a halo all around the head, with a few strands stubbornly clinging to the top of the skull along with a few decomposing leaves. The mat of hair and leaf debris surrounded the skull, burying it to about the level of the bottom of the eye sockets. The skull was tilted very slightly upward. A small amount of the hair that had fallen forward collected at the area that had been the nose. Even before the skull was removed, a length of shining gray plastic duct tape, about half an inch from the face of the skull, could be seen through the leaf debris. At first glance, there appeared to be more than one piece.

The rest of the skeleton was extremely scattered, having been distributed by animals as well as Central Florida's summer rains and flooding. Every summer during the rainy season, low-lying swampy areas and recesses take on an extra four or five feet of standing water, which slowly dries up in the late autumn. Decomposition causes the bones of the body to separate, and the effects of animal activity and flooding led to an overall dispersal of the bones. That made it difficult for the crime scene investigators, though it was not at all startling or unexpected. Over the next ten days they would find that the torso and most of the ribs had been pulled to a secondary location, and the vertebrae had been pulled to a third place. One specific bone, a hip bone, was buried in four inches of muck. This type of accumulation of muck could have occurred only through the movement of water over and around the bone once it had been moved to that location by an animal scavenging. Thus we were able to determine that the body had fully decomposed prior to the rainy season in July and Tropical Storm Faye, which hit in mid-August.

Beyond the actual bones, there was other physical evidence that had been buried along with the body. It appeared that the body had been wrapped in a baby blanket that had a Winnie-the-Pooh and Piglet pattern on it, and then stuffed in two garbage bags, one inside the other for extra strength, and all of that inside a laundry bag. About a foot to the left of the skull was a pair of shorts, size 24 months, with a kind of a striped pattern on them. Everything was pretty shredded up.

The obvious pieces were dealt with first. The medical examiner's investigator, Stephen Hansen, collected the skull with the tape, as well as the leaf debris immediately around it, as one item. Trying as best as he could to keep all the items in their original position, he also collected the bags, clothing remnants, and other debris in the immediate vicinity of the skull. Everything from the scene not collected by Hansen—from the shreds of the garbage bags to the tatters of clothes—was photographed and collected separately by the CSIs and later taken to the crime lab.

As the search expanded to try and locate the other remains, the entire crime scene was cordoned off and set up like an archaeological site. The search area started small, about twenty feet by twenty feet, and expanded as the investigators found more bones. It ended up about eighty feet by forty feet, extending back into the woods. The CSIs would scrape down three or four inches and sift the earth looking for remains. They had a lot of people out there doing it, including people from the sheriff's office, detectives from the FBI, civilian technicians, and crime scene investigators. The objective was to recover every possible bone of the little girl's body.

The conditions were horrendous. This area was obviously used by locals as a secluded area to dump garbage and lawn waste. The swamp was a pit of raging poison ivy, nasty insects, poisonous snakes, and disgusting muck. Many of the search team members got poison ivy, and a lot of them got sick. In the end, they recovered almost every single bone, all except two tiny bones from one tiny toe, an unbelievable success given the environment they had to work with.

THE DAY BEFORE THE DISCOVERY, Cindy and George Anthony were in Los Angeles for an appearance on *Larry King Live*. Once again Cindy had been taking to the airwaves to spread her message and had spent most of her time on *Larry King* denouncing the Orange County Sheriff's Office for their indifference to the search for Caylee as they focused instead on proving Casey's guilt. Cindy and George were in Los Angeles International Airport, ready to board a jet for their flight back to Orlando, when their lawyer, Mark NeJame, called them with the news that a child's body had been found not far from their home. They were devastated. Without a fraction of a doubt, it was Caylee. They made the long trip back to Florida overwhelmed by the news.

Casey got the news earlier than her parents. The body had been discovered around 9:30 A.M. Around an hour later, the police arranged for Casey to be brought to the clinic in the jail, where they would have a chaplain tell her the news per jail policy. There is a TV in the waiting room of the clinic, and the waiting room is monitored by video surveillance, so they recorded the scene in case the story about Caylee came on. That way, they could catch Casey's reaction.

Later on, this setup became a subject of great angst to the defense. They said it was a violation of Casey's constitutional rights. The videotape did not show that much, and we on the prosecution team did not introduce it at trial for precisely that reason. You couldn't see much because of the distance and the angle of the camera; perhaps most important, you could not clearly see Casey's face. Basically, she heard a newscaster saying there was breaking news about Caylee Anthony, she looked up at the TV set, and she put her head down and started to cry. Her body language could be equally indicative of "Oh crap, I'm caught" or "Oh crap, my daughter's dead." So in the end it didn't add much information either way. But apparently the defense thought differently, and they got the judge to seal it. I always thought it was amusing that their actions led the public to think the tape was so much more incriminating than it actually was.

Regardless of the videotape, investigators worked quickly to see if there was a link between what they'd found at the scene and the Anthony home. Back at the medical examiner's office, deputy chief medical examiner Gary Utz and investigators on the scene were inventorying the canvas laundry bag. The bag had a metal reinforced top and a brand tag identifying it as a Whitney Design. Along with the bag, they itemized the collar and tag from a size 3T shirt, as well as the iron-on letters that appeared to belong to that shirt. The letters spelled out the words BIG, TROUBLE, comes, and small. In addition, there were the remnants of a diaper or pull-up, a Winnie-the-Pooh blanket, and at least two black trash bags with yellow tie handles.

When the skull was examined more closely, the duct tape was found to be three partially overlapping pieces with the brand name Henkel and with the text "Consumer Adhesives Inc. max temp 200 f Avon Ohio 44011" stamped on the back. The three pieces spanned the area from the jaw just below the right ear to the jaw just below the left ear. Small strands of hair still adhered to the tape, and the lower edge of the lowest piece of tape was bent in slightly, as if it had been pressed under the jaw. Though the tape was not adhering to the jawbone (also known as the mandible), some strands of the tape were. Dr. Utz found it unusual that the jawbone was still in its natural position in relation to the rest of the skull. He would later explain that during decomposition, when the strands of tissue holding the jawbone to the skull decompose, it always separates from the skull. The only time the mandible and skull are found in proper position is when there is something keeping them in place throughout that process, which in this instance was the tape.

There was still a lot to comb through, but even just these pieces of physical evidence were enough for us to begin relating things back to the Anthony house. A search warrant on the home was executed that very afternoon, specifically looking for those kinds of things that had been recovered at the site: any and all varieties of garbage bags or laundry bags; adhesive tape to include duct tape; all photos and photo albums, videos or CDs containing photos; Winnie-the-Pooh clothing, towels, blankets, or similar cloth items; toothbrushes and hairbrushes; and components that could be used to make chloroform, such as bleach and acetone. Even though Dr. Vass had discovered large amounts of chloroform residue in the carpet sample taken from the Pontiac, police had not returned to the Anthony home to initiate a chloroform search. The December search turned up nothing except household bleach. No acetone was found.

During the search, detectives found a number of items that connected to the crime scene. A laundry bag of the same Whitney Design brand as the one with Caylee's remains was found in the garage. Whitney Design was a Target product, and the canvas bags lined with coated plastic were sold in sets of two, one rectangular and one cylindrical. Caylee's remains were in a cylindrical one. A rectangular one was found in the house. Cindy would later acknowledge having purchased the cylindrical bag as well. She said that a neighbor, Brian Burner, had given her a whole bunch of plastic balls for a ball crawl for Caylee, and Cindy had used the bag for the balls. However, now she couldn't say where it was.

Moving to the shed in the backyard, they found boxes of trash bags like the ones at the crime scene: giant-size standard black trash bags. Although they were the same kind, the product was so common that it would have been impossible to say definitely that the ones at the crime scene had come from the home. Perhaps more definitive was that they found the same brand of duct tape that had been attached to Caylee's skull. The tape from the crime scene had been Henkel, not a common brand, and the words stamped on the back made it fairly easy to match. This same information and logo appeared on a swatch of duct tape that was stuck to the vent hole on one of the two red gas cans in the Anthonys' back shed—the gas cans that Casey had taken from George when her car ran out of gas.

Venturing back to the house, the search warrant specifically singled out items with Winnie-the-Pooh and Piglet, based on the blanket found around the skeleton. The identical pattern of the two characters was in numerous places in Caylee's room, from her curtains to the bolster on her bed. Cindy would later acknowledge that a blanket that went with the bed set was missing.

The detectives left the Anthony house with bags and bags of evidence, not only items linking the two scenes, but also samples for fluid and DNA testing.

LINDA AND I HAD DECIDED not to attempt going to the crime scene for the first few days. We wanted to let the CSIs do their jobs, and there was enough craziness out there without having us in the way. But finally, on Wednesday, December 17, Linda, Frank, and I decided to go. We came to work in our jeans and headed over in one of the detective's cars. When we arrived, we were greeted by a horde of news trucks. The restricted zone had been moved back a hundred yards or so to the intersection with Hopespring Drive to keep the media and the curious at bay. The primary crime scene had largely been cleared of debris. Deputies were clearing additional areas, as dictated by the discovery of bones. A blue canopy had been erected over the primary dump site, as well as over the shifting area where technicians picked through debris in search of bones no larger than a dime. An RV, used as a command center, was parked on the road nearby.

An old homicide detective buddy of mine, Dave Clark, was there wielding a chain saw as he cleared away debris. Another, Don Knight, who had been a CSI years ago and now was a court deputy, was also out digging. It appeared that all hands were on deck for this one. A sifting station was off to the right, as well as an ever-increasing pile of debris. Though it had not rained since the day of the discovery, the ground was still moist. Surveying the landscape, it struck me just what a mess this place must have been during the rainy season. It didn't surprise me at all that it had taken this long to find anything out here.

We walked down the incline so that detectives could show us exactly where the remains had been found. Even though it was mid-December, it was still a little warm. Dave Clark was soaked in sweat. Linda and I stood for a time talking to Nick Savage from the FBI about the progress of the evidence that had been sent to the lab. Dr. Neal Haskell, a forensic entomologist we had enlisted, showed up at the scene shortly thereafter. Dr. Haskell had looked at insect evidence from the car and issued some preliminary findings. By coincidence, we had been planning for a few weeks to ask him to come down this week to inspect the car. It was fortunate that he could be here to see the scene firsthand. We had never met but had spoken on the phone several times and he seemed very likable. He was a barrel of a man, standing six feet two, with a broad smile and an enduring fascination with bugs. He looked every bit the Indiana farmboy that in fact he was.

After the site visit, Linda, Frank, Dr. Haskell, and I next went to the office of the medical examiner, where we met with Dr. Jan Garavaglia, or Dr. G, as we all know her. Dr. G is a force of nature. Bright, outgoing—she really commands a room. I had presented her testimony at trial in the past. She would never say more than the facts and science would support, and once she arrived at her conclusion, she was a rock. She took all of us into the biohazard bay of the autopsy suite, the one frequently used in skeletal cases. There, laid out before us on a steel table, was the almost complete skeleton of a small child.

Even now, almost three years later, I have difficulty describing what I felt looking down at that sight. She was so small. For so long we had known that one day we would find her, but I was still not prepared for this moment.

I had seen adult skeletons many times, but this was my first time seeing a child's. How could anyone just throw Caylee away like that, with a laundry bag as her coffin? For a moment, I allowed myself to hate Casey Anthony. It didn't help me to do my job—in fact, if anything, it made things harder. There was work to be done that required me to keep my emotions out of it. We had to examine the items found with her remains as clinically as possible, and Dr. Haskell picked through the items for bug evidence. Just as quickly as it had risen, I pushed that hatred away. But I will never forget what I felt in that moment, and how then, just as now, there was no doubt in my mind that Casey had killed this beautiful little girl.

Two days after our visit to the ME's office, Dr. Garavaglia completed her autopsy. Based on DNA analysis and all the supporting evidence, she positively identified the remains as those of Caylee Marie Anthony. That afternoon, the remains were released to the Anthony family. The body of the little girl with the big brown eyes was delivered to a local funeral home, where Dr. Werner Spitz performed a second autopsy. The remains were then cremated, per the wishes of the Anthony family. Casey had signed some paperwork to allow her parents to determine the disposition, but the family's decision was unanimous. With that, Caylee was officially discharged to the care of the angels before she even had three years on earth.

CHAPTER THIRTEEN

THE SWAMP

The discovery of Caylee's remains altered the case on a fundamental level. Where there had been relative calm, with both sides feeling each other out, figuring out the right strategy, suddenly all that changed. In short, all hell broke loose.

The problems began with Roy Kronk, the man who found Caylee's body, but they didn't end there. From the start, Kronk was an issue for the prosecution. My feeling about Kronk was that it was no coincidence that he called 911 on December 11, 2008, to say that he had come across human remains in a swampy woods not far from the Anthonys' home. The pretrial conference had just commenced, and once again Casey Anthony, suspected child murderer, was the biggest "true crime" news story out there. Kronk had a female roommate who he later would say was obsessed with the case. She watched it all the time on television. December 11, 2008, was the day Jose Baez went before Judge Stan Strickland requesting more time to prepare the case and waiving the right to a speedy trial. What I suspect is that Kronk must have been back in the Chickasaw neighborhood that day reading meters, and because the Anthonys were in the news again, he basically went back to see if the bag he had seen in August was still there—and it was.

Ultimately, though, Kronk being attracted by the attention the case was getting was not the real problem; the problem was the information that he misrepresented and withheld from investigators. For starters, that December morning, when the investigators responding to Kronk's 911 call arrived at Suburban Drive, Kronk did not mention immediately that he had been to the site in August and had called 911 three times over three days to report a suspicious bag next to a white object that looked like a skull. Maybe he was trying to protect the sheriff's office from an obvious embarrassment, or maybe he was embarrassed that he had let Caylee's remains lie there for that extra four months. In any case, by temporarily withholding the fact that he'd been to that spot before, he set himself up for a lot of speculation that he was up to something nefarious, maybe even removing the body and bringing it back. It didn't matter that the physical evidence proved that to be impossible.

Furthermore, his actual story of finding the body, supposedly for the first time, on December 11, was riddled with inconsistencies. On the afternoon of the discovery, Kronk sat down with Yuri Melich to give a blow-by-blow account in a taped interview. He said he didn't touch or disturb anything beyond using his meter stick, which had a hooked end, to poke and lift the laundry bag high enough for the skull to drop out.

Recounting the details for Yuri, Kronk said, "I took my stick and I hit it and it thudded. And it sounded like either plastic or like, you know, hollow bone or something. And so I took my stick, which is curved for pulling meter boxes, and I grabbed the bottom of the bag and I pulled it. And I pulled it the second time and then, uhm, a human skull dropped out with hair around it and duct tape across the mouth. And I went, 'Oh, God,' and immediately came up and called my supervisor and then called Orange County Utilities and notified them that I had found human remains and that I needed the police."

It was a story that would have fit nicely in an episode of *CSI*, but the facts at the crime scene made it unbelievable. This version in which he takes a leak in the woods, sees a bag with bones in it, picks at the bag with his meter stick, and watches a skull roll out could not have happened. The physical evidence showed that the skull had vines and vegetation growing through and around it when it was collected. The forensic biologist would address that in his report. Kronk seemed to be embellishing his story, for whatever reason. Personally, I don't believe that the skull was touched or moved at all; I just wish he had been more candid in his story about what really happened on December 11.

This flawed version of events, along with the fact that he hadn't informed investigators about his trips to the same spot in August, became hugely problematic for everyone. Things grew only more confusing a few days later when Kronk finally admitted that he had been the one to make the three 911 calls to police that past August. When Kronk came clean about what he'd seen in August, he also voiced frustration that the deputy who had met him, Richard Cain, had barely taken him seriously and in fact had berated him, making him feel that he was wasting the officer's time.

On December 18, Deputy Richard Cain had some explaining to do. During Cain's interview with Corporal Yuri Melich and Sergeant John Allen, he claimed that Kronk told him he saw a bag in the woods and that it had bones in it.

"So, we enter the woods, I saw a bag, it was not a big bag, it was like a trash bag, like a leaf bag."

"What color?" Melich asked.

Cain said it was a black plastic bag. He then said he went into the woods, careful of his footing, stepping where he could without falling in the water. "I reached down, lifted the bag up. It was pretty heavy. But when I lifted it up, it tore, you know, the bottom. All leaves fell out, some sticks.

"I took my baton out, I kind of poked around. I didn't see anything. And I went back to Suburban." Cain claimed that Kronk was right behind him when he entered the woods.

That was not the way Kronk told it. On January 6, 2009, Corporal Mike Ruggiero talked to Kronk with the objective of evaluating Cain's conduct. There was a disconnect between Cain's and Kronk's stories about what happened when they met by Suburban Drive that day. Cain's account had both men traveling into the marshy area together to look around. Kronk's version had neither man venturing in, scared off by a six-foot diamondback rattler Kronk had photographed two days earlier. Kronk said that Cain gave him the brush-off, was doubtful that there was a skull, threw a cursory glance into the woods, and somewhat rudely dismissed Kronk and his find.

A second deputy, Kethlin Cutcher, was also questioned that same day about Kronk's August 13 call to police. He confirmed Kronk's story, saying that Deputy Cain was already exiting the swamp when he arrived and that Cain had told him it was just a bag of trash in the swamp. Deputy Cutcher never entered the wooded area, but he was able to see some "black plastic bags around." At first it was hard to know for sure what happened that day in August, but eventually, too many discrepancies in Cain's story made his account unravel. He finally agreed that neither he nor Kronk had gone into the swamp the day he met the meter man by his work truck on the afternoon of August 13. He was suspended from his duties for not investigating a lead properly, and had a disciplinary investigation pending when he put in his resignation with the Orange County Sheriff's Office.

EVEN THOUGH IT SEEMED AS if Kronk's version of the events was correct, the original issues with his story of finding the body were glaring, and—perhaps most unfortunately for both Kronk and us—they gave the defense an opening.

Throughout the case, the defense had been floating different theories about what had happened to Caylee. Kronk's inconsistencies gave them a totally new narrative to grab hold of. Suddenly Kronk might have had something to do with Caylee's death. Suddenly Kronk could have planted the body in the swamp in the fall of 2008, after Casey had been arrested. Suddenly the defense had a whole new argument to obscure things with.

Between Kronk's disingenuous behavior and his exaggerations, the skeptics had a field day. At every turn, Kronk was vilified and had to defend himself. However, as bad as he got it from the media, the pundits, and the bloggers, nothing was as bad as the blindsiding he endured at the hands of Jose Baez.

It wouldn't happen until nearly a year later because it took until November 2009 for the defense to set Kronk up for deposition. On November 19, 2009, Kronk appeared in our office accompanied by David Evans, a local attorney representing him. David had originally been hired for Kronk by the county because of all the media attention, but he stayed on pro bono. During the meeting, Kronk was deposed at length by Jose Baez, who inquired in very general terms about Kronk's past years in the Coast Guard, his marriage back in the 1990s, and his son by that relationship. The process continued until 4:30 P.M., when the defense team abruptly called it a day, saying they'd pick it up again later that week, date to be determined.

None of us thought anything of it, but when the deposition was over, Baez quickly walked over to the clerk's office and filed a motion in limine, which is a generic motion that asks for a pretrial ruling on the admissibility of certain evidence. He attached affidavits from Kronk's ex-wife and every woman he'd supposedly ever wronged, statements filled with nasty stuff about him—he was a terrible person; he was a liar; fifteen years before he had supposedly used duct tape to restrain a girlfriend after a fight. The filing even went so far as to quote his ex-wife's statement that Kronk's sister wouldn't let him be alone with her daughter, implying some suspicion on the sister's part.

Their intent was to file the documents moments before the court closed but in time for the media to get their hands on them for the five o'clock news. This was classic Baez, filing motions without telling the prosecution just in time for the evening news and making headlines out of irrelevant matters. We were convinced that the only reason he had filed this was to publicly discredit Kronk, to get people talking and thinking that he was shady enough to at least take a second look at.

I didn't learn of the scurrilous remarks about Kronk until the next morning when I opened the newspaper and read them. I had even *been* at the deposition and it was news to me. The defense was giving information to the media I believed that they knew would never be admitted at trial, but they were using the court to promote their media agenda. It was one of the most disgusting abuses of the court system I had ever seen.

Not one word of it had anything to do with the case. I may have had my own concerns about Kronk's credibility, but the guy didn't deserve that—nobody did. Support for my belief that their intention was merely to throw mud came more than a year later when the defense waived its right to a hearing on the admissibility of the nasty hearsay evidence. They didn't even try to defend the evidence once its media relevance had passed, and of course the judge excluded it.

In the end, we wouldn't call Kronk in the case—not because of his past, but because of his words and his alleged "character" issues. That he embellished his story on December 11 was very frustrating for us, so we decided not to use him as a prosecution witness. We did not want to be vouching for his credibility when we didn't believe him ourselves. It would have hurt us more to put him on the stand. Of course, there was a hundred miles between embellishing a story to make it look better and the ludicrous claim that he took the skull home for three months and then brought it back—a claim which the defense eventually made.

In exchange for his public embarrassment, Kronk did not end up with the money that he had expected to get. He did not collect the $50,000 offered by bounty hunter Leonard Padilla for Caylee's discovery, because he did not meet the procedural requirement that he initiate the tip with Crimeline. Mr. Kronk had called 911. He did get $5,000 from Mark NeJame, the local lawyer with one client or another attached to the case, for his effort. And he collected $20,000 from *Good Morning America* for his photograph of the six-foot rattler and an interview.

AS THE DEFENSE TRIED TO cloud Kronk in suspicion, the main counter-narrative they stuck to was that the body had been planted. As they laid it out, this premise was based on the fact that in the weeks after Caylee was reported missing, the area where the body was found had supposedly been thoroughly searched, but the remains had not been found. Therefore, they concluded, when the body was found in December within a quarter mile of the Anthony home, it must have been hauled there and planted. Roy Kronk was now their best scapegoat for such an action. Of course, there was no evidence to implicate Kronk beyond his questionable behavior upon finding the body, but the defense's story did highlight an important question that the discovery of Caylee's body revealed: how could her remains have gone unnoticed for so long in an area so close to the Anthonys' home?

Rife with the prerequisites for a good place to hide a body—such as an almost impenetrable air potato curtain obscuring the site from the road—the swamp off Suburban Drive should have been one of the first places checked. It had near-perfect conditions to promote decay, not to mention that its unappealing landscape was scattered with its share of household toss-offs—from old paint cans and beer bottles, to a half-submerged television, to various car parts, hubcaps, and batteries. Amid this mess of artifacts, the laundry bag shrouding the tiny body was in perfect suburban camouflage. Still, it should have been found, because the area should have been searched. But it wasn't. In the end, Murphy's Law prevailed: everyone assumed that someone else had searched there, but in fact no one actually had.

One of the first groups to face scrutiny following Kronk's discovery was Texas EquuSearch, the volunteer search and rescue organization founded by a man named Tim Miller and based in Dickinson, Texas. EquuSearch had dedicated a huge share of its resources to the Find Caylee Marie operation, sending more than forty-two hundred workers and volunteers to Orlando and eating up close to half its annual budget. According to the mission statement of the volunteer group, "We are committed to providing experienced, organized and ethical volunteer search efforts for missing persons, utilizing the most suitable and up-to-date technologies and methodologies." Beginning in late August 2008 and again in November, three months later, teams from this organization were actively searching vast areas of Orange and Osceola Counties. I recall seeing footage of their efforts on the news in early September of 2008.

EquuSearch hadn't been able to get their initial teams set up until a week or so after August 20, 2008, when a huge rain maker, Tropical Storm Fay, dumped massive amounts of water on us. When they finally began in late August 2008, there were certain areas that they simply could not search because of the standing water. I recall Miller saying in an interview that they were going to search those areas at a later date. In my opinion, those eleven inches of rain worked in Casey's favor. Sometimes even bad people have a guardian angel, for whatever reason, and I think Casey had one in that circumstance. When EquuSearch came back, they scoured different areas altogether and never returned to Suburban Drive. And furthermore, nobody knew that was the case. Everyone, including law enforcement, assumed that the most obvious place had to have been combed and given the all clear—which just goes to prove the old adage about what happens when you assume. Everybody ended up looking like an ass and a nation spent an extra four months searching around the country for a lost little girl who was a quarter mile from home.

The sheriff's office was equally piecemeal in their efforts. They totally botched Roy Kronk's three calls. His third call had gone so far up the tip line that it had reached Yuri Melich himself. A Detective White, who had the role of reviewing the tips as they came in and passing them along, brought the Suburban Drive tip from Kronk to Melich's desk, but Melich told him that the searchers had already completed a sweep of that area. The sheriff's office was relying on the expertise of Texas EquuSearch, but not actually checking up on them. We all assumed that EquuSearch's record keeping was better than it was, but they were only volunteers doing the best they could. The case had begun as a missing child investigation, with the sheriff's office looking for a living child. When they switched the effort from rescue to recovery, the sheriff's office investigators worked with tips, not grid searches or sweeps. In hindsight, relying solely on a volunteer organization for field searches was probably not the best idea.

Still, a fierce debate began to rage about whether EquuSearch had in fact searched and cleared that area. The stakes were high, because the defense was trying to substantiate their claim that the body had been placed there while Casey was in jail. If, in fact, EquuSearch had swept that area and okayed it while Casey was in custody, it would lend credence to the defense. Shortly after Caylee's remains were identified, the defense began an attempt to obtain the records of EquuSearch. By this point, Tim Miller was represented by Mark NeJame, who had previously represented the Anthonys. Initially, Baez wanted the names and personal information of every single searcher who had volunteered in this pursuit. NeJame thought that request was too broad and offered to provide the information related to the swamp area in question, which was initially agreeable to all parties.

Later on, in August of 2009, the defense would go on to boldly announce, for the benefit of the press, that they had found a hundred people who had searched that area off Suburban Drive while Casey was in jail and had not found Caylee's remains. A week later, we called their bluff and filed a motion asking the court to require them to produce the list of witnesses. We didn't mind if the list fell short of a hundred people; we just wanted names so that we could depose them. The court granted the motion and set a February 2010 deadline for the defense to provide it. That deadline came and went, but we didn't start to get names until late that year.

In the months following the discovery of Caylee, the defense began to contact some of the searchers for interviews. Shortly after Caylee's body was found, a searcher named Joe Jordan e-mailed the sheriff's office to say that he had searched an area on Suburban Drive, and she had not been there. That e-mail was not followed up on initially, but later investigators would learn that the area Jordan referred to in his e-mail was different from the one where Caylee was found. Regardless, the defense contacted Mr. Jordan for an interview, and a date was set.

Jordan was apprehensive, however. He later told police he'd been hearing rumors from other searchers that a private investigator hired by the defense to look into the records of the searchers was pressuring people to remember things the way he wanted them to. With this in mind, when Jordan agreed to meet with the defense investigators, it was at the office of a local attorney he'd hired, Kelly Sims. This was probably a smart move on his part, but his next decision was not so smart. Without telling even his own lawyer, he brought a concealed tape recorder into the interview and recorded the entire session. The only problem was that by doing so he was unwittingly committing a felony.

After the interview, Jordan contacted Corporal Eric Edwards at the sheriff's office, and during their discussion he volunteered the information that he had recorded the interview secretly. Realizing that Jordan had just confessed to a crime, Edwards told him to retain the tape and moved on to the content of the interview. Jordan told Edwards that at the meeting the investigator for the defense, Mortimer Smith, had shown Jordan a document purporting to be an EquuSearch form that supposedly demonstrated his participation in a search of the area off Suburban Drive near where Caylee was found. The document listed the team leader's name as Laura Buchanan. Jordan informed Edwards that in his opinion the document was not genuine and that the search it purported to document never happened. He also related that he had received a phone call earlier from a woman claiming to be in law enforcement in Kentucky who identified herself as Laura Buchanan. She insisted to him that she had searched the area where Caylee was found and found nothing and that he had been involved with her in the search.

The recording complicated that case a bit for us. Since it was illegal, we were not permitted by law to listen to it or know its contents. The detective could listen to it as part of his investigation into that offense, but we did not feel that we could. Investigators wanted very badly to inform us of the contents of the tape or to have us review it, because they felt it revealed something important about the defense's tactics, but we would not permit them to discuss it in our presence. To this day we have no idea what the tape contains. All parties involved in the conversation declined to prosecute Mr. Jordan, so the case was not pursued. The defense then took the position that they wanted to review the tape, but we informed them that if we let them do so, we would be committing a felony as well. They repeatedly attempted to get the court to order us to release it to them, but the judge read the statute the same way we did and it remained unheard.

As investigators and the defense moved on from Jordan, Laura Buchanan became the center of scrutiny. Buchanan was the Texas EquuSearch team leader who Jordan said had called him. At the time of the search, Buchanan, actually a housewife from Kentucky, had been in Orlando with her husband who was on a business trip, and she had volunteered with EquuSearch in the late August searches. She injected herself into the case having followed it on the news and not having much to do in Orlando while her husband was at his meetings. She said she was in possession of field documents proving that she had searched the Suburban Drive area on or around September 1, 2008. She had also searched Blanchard Park, where, according to Casey, Zanny and Caylee had been frequent visitors. Buchanan went so far as to say that she and Jordan had searched together. She claimed that they agreed that no one had sent them, but they decided to search there on their own. When Jordan was later shown a photograph of Buchanan, he did not recognize her.

With all of this back-and-forth, it was clear we needed to get Buchanan on the record. She was set for deposition in New Jersey, where she had recently moved. We were attempting to utilize some new technology that would enable us to take depositions over the Internet, so Buchanan was in the office of her attorney while the rest of us were in Florida. During the deposition the witness referenced the EquuSearch document that she claimed to have given to the defense's investigator, which listed all the people who had searched the area off Suburban Drive. She also referred to a photograph on which the investigator claimed she'd marked the spot she searched.

As usual, the defense had not provided either the document or the photograph to us. Buchanan and her attorney tried to fax the document, but the copy was so poor it was illegible. Buchanan went on to make the claim that she had seen the area where Caylee was found on TV and remembered searching that area, but her exact description of the area was a little vague, and precision was hampered by the technology we were using.

We agreed that she would have to be deposed again. During the period between the first and second depositions, we obtained a good copy of the document in question. The detectives then began investigating and speaking to the people on the list. Some of them told the police that while they did volunteer for EquuSearch, it was not on that day. Others said they remembered searching with Buchanan but not at Suburban Drive. Still another remembered searching Suburban Drive, but only the portion near the school—not where Caylee was found—because it was underwater at the time.

It was beginning to appear from the witnesses' statements that the field document Buchanan had produced had been altered, which commenced a criminal investigation against her. She was under scrutiny for perjury and interfering with a homicide investigation. The second deposition was reset at our offices in Orlando, and she appeared in person and represented by a new attorney. This time her attitude was far different. In reference to the EquuSearch document, her story was that she had found it under the seat of her car months after the search, and when the investigator, Mortimer

Smith, called for an interview, she'd made notes on the document of people she thought were with her. She claimed that she gave it to Smith without telling him she had altered it.

Though we found the explanation a bit hard to swallow, at least the defense's balloon had been burst. Not only did they not have a list of people who'd searched that area, but Buchanan also testified that while she had been in the area off Suburban Drive, she had not searched the exact area where Caylee had been found. Just like all the defense's theories, this one began to unravel as well. Ultimately, based upon her statements at her second deposition and the police investigation, no charges were brought against Buchanan.

Linda continued to depose other searchers that the defense had listed. The defense said that each had given a statement saying they had searched the area and found nothing, but as Linda spoke to them, all but one acknowledged that the area in question was underwater and was not searched. The only one who didn't fold completely was a gentleman who said that after a night of socializing at a sports bar he'd visited the scene. At three in the morning and by moonlight, mind you, he could swear that no remains were present.

In the end, the defense's earlier claim that there were a hundred searchers, as well as their subsequent claim that there had been a dozen, were both a big fizzle. It had taken hundreds of hours of investigator time and dozens of hours of depositions to confirm what the physical evidence told us to begin with: for almost six months little Caylee had lain in that spot while literally thousands of people had passed by, never knowing that they were within feet of her.

I'm not convinced that finding Caylee in mid-August instead of mid-December would have made much of a difference forensically. In either case the little girl would have been completely skeletonized. But emotionally, we all wished she hadn't had to lie there among discarded trash for even a moment when all those who knew her wanted her home—that is, everyone except perhaps Casey.

CHAPTER FOURTEEN

LIFE OR DEATH?

Although a large amount of evidence was collected at the crime scene, the ravages of weather, water, and nature had rendered most of it relatively useless. The worst conditions for preserving DNA or fingerprints involve heat and water, and in the more than six months Caylee was there, we had an overabundance of both. The recovery team left no stone unturned, though. Every scrap of garbage within the search radius was collected, cataloged, and stored, and ultimately most of it was sent to the lab.

The remains themselves told us the most. It is a credit to the folks at the sheriff's office, in the Florida Department of Law Enforcement, and on the FBI's Evidence Response Team that they were able to recover almost all of Caylee's bones, some of which were smaller than a dime because of her age. If a bone was large enough to be spotted by the investigator, it was photographed in position and its location recorded both on a diagram and by the placement of numbered flags at the precise location. The information was also entered into a software program called Total Station, which combined that information with a topographical survey of the area so that the precise orientation of any object to any other object could be determined with a keystroke.

Those bones that were too small or too buried to be detected visually were discovered by a sifting technique. First the search area was divided into approximately four-by-four-foot squares using a grid. Each square was given an alphanumeric designation. The ground cover was then removed to a designated depth and placed in buckets marked as to location and depth. The contents were then sifted through two levels of wire mesh. Any objects of interest were tagged and the bag labeled with location and depth information. The system was set up with the advice and assistance of Dr. John Schultz, an anthropology professor at the University of Central Florida and a contract consultant with Dr. G's office. As suspected bones were found, they were shown to Dr. Schultz at the site, since he was often participating in the search, or in his absence they were given to Steve Hansen, the ME investigator, during his daily visits to the scene. It was through this rigorous combination of techniques that they were able to recover Caylee's entire skeleton with the exception of some of the smaller bones of the foot. We were all very proud of the men and women who were so dedicated to showing Caylee the respect that she deserved, even in death.

Once Dr. G arrived on December 12, she began the process of examining the remains. Unfortunately, the tape had already been removed from the skull by the time she saw it. Dr. Utz had thoroughly documented the condition of the tape on the skull from every possible angle. The FBI was eager to send the skull to the lab for analysis, but in retrospect I wish they had been more patient and waited for Dr. G to see it for herself. As much as we try to use photos as a substitute, there is nothing like seeing something firsthand. We didn't get good pictures of how the pieces of tape were configured over one another, since all the pictures were taken either after the tape was separated, or to provide exact measurements of the total width of the pieces together. Not having better photos hindered us somewhat in arguing precisely how the tape was placed on Caylee's face. Who knows if it would have made a difference, but it was a source of frustration as we were deciphering all that we could from the remains.

Once Dr. G had a chance to examine the entire skeleton, she said it really didn't tell us much. It was free of any evidence of injury and looked like the skeleton of a perfectly healthy little girl, but it was from this skeleton that Dr. G was tasked with discerning both the manner and the cause of death.

There is a difference between the manner of death and the cause of death. The cause of death is a purely medical determination of the biological mechanism that causes the body to cease to function. In a suicide by gunshot wound to the head and a murder by the same method, the cause of death is the same. The manner of death is a medical and legal determination that the medical examiner (ME) is required to make based upon both medical and investigative information. In the example above, though the cause of death is the same, the manner of death is different, since one is a suicide and one is a murder. It is not unusual for the cause of death to be undetermined but the manner of death to be homicide—in fact, in most skeletal cases or cases where the body has been incinerated, that is likely to be the case.

Such was the situation with Caylee. Dr. G rendered the opinion that the manner of death was homicide, basing that judgment mostly upon the manner in which the remains were found and the actions of the mother, but when it came to the cause of death, medically it could not be determined. The only things found with the body that could have caused her death were the tape and the plastic bags. Either one would have been sufficient to cause suffocation, but the state of the body prevented us from medically determining which one might have played a direct role in the death. That determination would have to come from the jury applying their common sense to the evidence revealed in the photographs.

Ultimately, most of the information we obtained from the remains was based upon where the bones were found. Dr. Schultz was able to learn a good deal from the distribution of the bones, allowing us to say more definitively that an animal had indeed been involved in their dispersal. He explained that when the body decomposes, the connective tissue keeps certain body units together even as other units separate from each other. The torso may separate from the head and extremities but still maintain cohesion as a unit for a bit longer. As decomposition continues, the torso

itself will separate into its component parts as well, until all the connective tissue has decomposed, leaving the individual bones free to be moved
about separately. In our situation it was apparent to Dr. Schultz that an
animal had moved the torso as a unit from the primary site to a location
about ten feet away. All the ribs were found in that area. Since the vertebral
column would have been the last to break down, it was later dragged a few
feet farther away, where the remaining connective tissue decomposed, leaving all the vertebrae again in the same area.

More important than an animal's involvement was that this dispersal
gave a better sense of the time period involved. Because of the way the
animal(s) had moved the body parts, Dr. Schultz felt that the body had
been placed where it was at some point during the decomposition process
but while the body was intact. His opinion was that the body could have
been completely skeletonized in as little as two weeks after death and most
certainly was only bones within a month, a time frame that sent Casey's
thirty-one days of lies shooting back into all of our minds.

One bone in particular was of interest to him in dating the placement
of the body. One of Caylee's hip bones was found several feet away from the
primary site. It had evidence of animal damage and was found up against
a palmetto trunk, buried in four inches of muck. For those not familiar
with the term, *muck* is the product of decomposing vegetation. It occurs
when the vegetation is somewhere between being identifiable as what it was
and being actual soil. When an area like the swamp off Suburban Drive
floods, this fine debris mixes with the water, and as the water recedes, it
leaves behind a layer of the fine debris in the form of muck. It is less dense
than soil, and in swamps it can be several feet deep. Occasionally, in an
extremely dry period, it can catch fire underground, which is what we call
a "muck fire." The fact that the bone was buried in muck meant that it had
been deposited in that spot before the rains of summer and in particular
before Tropical Storm Fay in August, which allowed the muck to settle
over the bone. Based upon his estimate of the time for decomposition and
dispersion of the bones, he placed the date of deposit of the remains in late
June or early July.

Dr. David Hall, a retired professor from the University of Florida and a renowned expert in forensic botany, was called to the scene to examine the plants growing in the area where the remains were found. He was also sent photographs of the remains and the items found with them. Dr. Hall noted significant plant root growth into some of the bones. The mass of Caylee's hair that had fallen around the skull was inundated with both small and large roots. Significant root growth could also be found in the baby blanket, laundry bag, and trash bag found with her. He issued an initial report expressing his opinion that the root growth through the items found with the remains would have taken at least four to six months. This was my first time dealing with forensic botany, so I was eager to meet Dr. Hall and explore his opinions further.

In February 2009, Linda, Frank, and I took a road trip to Gainesville to meet with a number of the experts we had working on the case. The University of Florida, my alma mater, has always been a valuable resource for prosecutors in the state of Florida. Over the course of this case, we would consult experts associated with the university in botany, toxicology, anthropology, hydrology, and law. We met Dr. Hall at his home in what appeared to be an older residential area not too far off one of the main roads past the university. His home sat on a multi-acre plot that could only be described as a botanical garden. Let's just say it made my meager attempts at landscaping look like a dying potted plant. He gave us a tour of the grounds, which included his own private swamp on part of the property. All of the plants were beautiful native vegetation. You could tell that botany was not only this man's profession, it was also his life.

Dr. Hall may have been retired and looked every bit the grandfatherly figure he had sounded over the phone, but his life was anything but that of a typical retiree. Between lectures, teaching, writing, and consulting, he had a full plate, and we appreciated the time he took with us. Taking us into a wood-paneled room that served as his library and office, he pushed aside the project he was working on—a treatise on some botanical issue I couldn't possibly understand—and sat us near his desk.

He explained to us that when a human body is in the process of decomposition, the fluids released are actually toxic to plants. If you were to find a body in the middle stages of decomposition, you would find the grass underneath it dead. The importance of that in this case was that the root growth wouldn't begin until the body was completely skeletonized, meaning that his four- to six-month time frame would have to be tacked on to Dr. Schultz's two to four weeks for decomposition. That was putting us right about the time Caylee was last seen.

He candidly admitted that there were no published studies on root growth rates that could apply to this issue; his opinions were based upon five decades of studying and working with plants, not on specific documentation. But looking at the man who sat before me and at the lush grounds of his home, I was confident that his opinion would be enough.

With the plant issue settled, we moved on to the insects. When forensic etymologist Dr. Neal Haskell completed his evaluation of the insect evidence at the crime scene, it also dovetailed with Caylee's body being deposited in the swamp during that midsummer period. Dr. Haskell discovered something else interesting as well, but to explain it I have to talk a little about bugs.

When a human body goes through the process of decomposition, it passes through a number of stages that involve different chemical processes. These five stages are referred to as *fresh, bloat, active decay, advanced decay,* and *dry remains*. I will spare you the disgusting details of each stage, but suffice it to say that different insects are attracted to remains at different stages of this process. At each stage the insect will deposit eggs in the remains, which will then hatch and consume the remains to support its maturation. Once mature, the insect will repeat the cycle. Each stage of that evolution leaves behind some remnant that etymologists can interpret. The first insects to be attracted to fresh remains are referred to as *early colonizers*.

What interested Dr. Haskell at the scene was what he *didn't* find. Had the body been placed in the swamp shortly after death, he would have expected to find evidence of large colonies of early colonizers. Instead he found evidence of very few, and though there had been both flies and maggots in the trunk, these fell into a separate category from the early colonizers that Haskell expected to find. What this indicated was that the remains had been stored in some other location and then moved to the swamp after a few days of decomposition. Even if the body had just been moved from one open area to another, he still would have expected to see evidence of early colonizers from the location. The only conclusion to draw was that wherever Caylee had been, the early colonizers had difficulty getting to her—like, say, if she were in the trunk of a car sealed in multiple plastic bags.

ASIDE FROM THE SCENE, THE items found with the body couldn't tell us much scientifically. Most of their value for us lay in our ability to connect them to the Anthony home and Casey. Investigators had obtained a warrant to search the Anthony house on December 11, the day Caylee was found, and returned again nine days later on December 20. The list of items they were searching for included shoes belonging to Casey Anthony; the original clothing Caylee had been wearing when George last saw her—a pink top, blue jean skirt, white shoes, backpack with a monkey design, and white-rimmed sunglasses; doll clothing that would fit the doll recovered from the Pontiac Sunfire; small plastic toy horses similar to one that had been found at the crime scene; and any prescription drugs, including amphetamines and narcotics.

Every scrap of plastic bag collected at the scene—and there turned out to be over three hundred of them—was tested for prints with no result. The duct tape and laundry bag tested similarly. No surprise there, given the abundance of water and heat, but they were checked anyway. Still, there was a consensus among all of us that the duct tape held a great deal of forensic potential.

When the duct tape arrived at the FBI laboratory, a decision had to be made about where to send it first. The condition of the tape was so poor that most of the adhesive was gone and much of the fabric layer had separated from the plastic. The general opinion was that there was virtually no chance of any DNA being found on the tape. As destructive as heat and moisture are to fingerprints, they are twice as destructive to DNA. The decision was made that the tape would go first to the latent print section to be photographed, then to the Trace Evidence Unit for removal of any adhering hairs or fibers, and finally to the Chemistry Unit for comparison of this sample of tape to that on the gas can.

The task of initially examining and photographing the tape fell to Elizabeth Fontaine, a fairly new examiner. One of the processes used in searching for fingerprints is to inspect the object using different wavelengths of light, some of which are beyond the human visual spectrum. During these examinations she observed no fingerprints, but she did notice a peculiar artifact on the tape, residue that appeared to be in the shape of a small heart. She would describe it as similar in appearance to what you would see after removing a Band-Aid that had been on your skin for a period of time: as if dirt had adhered to the residue of adhesive. She dutifully noted it in her report and showed it to her supervisor. Since there was no policy in place about photographing nonprint impressions, she did not photograph it, and instead she passed the tape along to trace. When trace returned it, she proceeded to the next stages of processing, using various chemicals to enhance otherwise invisible prints. The additional methods met with negative results as expected.

When news of the heart-shaped impression reached investigators, they asked Fontaine to try and photograph the impression. Unfortunately, by the time the attempts were made, the impression could no longer be detected. In an attempt to record the impression, the tape was diverted to Lori Gotesman, a documents examiner, to see if she could do anything with it. She was also unable to visualize the impression.

A big part of the investigators' interest in the heart-shaped residue was that a red heart sticker had been found at the crime scene on a piece of cardboard some distance from the primary site, a find that had raised eyebrows. Indeed, for this reason, among the list of items on the search warrant when investigators entered the Anthony house had been scrapbooking and arts and crafts supplies. The searchers did find a roll of heart stickers in Casey's room that were of similar size to the one found at the crime scene.

Despite the lack of clear connection to the Anthony home, this concept of the heart sticker resonated, both in the media and with investigators. It was a disturbing image, and combined with Fontaine's heart-shaped residue findings, it suggested a surprising possibility: someone, presumably Caylee's killer, had placed the heart sticker on the duct tape over her mouth.

· · ·

INVESTIGATORS CONTINUED TO SEARCH FOR a way to connect the Anthony home to the crime scene, and so the next step was to compare the tape at the crime scene to the tape from the gas can. The chemical comparison of the tapes from the scene and the gas can revealed that they were identical in composition and were manufactured the same way.

After those analyses were completed, it was determined that DNA testing should be attempted no matter how improbable, but in the end it only further muddied the waters. A foreign DNA profile was found on the sticky side of the tape that did not match any of the known samples submitted in the case. In addition, the opposite side of the tape had an indication of a very minuscule amount of DNA that was different both from that on the sticky side and from all known samples in the case. After testing the DNA of all those who had examined the tape, it was determined that the DNA matched examiner Lori Gotesman, the documents examiner, and the other trace was accounted for by a second examiner from the Chemistry Unit. The ability of DNA testing to detect extremely small amounts of DNA is both a blessing and a curse. Contamination, as hard as one might try to prevent it, is a fact of life. Forensically insignificant, but embarrassing to the FBI.

The last examination of the tape was done by Karen Lowe, the hair and fiber analyst who had originally examined the hairs from Casey's car. Lowe's report threw us for a bit of a loop. She compared the fibers in the tape found on the remains to the fibers in the tape from the gas can. Shockingly, even though the logos matched precisely, the fibers themselves did not match. The report said that the fabric portion of the tape from the scene was composed of only polyester fibers, while the tape from the gas can was cotton and polyester. After reading those words, I was quickly on the phone with Karen. I knew that the cotton in Caylee's shirt had completely decomposed, leaving only the lettering and the elastic collar. If that cotton had decomposed, wouldn't the same have happened to the cotton in the tape?

From the product information we'd received from the tape's distributor, it appeared that the tape was made only with both polyester and cotton. It did not appear that they manufactured tape using just polyester, but we didn't know for sure. I questioned Karen on the phone about the possibility of decomposition affecting the comparison, and she seemed unimpressed with the idea, but when I suggested that she call the manufacturer to determine whether the tape had ever been made with only polyester, she did not seem willing to investigate the matter more fully. It took me six months, a dozen calls, and actually sending a sample of the tape to the manufacturer to establish what I'd been suspecting since I first read Lowe's report: the tape from the crime scene had originally been manufactured as a cotton/ poly blend, and the cotton had merely decomposed. As such, it was a match to the tape from the gas can.

The duct tape was the smoking gun, or as close to it as we were going to get. It was the primary piece of evidence that led me to the firm conviction that Casey had committed premeditated murder. In my opinion, its position over the nose and mouth was no coincidence; it was murder. The jawbone being in the position it was, anatomically correct on the skull, proved this. For the jawbone to stay in place after decomposition, the tape had to be there before the decomposition began.

Part of interpreting a crime scene is eliminating things that don't make sense. You hope to convince jurors to use their common sense as well. So is there any reason someone would put duct tape over the nose and mouth of a *dead* child? Only if someone wants to make it look like a murder. But why would anyone want to do that?

People don't make accidents look like murder unless they are covering something up. If Caylee had died accidentally and Casey didn't want to take any responsibility, maybe Casey thought staging a murder that could be blamed on Zanny or a stranger could get her off the hook. That way, she'd be able to argue that someone else had abducted Caylee, suffocated her with duct tape, and dumped her in the swamp. But why do that, since the accident wasn't a crime?

Still, I didn't really buy her using the duct tape as a cover-up. In my mind, the only reason there was duct tape on Caylee's nose and mouth was to keep her from breathing. Preventing someone from breathing means premeditation, plain and simple. When I thought it through, it was the only reason that made sense to me.

College of the Ouachitas

There was one rather odd item of evidence from the scene. About a foot from Caylee's remains was a red Disney World bag. Neither the bag nor its contents was ever tied to anyone involved in the case, but they're odd enough that they bear mentioning. Inside the bag was a Gatorade bottle with a murky translucent liquid inside. When the bottle was opened at the lab, also found inside the bottle were a syringe and its wrapper. The liquid contents of the bottle were tested and found to be consistent with a cleaning product that contained trace amounts of chloroform. Dr. Michael Rickenbach, who had separately confirmed Dr. Vass's findings of chloroform in the trunk of Casey's car, attributed the chloroform in the bottle to a component of the cleaner.

Even odder was that the liquid, in small amounts, and the syringe showed the presence of four testosterone compounds. When I received Dr. Rickenbach's report, I did a little Internet research and discovered that the combination of compounds was found in a male hormone supplement that a young man might take to enhance muscle mass or an older one might be prescribed as a hormone supplement that is available legally only by prescription. I tried to trace the syringe through the manufacturer, but the items could not be tracked to the direct purchasers. We wondered if maybe it was tied to something George had been prescribed, but we found no evidence of it. Just a big ole red herring. Still don't have any idea how it got there or if it was related, but I sure would like to know.

The final items were Caylee's bones and hair. There was the formal matter of identification to be determined. One of the bones was transported to the FBI lab, where a portion of the marrow was removed and tested. The results were compared with a DNA test that had been performed on Caylee's toothbrush a month before as well as with Casey's genetic profile. A positive identification was made: the remains in the woods were Caylee Marie Anthony.

That would appear to be the end of the forensics on the crime scene, but sometimes peculiar things can be found in looking deeper into test results. For purposes of elimination, DNA samples were taken from Cindy, George, and Lee Anthony. Having done as many of these as I have, I am able to read and compare the profiles pretty well. The cops had always wondered if Lee or George was Caylee's father. They like to think the worst of people sometimes, and their opinion of the Anthonys was not great anyway. One look at the DNA profiles and I assured them there was no way. I had in the past been involved in two cases where these types of elimination tests of relatives had exposed some unpleasant surprises to men who thought they were the father of someone they weren't. One, tragically, was the father of a seventeen-year-old girl who had been murdered. Ever since then, I'd gotten in the habit of checking these things.

When I looked at Casey's profile, she checked out as the child of George and Cindy. Likewise, neither George nor Lee was Caylee's father.

Caylee's hair was the last to be examined. When it arrived, Karen Lowe was out of the lab so the case was assigned to Stephen Shaw, another hair and fiber analyst. The hairs on the body matched the hair from the trunk, in length, color, and microscopic characteristics, and they both had the death band. The only difference was that the hair from the swamp showed more advanced decomposition—after all, it had been there for almost six months.

EVEN THOUGH WE DIDN'T LEARN volumes from the remains, their discovery impacted every aspect of our case—especially our decision to seek the death penalty. Once Caylee's remains were found and analyzed, we had to make a sober assessment of the story the evidence was telling us and readdress the penalty issue.

A couple of months earlier, our decision not to seek the death penalty had been based largely on the fact that we did not have a body and didn't know exactly how Caylee had died. The discovery changed our decision on every level. A lot has been said about the decision to seek the death penalty, both before and after the trial. The death penalty is a visceral issue, and oftentimes it may feel as if the decision to seek the death penalty is made viscerally. Nothing could be further from the truth, no matter how horrific the crime. There are always arguments on both sides, but in the end the decision is always reached after we've weighed every aspect of the case. Such was the case with our eventual decision to pursue the death penalty against Casey Anthony.

In terms of the discussions that went into making this decision, the story behind those belongs to State Attorney Lawson Lamar. Lawson made the final decision and as such it was his to reveal as he saw fit. The questions he asked during our discussions and the answers we gave are kept in confidence. At the end of the day, only he knows why he made the decision that he did. I do, however, think I can help the public understand how the decision was reached by sharing my thought process.

First, consider the law. By Florida law, the death penalty is a possible sentence for any first-degree murder. But before the penalty can be imposed, certain additional factors must be present, and these were the factors that we considered when first making the death penalty decision prior to finding the remains. These factors are called "aggravating circumstances." They are very specific and precisely laid out in Florida's death penalty statute. Some circumstances depend upon facts about the victim: was she a young child, elderly and infirm, or a police officer or government official? Some deal with the issue of why the crime was committed: was it for financial gain, to eliminate a witness, or to disrupt the functioning of government? Some relate to how the crime was committed: was it committed during another felony, was it coldly planned in advance, was it torturous and cruel, involving conscious suffering by the victim? The last group of circumstances looks at the defendant's criminal record: was the defendant ever in prison, on probation, or does he or she have a past history of conviction for violent crimes?

There are certain cases in which, while the defendant may be guilty of first-degree murder, none of the aggravating circumstances are present. The death penalty can never be applied to these people. There are other defendants whose cases are so horrendous that the death penalty must always be an option. For those in the middle of the spectrum, it is not merely the existence of the aggravating circumstances that must be considered, but the weight of them.

Over the decades, our courts have refined both the definitions of the aggravating circumstances and the concept of weighing. They teach us that not all aggravating circumstances are given the same weight. For example, if a murder is committed during the commission of another felony, as in the course of a robbery, it is weighted far less heavily than a contract killing, coldly planned and executed. While it may seem odd to use such subjective criteria in the context of a legal determination that could result in a guilty person losing his or her life, it is the process mandated by the statute.

In addition, when deciding if going after the death penalty is appropriate, there is a vital linguistic distinction to be made. The media likes to use the phrase "the state is seeking the death penalty." When making the decision about whether to pursue the death penalty, the prosecution sometimes adopts a similar shorthand. More properly put, what we do is decide that the jurors should be allowed to consider the death penalty as an option based upon their individual interpretations of the facts. In other words, we say, "This case merits giving the jury the option of a death sentence." That distinction is particularly important in this case. None of us presumed to decide what Casey's fate should be. I have had cases in the past that were so egregious that I felt justice could be served only by a sentence of death, but I did not feel that way here. The real question for us was whether *we* should decide her fate, or allow a jury to make that determination. For that assessment, we must look to the facts.

It was against the backdrop of this body of law that we analyzed Casey's case. So what could a juror take from these facts? First, as to the category dealing with the victim, it seemed clear to us that Caylee was a child who'd been killed by her mother. That alone was an aggravating circumstance all by itself, but according to my interpretation of the case law, it was unlikely to be of sufficient weight to sustain the death penalty. I know many may be shocked by that comment, but in weighing the factors, we look to how common that type of crime is and how it is generally treated, a process the court refers to as "proportionality." Regrettably, infanticide is not that rare, and as such, it almost never results in the death penalty. So while that factor is entitled to some weight, it is not sufficient by itself. This was why we'd been unable to seek the death penalty prior to the discovery of the remains.

The new information we had to take into account concerned the remains and the condition in which they were found. I believed that if a juror saw in those photographs what I saw—three pieces of duct tape covering the nose and mouth of a two-and-a-half-year-old child—he or she would conclude that little Caylee was suffocated. "Suffocation while conscious" is considered by the court an unnecessarily torturous way to die. The physical pain and fear involved is unimaginable, and for a small child, unthinkable. So, if the jury were to believe that Caylee died by suffocation while she was conscious, then there would be two aggravating circumstances present, which would be in line with other death penalty cases the court had addressed in the past.

Of course, if the jury were to find that Caylee was unconscious at the time the tape was applied, then the "torture" aggravator would not apply. But why would she be unconscious? There were no skull fractures, so there was no evidence that she was rendered unconscious by blows to the head. How about the chloroform? The chemical element had been found in the trunk of the car and the word "chloroform" in Casey's hard drive searches. Yes, a jury could conclude that Casey knocked her out with chloroform and then applied the tape to humanely dispatch her daughter. If so, then the "torture" aggravator also would not apply, but the cold planning and premeditation could. So either way, we would be back to two aggravating circumstances and sufficient weight to justify death, if the jury should so choose.

Having determined the existence of aggravation, we must then look to mitigation, which generally examines the defendant's past: any mental health history or any surrounding context for the reason or the manner in which the crime was committed. To this point, we have still been given nothing to indicate that Casey suffered from any mental illness or personality disorders, other than appearing a bit of a psychopathic narcissist (just my opinion—not a professional diagnosis). So none of the mental illness mitigating factors applied. If the defendant has no criminal conduct in the past, this also would be considered mitigating, but since Casey had stolen money from her mother, her grandmother, and her friend Amy, that behavior ruled out "no prior criminal behavior."

Mitigation can also come from general factors in one's background, such as childhood deprivations or abuse. These are common family histories put forth as mitigating circumstances, but Casey's early interviews with the psychologists ruled those out. From all available evidence, not to mention Casey's own words to that point, she appeared to have been raised in a loving middle-class home, experienced no abuse of any kind, and been given every opportunity in life that her parents could manage to supply. I am sure the defense would dispute this, they always do. But it appeared to us that there was no obvious mitigation. Once that analysis was complete, it was clear that the death penalty would have been lawful under a view of the evidence that the jury could reasonably have taken.

Aside from the legal issues, there are practical issues to consider as well. A case in which the death penalty is sought involves a substantial expenditure of public resources, so my feeling has always been that, as with any other prosecution decision, the cost must be weighed. Any lawyer must consider the cost to his client of pursuing a course of action versus the potential for success. I believe all public officials who have the power to spend the public's money should take into account how much it is going to cost the taxpayers. However, it cannot be the driving force in any decision. Justice doesn't have a price. The two must be balanced.

Casey Anthony's case was a tough one for me to balance. On the one hand, the death penalty had been considered by juries in three cases that involved the murders of children by caretakers in my thirty years in the office. But all the defendants had been men, with prior criminal records. The jury voted for life in all three of those cases. The juries in our circuit have never given death to a caregiver who had killed a child. On the other hand, none of the caregiver defendants had planned and premeditated a murder, as we were intending to claim in the death of Caylee. While there had been other cases where mothers had planned and carried out the murders of their children, the mothers always presented pretty clear evidence of psychological and emotional problems, which were not present with Casey.

The most frustrating part of the analysis was that in reality, the issue that would most probably be in the minds of the jurors would be the very one they should *not* be considering: that Casey was an attractive, middle-class Caucasian girl. I believe you must always do a gut check in a decision of this kind and ask yourself, "Would my decision be different if the defendant were X and not Y?"

How would the jury view this if Casey were a father and not a mother? How about if she were African-American or Hispanic? What if she were poor or extremely wealthy? In the end, I concluded that under any circumstance, the death penalty could be lawfully sought in good faith. But based upon my experience, the odds of the jury actually voting to recommend it were exceedingly small. Ultimately, the decision of the state attorney was to go forward and let the jury decide. Since I was convinced we were on solid legal footing, and we were going forward in good faith, I was ready to proceed.

Ever since that decision was made and certainly in the aftermath of the trial, some second-guessers have claimed that Lawson should not have reintroduced the death penalty to the case, saying that its potential put a cloud over this case that might have impacted the outcome. To me, that position is more about people trying desperately to find something to say we did wrong, and I think it's highly unfair to Lawson. This jury had plenty of options that would have assured Casey's punishment short of death. First, they were told time and again that it would be their recommendation that would control her fate in the end. They were also given multiple options for lesser penalties, including offenses that could never have involved death. As a result, I have no difficulty in expressing my opinion that nothing in this case would have been different if death had not been an option.

At the same time, I've spent the last two and half years debating the issue of the death penalty in this case, and despite the multitude of reasons that I felt that a jury *could* have given the death penalty, I always came back to the reality that they never actually *would*. Lawson's decision was to allow the jury to decide, and I respect him for making it. Personally, I think I would have been happier if the death penalty had not been reintroduced into the case, even though on some level I think Casey may have deserved it. Simply put, I just didn't think the jury would go there. Later on, when we were picking the jury, I chose to keep a juror I liked, even though he was opposed to the death penalty. At that time, I remember saying to Frank, "it isn't going to matter, because she is not going to get it anyway."

SOME MONTHS AFTER THE DECISION was made, the defense challenged our legal basis for seeking the death penalty. The law is clear in Florida that absent a showing of "bad faith" on the part of the prosecution, the court may not second-guess the decision to proceed. *Bad faith* is defined in such a way that it is virtually impossible to prove, absent a blatant statement by the prosecutor showing that he or she is proceeding based solely upon racial or other unconstitutional considerations. We responded to the defense's challenge by citing the legal precedents on the issue, which prohibited the judge from forcing us to defend our decision.

Leading up to that challenge, the defense had been hitting us pretty hard in their statements to the media on this issue. We had made an office-wide decision not to comment during the pendency of the case, because we felt that silence was our obligation under the rules of ethics. However, I suggested to Linda that if they wanted to know why we were seeking death, I would give them the reasons in open court. And I was looking forward to it.

I spent a great deal of time drafting what I wanted to say. I wanted to make sure that my comments respected the presumption of innocence, but I still laid it out so that it would be understood in clear and certain terms why we felt the death penalty was a warranted option. I prefaced these comments with the caveat reminding all who would hear me that the defendant was presumed innocent.

"Caylee was almost three when she died with duct tape over her nose and her mouth," I began. "Any child of that age should have had the physical ability to remove the duct tape covering her airway and preventing her from breathing, and the evidence in this case would show that Caylee was, if not average, above average in that regard. A juror might conclude, then, that she must have been restrained, either chemically or physically. If chemically restrained, her killer prepared some substance in advance that would render her physically unable to resist, administered the substance and awaited its effect, and then methodically applied three pieces of duct tape to completely cut off the flow of air through her mouth or her nose and let nature take its course.

"At least Caylee wouldn't have had any fear," I continued. "How would the jurors apply those facts to the law that the court would give them? If she was physically restrained, her killer would have to restrain her arms by some means, applying tape while she was conscious as her killer looked into her face. Maybe her killer even saw her eyes as the tape was applied.

"First, one piece; then two; then three, so that no breath was possible. Could Caylee have understood what was happening to her? Did she try to resist? Could her killer see the fear in her eyes as the tape was applied?

"These are questions only the jurors will be able to answer in this case. One thing we do know is this: If we have gotten to this stage, those same jurors have already decided that the face that Caylee Anthony saw in those final moments of her life was her mother's face. Anyone who contends that no juror could find that these conclusions call for a sentence of death is only fooling himself."

As I was reading these remarks, the courtroom was silent as a tomb; all I could hear were movements at the defense table. Casey was in the courtroom when I read my remarks, but I was looking directly at Judge Strickland. I was told by observers that she had a dramatic reaction to my comments, so I reviewed the video of the hearing later. At the beginning of my statement and through the portion where I referenced someone administering the chemical substance, Casey looked angry. Her jaw locked in a scowl. Jose then leaned over and rather forcefully whispered something to her. Within five seconds, her demeanor changed. She began to shake her head no and cried, then continued crying for the remainder of my remarks.

In my opinion, for those first few minutes we saw the real Casey Anthony, the one who was angry with me for telling the truth. The transformation from that Casey Anthony to the crying, grieving mother was amazing to me, but it didn't compare to the performances we would see in the years to come.

———

CHAPTER FIFTEEN

LYING TO THEMSELVES

While Caylee's remains impacted everyone involved with the case in different ways, no one was more upset than George and Cindy Anthony. The find confirmed all their worst fears: their precious granddaughter was not missing, she was dead, and making matters worse, now more than ever before the finger appeared to point to Casey.

It didn't take long for us on the prosecution to begin speculating about how George and Cindy would react to the news. For so long, everything about their public personas had been singularly devoted to the idea that Caylee was alive. Now that everyone knew for sure that she was dead, none of us could say how that would change George and Cindy's attitude toward their daughter. Our hope was that they would suddenly wake up to the reality of the situation and choose Caylee over Casey. Of course that was a pretty small hope.

While law enforcement was searching their home on December 11, Cindy and George had just stepped off a plane from Los Angeles where they'd been guests on *Larry King Live* the previous evening. They'd used the appearance to proclaim that Caylee was still alive and to criticize inves-

tigators for persecuting Casey. When they landed, they were whisked away
to the Ritz Carlton Hotel in Orlando, which was paid for by an unknown
benefactor. While searchers with warrants combed through their home
for evidence, they joined Jose Baez and a few other supportive people for
dinner at the hotel restaurant. The search proceeded smoothly.

Our first indication that little in their attitude was going to change
occurred when the searchers returned to their house on December 20, and
the Anthonys were borderline hostile. They were annoyed at the mess and
chaos the prior search had caused, but more importantly, they seemed angry
that now Casey was the only suspect. As far as they were concerned, yes,
Caylee was dead, but their daughter didn't do it. The search had brought
the investigation to their doorstep, but they were still of the opinion that a
stranger had killed their precious angel.

Over the next several months, we prepared for the depositions of
Cindy, Lee, and George. The stretch of time seemed only to entrench
their attitudes. During those months, both Cindy and George remained
obstinate toward the investigators and the prosecution. Cindy continued to
make statements about Casey's innocence or offer her latest theory about
what was going on. Ultimately, we didn't speak with Cindy directly until we
scheduled a deposition with her during the summer of 2009.

On July 28, 2009, Cindy was at our office for a deposition. She came
with Brad Conway, the lawyer who was now representing her, and the usual
additional parties were present. Cindy had been subpoenaed, so she had to
come, and while she was obligated to answer our questions, she had immunity for herself if she said anything incriminating. But that did not mean
that anyone else was protected from what she said.

From the start of the deposition it was pretty clear that Cindy's
demeanor was largely the same as it had been over the previous year. She
remained in denial. Although at least this time she was willing to admit
some of Casey's shortcomings—lying, stealing, and so forth—she still
could not confront the reality of Casey's behavior. She stuck with her story
that Casey was a good mom and they were the best of friends, even telling
us how, the night before Caylee went missing, the three of them curled up
on the sofa together to watch TV.

Linda led the questioning. She began by asking Cindy about her well-being, and Cindy responded that she hadn't had a full night's sleep in a year, since Caylee went missing. She had slept four hours the night before, so that was good, she said. Cindy then gave us her biography. She was fifty-one, born and raised in Warren, Ohio, not far from the Pennsylvania border. She had three older brothers: Dan, Gary, and Rick. She was the only girl and the baby of the family. She went to three years of nursing school, graduating as an RN. She first specialized in pediatrics, and later orthopedics. She met George when he came to visit his sister at Trumbull Memorial Hospital, where his sister was one of her patients.

The two were married in a church wedding in Niles, Ohio, in 1981. The marriage was Cindy's first, George's second. George was seven years older than she. He was a detective with the Trumbull County Sheriff's Office, working in the homicide division. He eventually reached the rank of deputy sheriff. After thirteen years of service, he left the force at Cindy's urging. He was getting hurt a lot, and friends of his had even been killed. The job was dangerous: "car accidents, and people throwing bricks through windows, and things like that," she said.

George briefly joined his father in the family car business, Anthony's Auto Sales, before he became a proprietor of his own dealership. In 1989 the family relocated to Orlando. George's business was dissolving, and Cindy used the chance to be near her parents, who had recently moved to Mount Dora, Florida. Lee was seven and Casey was three. She chose Orlando because she thought it would have lots of job opportunities for both of them. Her job at Gentiva Heath Services, where she still worked, began in 2002. She managed a caseload of 120 patients.

Linda brought the questioning back to Casey, Caylee, and the recent past. We noticed that Cindy told the truth about all the important stuff that connected Caylee's body to the house. In fact, she went on to tell us that the duct tape from the house, which matched the tape on the body, had been used at a command post that was established to coordinate getting the word out about Caylee during the days and weeks after they discovered she was missing. This tip about the duct tape would later lead us to a TV news video that showed the same unique Henkel logo on duct tape that had been used to post a "missing child" flyer of Caylee. The ironies in the case never cease to amaze me.

Cindy's helpfulness in the deposition didn't last long, though, once we got to the search for chloroform on the home computer.

"All right. There is a search for how to make chloroform on your desktop computer," said Linda. "Did you make that search?"

"I'm not sure," Cindy replied.

"Why not?"

"Because I remember looking up chlorophyll back in March of last year, and I am not sure if I looked up chloroform as well. I looked up alcohol and several other things like ethyl alcohol and peroxide, too."

"Why?" Linda asked.

"I was researching things that—as far as the chlorophyll—and possibly chloroform—because of my animals. Because my cocker—or my Yorkies—would eat a lot of bamboo leaves and I know there's chlorophyll in those leaves and they were getting sick, quite sick.

"And I had previously lost two cocker spaniels, and I wanted to see if there was any tie. I had never thought about that with the cancer and stuff that I lost the cocker, so I started researching different things."

"Do you believe that you could have accidentally looked up how to make chloroform?" Linda asked.

"Chloroform. I may have looked up the ingredients, but not how to make it."

"Okay," Linda paused. "What did you learn about chlorophyll?"

"It can make an animal sick, but it wasn't—it didn't have, like, drowsiness effects and things that I was concerned with. It did not."

When Linda started asking her how she spelled *chlorophyll,* she stammered, and Baez got involved. Linda handed her a piece of paper and Cindy proceeded with the exercise by spelling it out in longhand.

"C-h-l-o-r-o-p-h-i-l," she wrote.

At this point my reaction was "You've got to be kidding me." Of all the stories we'd heard since this began, this was the lamest one yet. It amazed me that she was being truthful about things that really implicated Casey but then helping her out about something so stupid. It seemed rather desperate. Linda, being the wonderfully tenacious attorney that she is, sensed that the truth was slipping away. She zeroed in on the time of day that Cindy would have done the search. "Now, this computer search you did for chlorophyll . . . what time of day would that have been done?"

"I do not recall," said Cindy. "I just remember sometime in March or—I believe sometime in March. I don't believe it was April. I believe it was March or—"

Linda jumped in. "By time of day I mean would it have been first thing in the morning? In the evening?"

"I couldn't tell you."

"Do you work?"

"Yes," said Cindy. She agreed with Linda that she worked full-time.

Linda, Frank, and I knew right then that Cindy would go to great lengths to cover for her daughter.

The next day, Lee Anthony came to our office for his deposition. The same parties were present. He was cheerful and cooperative. On the whole, there wasn't that much that we hadn't heard before from him, but he did tell us yet another version of the events from the day Caylee went missing. This was something he'd heard from Casey herself when she was out on bond in August 2008. He recounted Casey's new, very elaborate story about what happened at Jay Blanchard Park, which was where she was supposedly meeting Zanny on that Monday.

"So she goes to Jay Blanchard Park and brings Caylee. . . . Zenaida is there with her sister, as well as her sister has two daughters. I can't remember the sister's name, I think it is Jessica or something like that. Jessica was there with her kids, and Casey drops off Caylee, and sits down in the park there with Zenaida."

Lee said that Casey and Zenaida were watching the kids playing when the nanny grabbed Casey, threatened her, and told her she was a bad mother. She said she was going to take Caylee as punishment.

Lee said that Zenaida told Casey, "I need to teach you a lesson. I will return her to you, but you've got to do something for me. You cannot go to the police, can't tell anybody about this. If this happens, if you do go to the police, if you tell somebody about this, you know, I know where your parents live. I know where your brother lives. I have Caylee, and you don't want me to find out you told somebody something."

Hearing this new version of events, I suddenly found myself thinking about the hallway at Universal. In the weeks while she was in jail, the cops had completely debunked her story about dropping Caylee off at Sawgrass and Casey taking on her "own investigation" to find them. That story was no longer tenable. So what did Casey do? She made up a new lie, Casey 3.0. By shoring up the kidnapping story, Casey was finding a way to justify why she didn't tell anybody why Caylee was missing all that time.

GEORGE ANTHONY HAD HIS TURN on August 5. His attitude from the time his granddaughter's body was found until the case went to trial changed from friendly to adversarial and back again. The first time I'd talked to him had been before he testified at the grand jury, when he was more than willing to help. I hadn't spoken to him since then, so I was taken aback when he started giving me a hard time during the deposition. Now I was more like the enemy. That Caylee was dead and we had our sights on his family wasn't sitting well with him.

In all fairness, the intervening months had been difficult for him. After Caylee's body was found, his life had been like a cliff jump. In January 2009, he had made a serious attempt to kill himself. The suicide attempt was an eye-opener for me. I came to realize just how despondent he was. His world had been torn to shreds and was as public a spectacle as the OJ trial. He didn't want to live without his granddaughter. He was overwhelmed with tremendous guilt and pain.

I felt really bad for him. I am a father of six, and have never had a situation close to as despairing as his, but I could only imagine the pain he must have been in, having his granddaughter die and his daughter the only suspect. The Anthony family lawyer, Brad Conway, was the one to call 911 on Saturday, January 22, with the alarm that George had left the house at 8:30 that morning with several bottles of prescription medication and some photos. No one had seen or heard from him since. "We are worried that he has done something to himself," Conway told the dispatcher.

The following day George was located by police in a motel room in Daytona Beach. He was despairing and barely coherent. A six- to eight-page suicide note addressed to his wife was unfinished. In it, he apologized to Cindy for all the disappointments he had caused her over the years.

"This should be no surprise that I have decided to leave the earth, because I need to be with Caylee Marie. I cannot keep on going because it should be me that is gone from this earth, not her.

"I have lived many years, I am satisfied with my decision because I have never been the man you, Lee, Casey & especially Caylee Marie deserved."

George blamed himself for the child's death and Casey's incarceration. "For a year or so I brought stuff up, only to be told not to be negative. . . . I sit here, falling apart, because I should have done more. She was so close to home, why was she there? Who placed her there? Why is she gone? Why? . . ."

George was taken to a medical center for evaluation and held for a short time before he was released and returned home to Cindy. The next time we spoke was at his deposition in August 2009.

George had been cooperative with law enforcement when Caylee was first reported missing. His early statements and the fact that he'd sought to speak to investigators without Cindy present reflected the conflict between the logical assessment of facts from the view of someone with law enforcement experience, and the desperate hope of a loving father and grandfather. Emotionally, he hoped that his granddaughter was alive and well and his daughter was not some murderous monster. But logically, especially from the perspective of someone with a law enforcement background, things looked dire.

I have always believed that there came a point when, either consciously or unconsciously, George was faced with a choice: either to follow the facts and fight for the truth or to drink the Kool-Aid that Casey was serving and Cindy was enjoying, to buy into Cindy's denial and let the truth be damned. If he followed his intellect, it meant that he had lost his granddaughter to the grave, his daughter to prison, and his wife to her unfounded theories— which might lead to divorce.

As days turned to weeks and weeks to months, George's choice became clear. During his recovery following his suicide attempt, he had apparently made the decision to get behind his wife and daughter. In public appearances, he always stood at Cindy's side and supported her in her denial. When he spoke, he echoed her sentiments, although with a little less conviction. His relationship with law enforcement and the prosecutor's office became more adversarial.

He demonstrated this in his attitude at his deposition. The duct tape on the gas can in the shed was a perfect example. When Caylee went missing, the police had asked George about any unusual activities around the property in the prior month. He told them about the stolen gas cans he had reported to the police, which Casey had then returned to him.

As a result of that information, the cans had been photographed at that time during the summer. In December, after it was clear that the tape on the cans matched the tape at the crime scene, the cans were seized because of the tape. Obviously the tape had been on them since June.

But when I asked George about the tape on the cans during the deposition, he was evasive. He admitted that it was his habit to cover the vent hole of the can with tape since he had lost the plug.

But I wanted him to confirm the obvious: that the duct tape on Caylee's remains came from his home. I showed him photographs of a number of items involved in the case, including the two metal gas cans. George knew that the tape was a key element in connecting Casey to Caylee's body and was ready with a surprising explanation.

Identifying the gas can with a small piece of tape, I asked, "Now, that gas can appears to have a piece of duct tape on it. Do you recognize that?"

"I didn't put the duct tape on there," George responded.

"Do you recognize it, though?"

"I recognize this can, but I didn't put that duct tape on there. I wouldn't do a sloppy job like that."

"Okay, have you ever seen that piece of duct tape on that can before?" I prodded.

"Not this particular size, no. No, sir."

Rather than argue with George, I backed up. "So, at some point, you say you had put a piece of duct tape over the vent of that can; is that correct?"

"Uh-huh . . . I don't know when I specifically did that, but I know that

I did it. Because whenever I put the duct tape over that particular vent hole that you've described or told me about, I did it very neatly. That's not my style," he explained.

"What's not neat about it?" I asked.

"It's too big. I wouldn't have done that. I wouldn't have put the tape there. I would have been neater than that. I would have cut it neater, more precisely than that to just cover the hole."

It was a strange statement, one that between the lines pretty much accused the police of planting the piece of duct tape on the can. I pointed out that in August, when the police first photographed the cans, the police had no reason to believe the duct tape had anything to do with the case. Caylee's body hadn't even been discovered, so it wouldn't have made sense for them to plant it. He had no real answer for the question, and the look on his face told me he knew he had nowhere to go with his story.

He next tried to deny using the cans from that date in June until the first of August, when he gave them to the cops, but he missed the fact that he would have had to mow the lawn in that period of time. When he realized the mistake, he tried to bring two supposedly newly purchased cans into the story. But when I asked when he had purchased the new ones, he had to admit that he'd bought those before the old ones were taken, which made no sense.

I asked him, "Okay, but why did you buy them if you did not yet know that these were missing?" I asked.

"Okay, I'm going to be very, very blunt with you," George responded. "Don't try to confuse me."

It was sad to witness how much George wanted to protect his daughter. Instead of changing course, though, he just looked at the table and stuck to his answer. This was not an argument that logic was going to win. He was trying to help Casey, much as Cindy had when she tried to take credit for the searches for chloroform. The tape on the gas can was one of the most important pieces of evidence, and he was trying to keep it from being connected to the crime scene. Suggesting that the police put it there was his only option, and it wasn't a particularly good one. While he didn't go as far as Cindy had, he was walking a questionable line.

It was easy to see that the cornerstone of the Anthony family dysfunction was Casey. If one looks at the Anthony family dynamic without Casey, they were really quite normal. Both Cindy and George had steady employment, working for many years in their fields. They were both well liked at work, in their neighborhood, and in general. Nobody came forward with any horror stories about either one of them. When you listened to friends, family and coworkers, they were the picture of a loving and committed couple raising two children into young adulthood. Even Lee seemed a genuinely well-adjusted young man. Indeed it was Casey alone that appeared to be the anomaly.

It's hard to say what it was about Casey that impacted everyone in the family so dramatically. My feeling is that Cindy's very real, very serious issues with denial when it came to Casey infected the entire family. When George would attempt to explore Casey's lies, Cindy would stymie him at every turn, telling him to "stop being a detective." I felt that Cindy was scared of pushing Casey too far because she didn't want her daughter to take Caylee out of her life. It was a misdirected love, and Cindy didn't want to lose either of them—Casey was her daughter and Caylee was her light and joy.

As a parent, I can only imagine how difficult a situation it is to look in the mirror and entertain the possibility that your daughter killed your granddaughter. There's no protocol for that . . . no guidebook for the correct emotional response. As irrational as the responses of Cindy and George were, I always tried to remind myself that I was not in their shoes. Still, it was hard to fathom the lengths they seemed to be going to in order to disrupt the conversation. As an attorney on the other side, it was hard to watch them fight us like this. If Cindy and George were lying to us, they were laughably incompetent at it; they'd had a lot more practice lying to themselves.

CHAPTER SIXTEEN

BEHIND THE DEFENSE

The chaos brought on by finding Caylee's body also spilled over to the defense team. The introduction of such vital evidence, along with our decision to make this a death penalty case, fundamentally changed the faces on the defense team. Yet through all the shifts on the defense, Jose Baez remained constant.

Linda, Frank, and I decided early that part of my role in the prosecution was to be the person to do battle with Jose. That way, Linda and Frank could try to maintain a working relationship with him and keep the channels of communication open. That's not to say that Linda didn't also have her fights with him, but I was his main adversary. As such, it won't surprise you that I must begin this portion of the story with a disclaimer, an admission of bias: I genuinely dislike Jose Baez. He has a great deal of superficial charm that can easily be appealing at first glance. I am a big movie fan, I even like musicals, and there is a line from *My Fair Lady* that has always reminded me of Jose. It comes when Henry Higgins describes Zoltan Karpathy, a gentleman of his acquaintance, thusly: "Oozing charm from every pore / He oiled his way across the floor."

It just seemed to fit.

There is an unearned air of arrogance about the man that is incredibly frustrating to witness. I say unearned because there are lawyers who either by accomplishment, reputation, or experience have earned the right to a bit of swagger. It's not always pleasant to be around, but at least you know that swagger comes from having done something special or at least having the reputation for being capable of it. Those who claim the right to that arrogance without the accomplishments to back it up deserve to be exposed. When we looked behind the extravagant claims, we found Baez to be a man of rather pedestrian accomplishments, with precious little experience or knowledge to back up his swagger.

Like most people, I had never heard of Jose before this trial, but not long after I joined the case I'd poked around to get his background and learned that he was a thirty-nine-year-old criminal lawyer based in Kissimmee who'd been admitted to the Florida Bar relatively recently—after difficulties with his background investigation for eight years running. According to reports in the media, it had to do with failure to pay child support and financial irresponsibility.

Baez was raised in New York City by a single mother. They later moved to South Florida, where he attended high school but dropped out in the ninth grade. At age seventeen, he was married with a child. Then he got his GED, joined the U.S. Navy in 1986, and was stationed in Norfolk, Virginia, for three years. After leaving the service, he attended Miami Dade Community College and the University of South Florida and went to law school at St. Thomas University School of Law in Miami.

As the press reported it, after he was denied admission to the Bar, he tried a few unsuccessful business ventures, including two online bikini businesses, Bon Bon Bikinis and Brazilian-Bikinis.com. He also worked in some paralegal/investigator role with the Miami-Dade Police Department. Given his limited experience in the courtroom prior to this case, I figured that paralegal/investigator role was where he got the exaggerated trial experience he had listed on his law firm's website when he began representing Casey.

Some people go into law because they are fascinated by some aspect of the profession and love the law. For others it's the complexity of the tax

This shot of Casey out partying was taken three days after June 16.

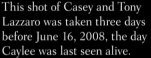

This shot of Casey and Tony Lazzaro was taken three days before June 16, 2008, the day Caylee was last seen alive.

Casey spent much of the thirty-one days that Caylee was missing with Tony. Whenever Tony would ask where Caylee was, Casey always had a story.

One of the infamous "party pictures" taken during the nights when Casey was out at the club Fusian following Caylee's disappearance. As a prosecutor, as a parent, as a person, it just didn't make sense to me that any mother could act the way Casey did after the accidental death of her child.

During the thirty-one days that Caylee was missing, Casey got a tattoo that read "Bella Vita," or "beautiful life" in Italian, which the sheriff's office documented upon court order. *Courtesy of the Orange County Sheriff's Office*

A photo of Casey taken by investigators after their interview, but before her arrest. They told her they were going to use it on a missing persons poster. Both before and after her arrest, there was little in her attitude that suggested she was grieving for her daughter. *Courtesy of the Orange County Sheriff's Office*

This overhead map of the Universal Studios office complex, which we introduced as evidence during the trial, shows the route that she took investigators on once she was through the security gate. It was a bizarre episode that left the police mystified, but perhaps the strangest thing was how much confidence she had in the lie—up until the very end. *Courtesy of the Orange County Sheriff's Office*

The hallway at Universal Studios where Casey finally turned around and admitted she didn't work there. This idea of her reaching the end of the hall became hugely symbolic for our prosecution team. Whenever we saw Casey run out of room on one lie and quickly latch on to a new one, we'd say, "She reached the end of the hall." *Courtesy of the Orange County Sheriff's Office*

The room at Universal where Detective Melich, Detective Appie Wells, and Sergeant Allen questioned Casey. After catching her in the Universal Studios lie, they thought they'd be able to get her to admit to the other lies that she told them. Unfortunately for everyone, Casey would not fold so easily. *Courtesy of the Orange County Sheriff's Office*

The Anthony home on Hopespring Drive. When everything began, their house was prettier than any other on the block, with meticulous landscaping and a front yard with nary a weed. It wasn't long before their pristine front lawn was taken over by news trucks and angry protestors, many of whom grew increasingly irate as the truth about Casey's deceptions came out. *Courtesy of the Orange County Sheriff's Office*

The playhouse that George Anthony assembled for Caylee. Once the defense made it clear that they planned on implicating him, this playhouse became an important symbol for our team. He'd built this house for his granddaughter, right down to the little mailbox in front of it. *Courtesy of the Orange County Sheriff's Office*

A view of the Anthony patio with the bamboo on the right for which Casey claimed she needed a shovel. In the background is the Anthony's pool with the ladder clipped over the side. *Courtesy of the Orange County Sheriff's Office*

Inside the Anthonys' living room, looking toward Caylee's bedroom. *Courtesy of the Orange County Sheriff's Office*

The interior of Casey's bedroom, taken not long after Caylee was reported missing. Later on, when Casey was released on bail and living at home, she would move her bed farther away from the window and from the protestors right outside. *Courtesy of the Orange County Sheriff's Office*

This shot of Caylee's bedroom was taken by police. Seeing this photo always reminds me that, regardless of which side you're on, a terrible thing was done to an innocent little girl. There's no disputing that tragedy. *Courtesy of the Orange County Sheriff's Office*

The Pontiac that Casey was driving when Caylee disappeared. The car belonged to Cindy and George Anthony, and Casey abandoned it in a parking lot during the thirty-one days Caylee was missing. After Cindy and George recovered the vehicle from the tow yard, they realized something was terribly wrong. *Courtesy of the Orange County Sheriff's Office*

From the moment George approached the car at the tow yard, the odor coming from it was putrid. As he would later say to police, "When I first went there to pick up that vehicle, I got within three feet of it, I could smell something." *Courtesy of the Orange County Sheriff's Office*

The trunk, pictured here, was the principal source of the odor. Working with Dr. Arpad Vass, a forensic anthropologist, we tested the smell, finding many of the chemicals common to human decomposition, as well as an unusually high level of chloroform. *Courtesy of the Orange County Sheriff's Office*

The defense tried to argue that the odor in the trunk had been produced by a bag of garbage that had been thrown into this Dumpster, pictured here, while the car was in the tow yard. *Courtesy of the Orange County Sheriff's Office*

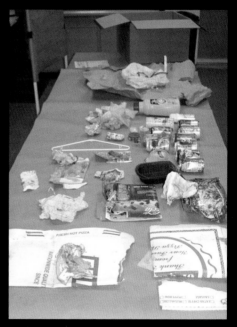

The police retrieved the bag and itemized all of its contents. There was nothing in the bag producing an odor like the one that existed in the back of the car. *Courtesy of the Orange County Sheriff's Office*

The inside of George Anthony's tool shed, which Casey broke into so she could take his gas cans. They are seated on top of the "ABC" box on the left. The "No Trespassing" signs in the middle were bought to keep members of the media and protestors off of the Anthonys' property. *Courtesy of the Orange County Sheriff's Office*

An aerial shot of the wooded area where Caylee's body was found by Roy Kronk, a meter reader who worked in the neighborhood by the Anthonys' home. *Courtesy of the Orange County Sheriff's Office*

Another shot of the crime scene from the air. In this shot you can see just how close to houses the body was left. *Courtesy of the Orange County Sheriff's Office*

A view of the crime scene from the road. *Courtesy of the Orange County Sheriff's Office*

Looking toward the crime scene from the road. In a totally random yet unsettling coincidence, the yellow sign on the ground is advertising a day-care center. *Courtesy of the Orange County Sheriff's Office*

In this shot, looking from the spot where the body was found back to the road, you can see just how close to the road the site actually was. That was one of the things that struck me right away—the laziness of the placement. *Courtesy of the Orange County Sheriff's Office*

The spot on the ground where Caylee's remains were placed. *Courtesy of the Orange County Sheriff's Office*

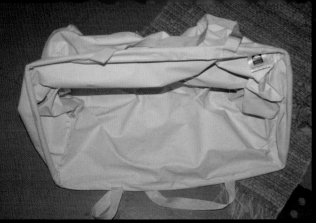

This laundry bag (left) was taken from the Anthony home. It is the sister bag to the bag in which Caylee's remains were found (below). *Courtesy of the Orange County Sheriff's Office*

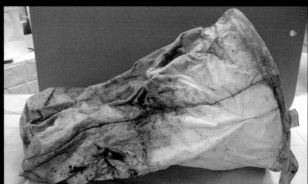

The matching tags from the bag from the Anthony home (left) and the bag from the remains (below). *Courtesy of the Orange County Sheriff's Office*

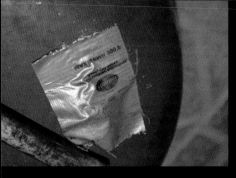

A sample of the duct tape that had been used in the Anthony home on a gas can (left), and a sample of the duct tape found at the crime scene (below). The brand is identical. *Courtesy of the Orange County Sheriff's Office*

On the left, a photo of Caylee and Casey in which Caylee is wearing a shirt that reads "Big Trouble Comes in Small Packages." Below are the remains of that shirt that were found with the body. *Shirt remains photograph courtesy of the Orange County Sheriff's Office*

Caylee's Winnie-the-Pooh bedding, as photographed in her room. *Courtesy of the Orange County Sheriff's Office*

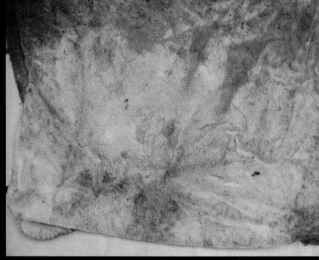

A very faded Winnie-the-Pooh blanket, which was found with Caylee's body. *Courtesy of the Orange County Sheriff's Office*

A shot of the overgrowth on the blanket by the time it was found. *Courtesy of the Orange County Sheriff's Office*

Once the crime scene unit moved onto the scene, they were remarkably careful with every aspect of the site. *Courtesy of the Orange County Sheriff's Office*

They painstakingly documented everything to make sure that no aspect of their work was subject to question. *Courtesy of the Orange County Sheriff's Office*

One of the crime scene workers laboring over the site. *Courtesy of the Orange County Sheriff's Office*

This was the white dry-erase board that we used to help us organize and get prepared for the trial. Everything from setting up our order of witnesses and structuring our argument was mapped here.

This shot of me, Frank, and the defense team was taken during the jury selection at the Pinellas County Criminal Justice Center. From left to right: me, Frank, Jose Baez, and Cheney Mason. *Used with permission of the* Orlando Sentinel, © 2011

In this photo from the trial, Linda, Frank, and I are sifting through the garbage that was in the back of the Pontiac so that I could counter a point made by a defense witness who had testified that there was an actual piece of meat in the garbage. As I quickly pointed out, what he was calling a piece of meat was just a piece of paper—nothing that could have produced the strong odor found in the car. *Used with permission of the* Orlando Sentinel, © 2011

A shot of the team taken at my retirement party. Unfortunately, Frank wasn't able to make it. I'd put off my retirement for six months to see this trial through until the end, and I couldn't have found a finer group of people to do it with. As much as it didn't end how I would have liked, I was ready to move on (from left to right: Yuri Melich, Linda, me, John Allen). *Photograph by Rita Brockway Ashton*

At this point, I don't think we'll ever find out what really happened that night. As I've revisited the verdict in the months since, I think somewhere along the way everyone—from Cindy and George Anthony to the media to the people trying the case—lost sight of Caylee. That, along with her death, is perhaps the greatest tragedy of all.

code, the chance to command a courtroom with their eloquence, or a passion to help the helpless that draws them to the law. Some people go into the profession as a business decision. I always figured Jose was in the latter group. Just as if he was selling the bikinis in his previous career, he was a consummate salesman—I have to give him that.

That said, he was not the first attorney I've met whom I would describe as I have just described Jose. There's nothing wrong with being in this job for the money or the spotlight—plenty of people are and I've worked with a lot of them. There are many lawyers whom I've done battle with in court, but when we step out of the courtroom, we are friends. Baez was not one of them—not because I disagreed with the cause he was championing but because I disagreed with the manner in which he went about doing it.

Part of the obligation of any good attorney is to advocate for his client no matter how unpopular that cause may be. Many times that requires an attorney to passionately argue his or her client's innocence even when the attorney may not subjectively believe it. I have no respect for a lawyer who would do any less. Between lawyers, though, honesty is key. Outside the courtroom, a lawyer's word should mean something both to other lawyers and to the public in general. Even if you're on opposing sides, you can't work with someone you don't trust.

In my dealings with Jose, though, he sometimes seemed recklessly unconcerned about the accuracy of what he was saying, frequently filing motions he had not adequately investigated and that were not true. The word I always use in describing Jose is smarmy: somebody who is slick, underhanded, and doesn't shoot straight.

I tried to like him in the beginning, but every time I saw him in the media I found the appearance unethical and unprofessional. Our rules caution attorneys to avoid statements that have a likelihood of affecting potential jurors and, in fact, make it an offense subject to punishment. Unfortunately, it is a rule that, in my opinion, is rarely enforced as it should be. That is one of the reasons why we requested a gag order early in the case, which sadly was denied.

The discovery of Caylee's body put more of a spotlight on this already sensational case, giving more opportunities for Jose to thrust himself in

front of the camera. Suddenly the stakes, already huge, grew even bigger—
for everyone on both sides. We knew it, and so did the defense.

PRIOR TO THE DISCOVERY OF the remains, a handful of lawyers had been
involved with the case but nothing extraordinary—mostly Jose and a couple
of associates. Adam Gabriel and Jose Garcia were associates of Baez's firm
who were each involved early on. In addition, there were Michael Walsh
and Jonathan Kasen, who would later be involved in a related civil case
filed by Zenaida Fernandez Gonzalez against Casey. Both Walsh and Kasen
appeared briefly, but I was never really sure if they worked for Baez's firm
or just what their roles were. The bottom line was that Baez was in charge.

The first real legal addition to the defense team came in the form of
Terrie Lenamon, an experienced capital defense attorney from Miami,
who joined the case in the fall of 2008 when we were originally debating
whether to pursue the death penalty against Casey. At that point, of course,
we didn't have a body, but we had told the defense to provide us with any
information they would like us to consider regarding the death penalty.
Lenamon gave us a brief, which basically argued that Casey was a good
mother and had never done anything wrong before, so therefore if Caylee
was dead, the death may have been accidental. The document was not particularly helpful, since it didn't provide any new information or allege any
particular mental health concern that might have explained her behavior.
In the end, it didn't impact our decision not to seek the death penalty, and
after we announced that decision in October 2008, Lenamon left the case,
leaving Baez to do as he pleased.

All that changed when Roy Kronk stumbled back into that Florida
swamp. On December 11, 2008, the day Caylee's body was found, Linda
Kenney Baden entered the case. A defense attorney from New Jersey who
was heavily involved with the forensic science community, Baden was the
wife of Dr. Michael Baden, a celebrity forensic pathologist who was always
on TV. I'd heard her name, but had never worked with her before, and my
initial impression of her was not favorable. A month or so after she came on
board, her new book, *Skeleton Justice*, coauthored with her husband, was

released with much fanfare, so it was easy to speculate that she was chasing the spotlight. However, after taking witness depositions with her, I came to respect that she knew what she was doing and ended up enjoying her as opposing counsel.

During the early days of Baden's involvement, Baez filed more than twenty "emergency" motions with the court, attempting to involve his experts in the processing of the crime scene and the evidence. One motion asked that their forensic pathologist observe our medical examiner, Dr. G, during her autopsy and for a second autopsy. The second autopsy was no problem for us, but Dr. G didn't need any rubberneckers. Baez and Baden suggested that a forensic expert be appointed by the court to control the processing of the evidence. They also wanted what is called a special master, sort of an extension of the judge's authority, to preside over their examination of the evidence, a process from which we would be excluded.

By January 8, we were in court hearing those and sixteen other "emergency" motions, most of which were either for materials they would have eventually received in the normal course of discovery or things they would never be entitled to anyway. We figured that most of the motions were drafted by Baden since they didn't seem to show an in-depth understanding of Florida law. Ultimately, the majority of them were denied, but we agreed to give the defense access to the crime scene when the sheriff's office was done.

Meanwhile, we filed a motion of our own to restrict the disclosure of photographs of Caylee's remains. A while back we'd heard rumors that Jose had engineered Casey's sale of photos of Caylee for $200,000 to ABC, and we did not want to see photos of Caylee's body end up the same way. The defense agreed to the motion and so those photos were not seen in public till the trial.

Whenever an attorney becomes involved in the financial affairs of a client aside from the payment of fees, it is a matter of concern. We had no specific information, but our concern was that if something inappropriate had occurred that Casey didn't know about, our entire effort might be undermined. Suddenly she would have a postconviction claim against her attorney because of conflict of interest.

We filed a motion asking the judge to hold a hearing in chambers to inquire and make sure that whatever deals had been struck, the defendant knew about them and waived any conflict. The defense was furious, and filed the first of many pleadings calling us every despicable thing you can think of. I remember that the judge seemed annoyed that we had raised the issue, but in the end I think he saw the wisdom in the precaution. The court had an obligation to ensure that counsel was free of conflict, so Judge Strickland set it for hearing.

We all went into the jury room on the twenty-third floor of the court-house. Altogether there were the three of us along with Baez, Casey, Judge Strickland, and the court reporter. First, Judge Strickland inquired about the sale of photos and confirmed that Casey had sold the photos and videos of her daughter to ABC for $200,000, which was being used for her defense. Baez claimed the money did not go directly to him but was eventually deposited in his trust account, saying that his fee was $89,000 and change, and the rest was for expenses.

Baez stated that Baden had a separate contract with Casey directly, but that she had received no money yet. He indicated that he had no deals finalized for right to publication of any story nor did Casey. The judge did not make any more detailed inquiry into potential negotiations, but Casey did confirm the information provided by Baez that she had sold the photos.

I was so disgusted by her at that moment. At the time when the sale had taken place, I was confident that Caylee was already dead and that Casey knew it. What kind of mother would sell pictures of her dead child for profit? I was also upset with ABC for participating in such checkbook journalism. I would have liked to inquire further about potential deals being cut, but clearly the judge felt that was enough and was not in the mood to press further. Ultimately, I was satisfied that we had done all we could to avoid that potential land mine.

When Baez and company finally ran out of money in March 2010, and Casey was found indigent, it was clear that the State was not going to pay expenses for out-of-state attorneys to travel. We suspected that Baden would probably bail out, but to her credit, she stayed on through the completion of the depositions of the forensic experts, and finally withdrew in October 2010.

EVERY TIME A NEW ATTORNEY joined the defense team, Baez touted him or her as having special expertise, whether it was in forensics, cross-examination, or procedure. The media ate it up. It seemed as though every-one who hooked up with the defense was suddenly anointed a great lawyer and part of the "dream team." But O. J. Simpson's, this defense was not.

Perhaps the strangest entrant to the case was Todd Macaluso, a per-sonal injury shark from California. As required of any attorney from another state who is not a member of the Florida Bar, Macaluso filed a motion seek-ing the court's permission to enter *pro hac vice,* or "for this occasion." These are motions by lawyers who have not been admitted to practice in a certain jurisdiction, but are allowed to participate in particular cases. In the filing, Macaluso was required to state that he was a member of the California Bar, in good standing, without discipline pending.

He filed that form making that declaration, but Linda went online with the California Bar and discovered that he was under investigation for some questionable acts with clients' money. One of our local reporters also dis-covered this, and asked Baez about it before we could spring it on them in court. Macaluso filed a corrected pleading, blaming his secretary for the oversight. Judge Strickland let him be involved in the case despite the pending investigation.

Later on, at the indigency hearing where we learned that the defense was out of money, we also found out that Macaluso had bought his way into the case by giving the defense $70,000. In truth, he had very little actual involvement in the case. He spoke only once in court, to make a claim about how many searchers had looked in the area on Suburban Drive. He was eventually suspended in California over the discipline issue and with-drew from the Casey Anthony case in April 2010.

In April 2009, when we announced our decision to seek the death penalty, the defense was required by law to have a qualified death pen-alty case lawyer on its team. There was talk that Terrie Lenamon would reenter the picture, but he did not want to come back on board. In an interview with *Orlando Sentinel* columnist Hal Boedeker in May 2009, Lenamon explained his decision. For starters, he had had few interactions with Casey. He also said that he and Baez had "a disagreement over strategy over mental-health mitigation," a statement that I interpreted as meaning that Lenamon had suggested a route to take and Baez had disagreed with him. Because Baez was lead counsel, his way prevailed.

In his interview with Boedeker, Lenamon went on to say that he felt media attention was going to be a problem for the case. Furthermore, Lenamon expressed concern that "the death penalty lawyer who will be brought in will be rubber-stamping a preplanned defense." He then went on to add that "whoever that [death penalty] lawyer is has to be independent of the strategy in evaluating the case."

"I am hopeful they bring in some big-shot death penalty lawyer," he said. "I will be the first one to say it's the best move Mr. Baez has made since bringing me in."

In the end Baez did just that, as another lawyer, Andrea Lyon, joined the case. Andrea was a capital death penalty attorney in Chicago and a true believer in the abolition of the death penalty. She was a clinical professor at DePaul University in Chicago, and was the director of the Center for Justice in Capital Cases there. We would later learn that the center had added funds to Casey's defense pot.

From the start Lyon seemed quite capable; she is a big woman with a forceful presence. I remember one of my first conversations with her. Linda, Frank, and I were in the elevator and she told us that the defense wouldn't be having any more of those unseemly press conferences that Jose was so fond of. I was briefly optimistic that perhaps things were changing. Then they quickly proceeded to hold a press conference, and then another, and many, many more. Lyon, like Baden, also had a book coming out, *Angel of Death Row: My Life as a Death Penalty Defense Lawyer,* coauthored with Alan Dershowitz. In January 2010, she told *Today* show host Meredith Vieira that Casey "didn't kill her kid." But Lyon declined to discuss any evidence she had seen to support her claim. I thought that Illinois had the same rule as Florida against making pretrial statements; oh well, I guess I was mistaken.

An Orlando defense attorney got in trouble with a local defense attorneys' association for leaking a speech Lyon made at a death penalty conference, Life After Death, held in Orlando in 2008, where she made a very unflattering sexual reference to female prosecutors going home and putting on their "strap-ons." We took it as a reference to a dildo—classy broad. The press had a field day, especially since the lead prosecutor in the Anthony case was a woman. Other statements Lyon made at that conference also created a stir, including her comments that judges are "ugly" and jurors are "killers."

To familiarize herself with Lyon, Linda reviewed the entire speech. Within the speech Lyon made repeated reference to her preferred defense tactic, creating an alternative suspect. Linda was of the opinion that Lyon was behind the defense's campaign to attack Roy Kronk, the utility worker who had found Caylee's remains. Shortly after Lyon entered the case, Mortimer Smith, an investigator who worked for her center, was digging into Kronk's past.

While Lyon was quite a charismatic adversary, the lawyer who, aside from Baez, would be there the longest arrived in March 2010. Cheney Mason was an Orlando lawyer touted in the press as having a stellar reputation. He'd made statements to the press in the past as a consultant, in which he questioned some of the things Baez was doing, so we were a little surprised, but we all knew Cheney and knew he craved the limelight. Linda, Frank, and I had each known Cheney for years and thought well of him. I can't recall if I had ever actually done a trial with him, though I had watched Linda in trial against him a year or so earlier. Cheney was in his sixties by then and quite a character. He probably won't like this, but we had always referred to him as Foghorn Leghorn, in that his accent and speech pattern were a spot-on match to that lovable Looney Tunes rooster. Cheney tended toward the bombastic—not really a details guy on either the law or the facts, but he could be very persuasive.

Most of all, though, he was experienced and pragmatic. When he first got involved, I think he wanted to ride in on his white horse and resurrect this failing defense. We always hoped the addition of a new, reputable attorney would class up the defense team's tactics. Unfortunately, we would find in the weeks and months ahead that instead of Cheney raising Baez to his level of professionalism, Baez seemed to bring Cheney down to his.

The first time I saw Mason in court with Lyon, I knew they were oil and water. Mason was an old Southerner type who seemed fine with women in certain roles, like being protégés, but seemed to have trouble with women who were his professional equals. He showed that side in his dealings with Linda once, not a mistake you want to make twice. Lyon, meanwhile, was a big-city lawyer who could give as well as she took. Big city versus old country, we on the prosecution team knew this would be fun to watch. He would say disrespectful things to us about motions Andrea had filed, such as how ridiculous they were. You could tell they would never get along. As predicted, Lyon would leave the case as soon as the death penalty motion was argued, citing cost issues.

Ann Finnell entered the case in September 2010. Ann was a very experienced capital litigator, much like Andrea Lyon, only less abrasive. I actually liked working with Ann, though I am sure she was not happy to be working on Baez's team. There were a number of occasions when she would lament to me privately about what an insane situation this was, referring to the lack of coherent management in the defense team and how she regretted getting involved.

The last to enter was Dorothy Sims, a civil lawyer from Ocala. She was touted as an expert in cross-examination of medical experts. During trial, however, she was relegated to the role of hand-holder and gal Friday. I thought Baez and Mason treated her very disrespectfully.

Ultimately, this defense team was not Kumbaya. It was all about who could survive in what was undoubtedly a difficult atmosphere, one in which Baez would perpetually govern every decision. When the dust settled there were four left standing, the four that would be our opposition for the trial: Baez, Mason, Finnell, and Sims.

CHAPTER SEVENTEEN

ORDER IN THE COURT

Shortly after Cheney Mason officially joined the case in the spring of 2010, the defense filed a motion to disqualify Judge Stan Strickland. Their reason for the recusal was that a blogger named Dave Knechel, known online as Marinade Dave, had engaged in conversations with Strickland about the Anthony case. The defense found that this showed a bias and said the judge should withdraw. They also accused Judge Strickland of being a publicity hound, which, in my opinion, was an accusation more applicable to them. It was not lost on Judge Strickland that the defense filed its motion at 4:48 P.M. on a Friday, just as it had done with the Kronk blindside. As we had seen before, no one from the Anthony defense team provided him with a copy, so he learned about it on the news. This was Baez's MO.

In his response to the allegations, Judge Strickland said that the accusation that he was biased in favor of the prosecution "must serve as a source of bemusement" to Linda, Frank, and me. "Each of whom has verbally sparred with the court many times. . . ."

Ultimately, Judge Strickland did recuse himself, as he should have, given the circumstances. In his order, he said, "At its core, defense counsel's motion accuses the undersigned of being a 'self-aggrandizing media hound.' Indeed, the irony is rich." On that, we agreed.

The fact that Baez and Mason had Judge Strickland removed from the case only to be replaced by Judge Belvin Perry was the stupidest move anybody in the Florida legal community had ever heard of. I loved the news.

For a while I had been frustrated that Judge Strickland wasn't doing enough to rein in Baez. Jose would take any opportunity to use a hearing as a forum to bash the sheriff's office or us. I knew that Mason wasn't going to be any better. Judge Strickland's style was laid-back and hands-off, which would be fine for most cases, but I was having nightmares thinking about what a circus the real hearings and trial would devolve into with Jose and Cheney in the ring.

I confess that I am a fighter. It's one of my faults and one of my strengths. If the judge wasn't going to control the defense, I knew the task would fall to me, which meant a free-for-all with everybody's gloves off. I wasn't going to let Baez or Mason own the courtroom. It is not in my character to take punches. During one venting session with Linda, I commented, "Can you imagine what this would be like if Belvin Perry was the judge?" Wishful thinking at the time. Little did I know I'd actually get my wish.

When Judge Strickland recused himself, Judge Perry, the chief judge of the Ninth Judicial Circuit, had the power to assign a new judge. He picked himself. It amazed us that Mason would have Judge Strickland recuse himself without the foresight that he was going to end up with Belvin Perry, a much stricter, letter-of-the-law kind of judge. Judge Perry and I had done many high-profile cases together over the years and I had always found him to be extremely fair and knowledgeable about the law. Furthermore, he loved complex, high-profile death penalty cases. Even as chief judge, he had continued to take those cases when the opportunity arose. It seemed like a no-brainer that he would assign himself to this. Linda, Frank, and I were delighted.

Some people go into law because they love law, and Judge Perry is one of those people. He lives and breathes law with every case he hears. In 1977 he got his Juris Doctorate degree from Thurgood Marshall School of Law at Texas Southern University. After, he became an assistant state attorney for the Ninth Judicial Circuit Court of Florida. He was elected a circuit court judge in 1989 and chief judge in 1995, and again in 2001. His father was one of Orlando's first African-American policemen.

Judge Perry is a big man for standing only five foot two. He is a huge presence, and it always surprises me how controlled he is, even when he is exasperated—Lord knows I have exasperated him more than once. He is a unique mixture of the legal mind of U.S. Supreme Court Justice Thurgood Marshall, the charisma of Rat Pack sensation Sammy Davis, Jr., the fire of actor Jack Nicholson, and the facial expressions of Bill Cosby thrown in for good measure. He doesn't take any crap from attorneys, regardless of whether they're on the defense or the prosecution. But his patience was about to be tried with the likes of Jose Baez and his "dream team." Of course, he was going to have his fair share of exasperation with us on the prosecution, too.

IN EARLY 2010, BEFORE MASON and Judge Perry came on board, we became concerned that the discovery stage of the case could go on interminably if Baez were left to his own devices. We suggested to Judge Strickland and the defense that the court enter an order setting a deadline for everything from depositions to filing the hearings on motions. Linda and I spent a great deal of time breaking down all that needed to be done by both sides prior to trial and assigning each to a category. The deadlines were staggered based upon the complexity of the issue. We then submitted it to the defense, and they requested a few changes that we agreed to, submitted it to Judge Strickland, and he signed it. Finally we had a trial date: May 9, 2011. It was more than a year away, but at least we had it set.

We spent the next year getting ready for that date. It was all the grunt work that goes into getting ready for a trial and sorting through what needs to be done. It's a process that I like, but there's always stress involved. Most of our hearing time was occupied by common death penalty motions that get filed in capital cases. The defense usually files a couple of dozen motions, all of which are routinely denied.

One thing we noticed was that with Judge Perry at the helm the hear-

ings tended to be shorter and involved much less posturing by the defense.
I recall with great affection the first time Judge Perry interrupted Baez and
politely insisted that he stick to the topic at hand. In that one statement,
it was instantly clear that Judge Perry was not going to let Baez get away
with the stuff he'd been pulling with Judge Strickland. Not long after, Baez
and Mason attempted to get Judge Perry to rehear several issues that Judge
Strickland had already ruled on. Judge Perry simply looked at them and
maintained all the rulings. Much to our satisfaction, Judge Perry also reaf-
firmed the discovery and motions deadlines that Judge Strickland had set,
meaning that our May 2011 trial was going to take place on schedule come
hell or high water.

Not surprisingly, the defense team's out-of-court shenanigans didn't
stop with the introduction of Judge Perry to the case. Ever since Casey had
been indicted by the grand jury, the pretrial preparations had been a constant roller coaster of Jose's noncompliance. Deadlines would be set, then
ignored. If and when they were finally met, there was little or no acknowl-
edgement of the fact that they had been met late. It was a frustrating cycle
for all of us on the prosecution, and it didn't bode well for the run-up to
the trial.

Of all the ways that the defense made the pretrial phase harder, perhaps the most glaring was that they did not have much respect for the
rules of discovery. When it came to evidence, Baez had a reputation as an
ambusher. Prosecutors who'd had cases with him in the past said they had
been ambushed with last-minute evidence. In a case in Lake County, he
had been reprimanded by the judge for this behavior. Mason, on the other
hand, was a reasonably straight shooter, so our hope was that they would
balance each other out.

When it came to the discovery phase, our first major issue with compliance started innocently enough. By November 2010, Jose had given us
a list of several expert witnesses, but he had said nothing about what the
subject of their testimony would be. Because the rules of discovery require
both sides to turn over the reports of experts, defense attorneys generally
tell their experts not to prepare reports so that there is nothing they are
required to turn over. But even though the prosecution doesn't have the

actual reports, we typically are given an idea of what the experts are going to say. In this case, however, Jose gave us nothing to go on.

In an attempt to get something to use to prepare for the depositions of the experts he had listed, I filed a motion requesting a number of different documents I suspected the defense might have—letters, e-mails, contracts—that would help explain the purpose of calling the various experts. At the hearing on the motion, Judge Perry denied most of what I was asking for but added something I hadn't asked for. He told Baez to file a document by a certain deadline that would give some general information about the background and expertise of the experts. He also added that Baez needed to provide a statement of the "subject matter" of their testimony. A rather modest order, I thought, but helpful nonetheless.

The deadline came and went with no filing. Once the deadline passed, I called Baez about it and he claimed he had forgotten. The next day his filing arrived. It contained some minimal information about the experts, pretty much what I had already found on the Internet, but nothing about the subject matter they would be discussing. I pointed this omission out to Baez, and some e-mails passed between us disputing the language of the judge's order—but still no compliance.

I filed a motion asking the judge to clarify what Baez had to file, though it seemed crystal clear to me. The judge apparently believed that the words were clear as well, and so he upped the ante. Judge Perry listed five specific questions that the defense had to answer about each expert, including every opinion they would give at trial and the factual basis for each of them. He then gave the defense another deadline.

When that deadline arrived, I received another filing. It contained mostly sarcastic comments about me, but little new information and nothing to clue us in about what opinions the experts would enter. I couldn't believe that Baez had essentially dared Judge Perry to enforce the order. It was like my eight-year-old son—you tell him to hurry up and he slows down just to be defiant. Since Baez had been given two opportunities to comply and was still refusing, I filed a motion asking that he be held in contempt and be fined for every day he failed to comply.

At the hearing, Baez had no real response except to attack me. Judge

Perry found that he had not complied with the prior orders and was in violation of the discovery rules, but rather than hold him in contempt, he ordered that the experts file reports that would provide essentially the same information that was supposed to have been in the prior orders. He also made Baez pay the state of Florida for the time I had spent preparing all these motions. It ended up being almost six hundred dollars. Eventually we got reports that appeared at the time to comply with the order.

The issue would arise again less than a month later. Baez had filed a motion requesting a Frye hearing to determine the admissibility of Dr. Vass's odor analysis testimony. The motion was no surprise. We had all been expecting it for over a year. After I read his motion, though, I couldn't figure out exactly what he was arguing was new or novel in Dr. Vass's work. Certain things Vass did were indeed new, and we were prepared to argue those. But the way Baez had written his motion, I could see an ambush on the horizon, if all of a sudden he started arguing about an issue that I thought would not be challenged because it was already a commonly accepted technique.

I raised the matter with the judge, and upon reviewing the motion, he agreed that it was not sufficiently specific. In open court, he asked Baez what he was challenging, and Baez gave an answer that I felt adequately limited the issue and gave me what I needed to be prepared. Perry then ordered Baez to file the motion again, and essentially just repeat what he'd said in court. Instead of listening to the judge, Baez filed a response to Judge Perry's order that once again was completely vague and had little connection to what Baez had said in court.

It was maddening. After the last round with him about the experts, it was apparent that this wasn't just an issue of misunderstanding; it was obstinacy. As familiar as I was with Baez's game, I was annoyed enough to file my own motion.

"Judge, he is not following your order again," I stated. "You should hold him in civil contempt." If Judge Perry was to find him in contempt, Baez would have to pay a fine or be jailed—no more wasting time waiting for him to comply. In response to my motion, Jose filed a response filled with attacks. This one went above and beyond anything he had said to date, specifically singling me out, calling me a liar, making accusations that were very personal, very nasty, and very much directed at me rather than at the team.

At the conclusion of other hearings one day, it was time to take up the issue of contempt. Judge Perry said to both of us, "I would prefer that y'all work it out, but I am willing to hear your motion."

Everybody went into a side room: Linda, Frank, Baez, Cheney Mason, Dorothy Sims, and me. They were desperate to avoid a public hearing on the second contempt charge against Jose, since they knew that Jose had stubbornly failed to comply with the prior order. This could only make them look unprofessional—it was a lose-lose as far as they were concerned. Cheney began the discussion.

"What do you want to resolve this?" he asked as Jose sulked in the corner.

I told him that I first wanted Baez to file a pleading in court detailing what he intended to challenge, in compliance with the court's original order. I suggested that it was as easy as repeating the language he had spoken in open court. Also, I wanted an apology for the personal attacks Jose had made on me.

"If that is done, I will withdraw my request to find Mr. Baez in contempt of court," I told Mason. "But Jose must apologize in open court, and I will be happy to withdraw the contempt request." I'd had enough. For two years I'd been putting up with his abuse, while he said whatever he felt like saying. He was going to apologize to me in the same place where he had attacked me so many times before.

I had to hand them a copy of the transcript of the prior hearing, and Dorothy Sims wrote out in longhand on a piece of yellow legal paper exactly what Jose had previously said in court on the matter. The handwritten paper served as the new motion. It was presented to Judge Perry, and Baez, as the lead defense counsel, signed it. I looked it over and said I was fine with that.

Back in court before Judge Perry, I explained to all the people present, "Judge, we've resolved the matter. We have agreed that if Mr. Baez apologizes and complies with the original order, we will agree to drop the contempt motion. The defense is going to file a pleading in compliance with the court's order."

Baez then presented Judge Perry with the signed yellow piece of paper, which documented that Baez would limit the scope of his challenge to Dr. Vass. He stood before the court and apologized for what he had said about me, crediting it to the deep passion he felt for his client. While it hadn't started out as much of an apology, he did acknowledge that the things he'd said were not appropriate or true. I accepted his apology and shook his hand, thinking the issue was resolved. I could now prepare for the Frye hearing knowing exactly what the issues were. Or so I thought.

When the Frye hearing came along in early April 2011, I experienced the most bizarre episode in my thirty years in court. As the hearing progressed, Baez began to challenge everything Vass had done, as I had originally feared he would do. He completely abandoned the limitations he himself had placed on the issues when he'd signed that handwritten piece of yellow legal paper. I was dumbstruck, and so was the judge. After two or three attempts to broaden the scope of the issue were denied, Baez actually complained that he had been coerced into signing the yellow piece of paper that Dorothy Sims had given him, and that he should not be held to what it said. He even claimed that I had coerced him into signing it.

My jaw dropped. He had lost that little battle of wills with the judge and me a month earlier, and now he stood in front of the court to whine about it. Words escape me at times like these, but they did not escape Judge Perry. "Well, I guess I can't trust any stipulation you get," Judge Perry said.

In the end, the court ruled that Dr. Vass's opinions were based upon generally accepted scientific principles, so Vass would be permitted to testify. It was an important victory for us, but we didn't have too long to savor it. The trial was a little over a month away—more than enough time to get one final, massive curveball thrown our way.

CHAPTER EIGHTEEN

———

THE NUCLEAR LIE

Eight weeks before trial, Linda, Frank, and I were reviewing every defense action that Jose and his dream team might come up with. We had long expected what Linda would call the nuclear lie, the big one. Our job was figuring out what that might be.

With Caylee's remains found and the crime scene tied to the Anthony home through the duct tape, the argument of abduction by a stranger had become hard to maintain. As late as the late winter of 2011 the defense was still trying to support the theory that Caylee had been alive, abducted by persons unknown, when Casey went to jail. That theory held that Caylee had been killed during Casey's incarceration and her body then deposited in the Suburban Drive swamp. In this scenario, Casey's alibi was irrefutable. She was in jail so she couldn't have murdered her daughter. The poor child's killers were still at large.

As their Texas EquuSearch witnesses fell apart one by one, the three of us on the prosecution knew that this version of Casey's lie was dying its inevitable death. In the two and a half years we'd been on this case, we'd seen this all before, whether it was during the role-play with Lee when Casey had first developed the kidnapping story and Casey 2.0 was born, or at Universal Studios, when she'd reached the end of the hall, or when she'd created the Blanchard Park variation of the kidnapping story, Casey 3.0, for Lee. She had nowhere else to go with the mysterious abductor story, so she needed a new narrative. We'd seen it before so many times, we could almost smell it. All the telltale signs were there that Casey's story was about to change. It had to. But the nuclear lie that was about to be dropped was beyond even our wildest imaginations.

With the Frye hearing finally over, Linda, Frank, and I had submitted the state's list of witnesses and the defense had submitted theirs. All motions about discovery had been resolved. There was nothing left for either side to do but plan for the logistics of the trial itself.

Yet one complication remained. During the Frye hearing, we'd received a new witness list from the defense with two new names: Dr. Jeffrey Danziger, a psychiatrist from Orlando, and Dr. William Weitz, a psychologist from the Fort Lauderdale area. I had known Dr. Danziger for many years. He was a forensic psychiatrist, and part of his practice was forensic evaluations. He was one of the two doctors who had originally examined Casey in July 2008 by order of Judge Strickland, who had asked both doctors to do a basic competency evaluation. At that time, the only significant finding had been that she was unusually happy for somebody in her circumstances.

Baez had not filed anything about the content of what these two mental health experts were going to testify to, so all signs pointed to another Baez ambush. At the end of the Frye hearing, we raised the issue with Judge Perry: the court had previously ordered that all experts had to provide reports, so we were expecting reports from Danziger and Weitz.

For the defense, Ann Finnell said she was going to contact these doctors and have them submit reports by that Friday, April 8. We had only four weeks till trial, so even Friday was pushing it. We needed to decide if we were going to depose them, but we didn't know what they were going to say.

That afternoon I was running out of the courtroom to pick up my children from day care. Linda and Frank had already gone home. When I got outside the courthouse, I remembered that my wife was on pickup duty so I slowed my pace. My cell phone rang just as I reached the parking garage. Ann Finnell was asking me to come back upstairs to the courtroom. I walked in to find Finnell, Mason, and Baez standing in the courtroom.

Ann told me she had contacted the two doctors and there was no way they could get their reports to her by Friday. She wanted to go before Judge Perry to explain the delay and she needed a member of the prosecution team in court. We called the judge and he reentered the now empty courtroom, without a court reporter, to see what was up.

We all stood in the courtroom near the jury box as Ann explained the issue with the report. I didn't have a problem with a slight delay, but time was of the essence.

"What is this about?" Judge Perry demanded. "Why don't you just tell? Why do we have all this mystery?"

All of us, including Judge Perry, went together into the back jury room. We took seats around a small table. Finnell started by saying that the doctors were important to explaining Casey's failure to report Caylee's disappearance for the thirty-one days.

I looked at them in disbelief and said, "Why don't you quit playing around and tell us what the story is?"

Jose smirked, and said that the story was going to be that Caylee drowned by accident and Casey trusted someone she shouldn't have to take care of it. I was dumbfounded by both parts of the premise. They were going to concede that Casey knew Caylee had died from the beginning, and they were going to implicate someone else in the cover-up.

"Who would that be?" I asked.

"George," he replied matter-of-factly, as if this were somehow an obvious answer.

I looked at him and broke out in laughter. "Just bring it on," I said. "I can't wait to cross-examine Casey." It was not my proudest moment, but it had been an exceedingly long day and my feistiness was showing.

I thought it was a complete crock of crap. For ages I'd assumed that Casey was going to implicate someone beyond herself as a way to deflect blame. Linda, Frank, and I had been debating for years what her next story was going to be. What was shocking was not that she had a new lie, but that this lie contained the combination of Caylee drowning and Casey blaming George. We had considered both separately, but we had never thought she'd put them both together in the same story.

I left the conversation, went downstairs, and called Linda. I got her answering machine and left a cryptic voice message. "I know what her story is," I said.

Linda called me back right away. "You've got to be kidding!" she exclaimed when I told her. Frank didn't get back to me until the next day, and he had the same response.

Sometime over the next day or two, Linda spoke to Jose and got a little more detail. The story was going to be that Casey had been awakened on the morning of June 16 by her father, saying that Caylee had drowned in the pool. Everything was on George. Casey took no responsibility whatsoever. That was always her position.

The following week, late as usual, we got the reports from the therapists. Dr. Danziger's report had a psychological evaluation of Casey and generalizations about maternal filicide. Dr. Weitz's report, also in very general terms, talked about the ideas of molestation, trauma, and denial. All of these allegations were not unusual to justify a crime. It seemed that Casey saw, as we did, that her prior lies weren't going to work, so it was time to come up with another one.

Although we will never know the genesis of Casey 4.0, since conversations between Casey and her lawyer are privileged, Linda had a theory. During a deposition of our medical examiner, Dr. G, back in September of 2010, Cheney had probed her about the possibility of drowning. Linda's theory was that he was exploring a potential defense in the case. Of course at that point, Cheney had still been pushing the stranger abduction story, so at the time it appeared to us that Casey 4.0 hadn't been born . . . yet.

In early 2011, something else had occurred which supported Linda's theory. Out of the blue one day, Baez called her. He was interested in discussing whether we would consider something called a proffer in exchange for taking the death penalty off the table. A proffer is essentially an offer of proof, so in other words, Casey would offer her story to us, if we would consider taking the death penalty off the table.

The conversation was incredibly vague. We had a closed door meeting with the defense during which they were evasive about the specifics of her story, but they felt it would be something that would convince us not to seek the death penalty. We discussed it with Lawson as well to get his take. At that point, we all wanted to hear what she had to say, but I must admit I think our motive was curiosity more than anything else. Much like everyone else, we wanted to know what the next lie would be, but of course we had to do what was best for the case, not what was best to satisfy our own interests.

Still, it was an intriguing possibility made all the more interesting because the offer appeared to be unconditional; we could hear the story she had to tell, and if we didn't buy it, we could still move forward with the death penalty. However, as with many things with the defense, their position changed over time. Eventually a huge caveat was put on their proffer: if we decided to hear her story out, we had to take the death penalty off the table. We had to take it sight unseen, or else the deal was off. In the end, none of us were comfortable striking this ambiguous bargain with a woman who had a documented history of lying, so we let the whole thing go.

But after we learned about the therapists' reports, suddenly these events from the months prior fell into place. Taken with Mason's comments about drowning at Dr. G's deposition, we could suddenly understand what they'd been up to. The way we figured it, Casey's version of events—blaming George for the abuse and the drowning—probably started coming together around fall of 2010. At some point before Baez called Linda about the proffer, that new version, Casey 4.0, had been pitched to the therapists. Once it was clear that they could get backing from the therapists on it, they tried to serve it up to us. When we wouldn't take the bait, they simply decided to use Dr. Danziger and Dr. Weitz as mouthpieces for Casey's story.

After we got the reports, we arranged sit-downs with the two new eleventh-hour witnesses. Dr. Danziger came first. On the morning of his appointment, he arrived before the defense attorneys. I noticed that Dr. Danziger was uneasy that morning. He expressed his apprehension in an odd kind of way. "I am very uncomfortable being the vector for this information," he said to me.

I was puzzled and went back to my office to look up the word *vector*.

I wanted to be sure of which definition he meant. The one definition that seemed most applicable was "a vehicle to spread disease."

When the defense attorneys got there, Dr. Danziger repeated his concern about being a vector. He added that he had difficulty being a mouthpiece for these "very, very serious allegations against someone in a situation where there is no other evidence he actually did anything."

I had known Jeffrey Danziger for twenty years. I had led him in testimony, as well as cross-examined him. He had testified in favor of some of my cases and against others. He had testified in cases where I felt the defendant was feeding him a line, and I called it for what it was. In still others, he had reported the symptoms displayed by a defendant, while questioning their genuineness and suggesting further observation.

And when he thought a defendant was honestly displaying symptoms, he said that, too. On our first case together, involving the brutal rape and murder of a ten-year-old girl, he gave the opinion that the defendant was insane but volunteered he had little factual support for his opinion. While I disagreed with him, I admired his frankness. You don't find that much in forensic psychiatry. When I did disagree with him, it was in cases where he believed there was genuine mental illness, and our disagreement went more to the legal significance of the illness than to its existence. Yet through all this disagreement, differing opinions, and professional respect, I have always known him to be an honest person—someone I respect immensely, even if I don't always agree with him.

In all of those years though, I had never seen him demonstrate the slightest reluctance to testify in any case on any issue. That day as we waited to begin the deposition, his demeanor was truly startling. In my opinion, he saw himself that day, not as a physician giving a diagnosis but as a vehicle for the transmission of a lie and I think the thought sickened him. I think he choose the word *vector* with great care. In his mind he was spreading the virus of Casey's lies. He knew that he was chosen because he would make the lie seem credible in a way she never could. In the end, I think he refused to allow himself to be used that way and he spoke his mind. I admire him for that because he was the only one who did.

We had asked Dr. Danziger to bring us copies of his notes from his interview with Casey, and we started out just going through them. A lot of them were biographical and background information, easy stuff. Then we got to the bombshell. Part of Casey's new claim was that at age eight, her father had begun molesting her. The abuse had included oral sex, vaginal— everything. It lasted until she was in her early teens, and then it stopped. According to Danziger's notes, her father was not the only abuser in the house. When she was a young teenager, her brother, Lee, had entered her room and felt up her breasts. She claimed she woke up and he was standing there, but he had not done anything other than that.

Then Danziger went over Casey's claims for the scenario that had played out on June 16, 2008. What follows is my best recollection of our conversation during the deposition with him. Casey was asleep in bed at 9 A.M. She was awakened by her father screaming at her, "Where is Caylee?"

Casey said that she would have Caylee sleep with her for Caylee's protection because she was afraid her father might try to molest Caylee. That morning, Casey slept very hard and very late for her. The subtext was that it was unusual for her to be that sound asleep, and we believed this was meant to imply that she had been drugged. Her father then began to search the house and he found Caylee in the pool.

Reading Danziger's report, we now had two versions of who found Caylee. Jose had told Linda that it had been Casey who found Caylee in the pool. But Casey's version to Danziger had George finding Caylee in the pool. In Danziger's version, George walked in with Caylee in his arms. She was dripping wet. He laid her on the floor and he began to scream, "This is your fault!"

Casey ran to her room, and that was the last she ever saw of Caylee.

Danziger said he interviewed Casey three times. We went methodically through the notes. During all three of her meetings with him, she consistently stuck with the exact same scenario.

That was the bombshell, but we still had the mushroom cloud.

Dr. Danziger went on to say that Casey told him she did not believe that Caylee drowned by accident. She did not believe that Caylee could have gotten into the pool on her own, because she couldn't have gotten the ladder up. Casey believed that her father drowned Caylee deliberately or drowned her while he was molesting her, even though she had no evidence that George had ever molested Caylee in the past.

This allegation of abuse was particularly alarming because in Danziger's interview with Casey when she was first arrested he had asked her specifically if she had ever been sexually abused and she had said no. Dr. Danziger had given her the Minnesota Multiphasic Personality Inventory (MMPI), a standard tool for a psychologist that he had taken special training to administer. Comprised of five hundred questions, the test is designed to discover mental illness or personality disorder. In all respects, she scored within normal ranges, Dr. Danziger said. He described her demeanor during the interviews as pleasant and happy, saying that the only emotion she showed was anger when she was describing her father.

That day, we did not complete Dr. Danziger's deposition, because we weren't anticipating the volume of information that he gave us. We agreed to reset it a few days later.

We didn't have much time to process everything we had heard. Dr. William Weitz was scheduled to talk with us that same day after lunch, and to the best of my memory, that deposition went like this:

We went through the same procedure with him as we had with Dr. Danziger, slowly and carefully reviewing his notes. He did not have the same reluctance as Dr. Danziger to relay his information to us.

As far as molestation went, Casey had basically told him the same story she had told Danziger: the abuse started when she was eight and included all manner of sexual activity. But she told him that the sexual activity continued into her late teens, which was longer than in her other account. She also said she had been concerned that George might be Caylee's father until the DNA test done by the FBI ruled out that possibility. Casey also told Dr. Weitz about Lee. She said she had tried to tell her mother about some aspect of the abuse, but Cindy had called her a whore.

As to the day of the tragedy, she added a few additional details to the version she'd told Danziger. She began by talking about being awakened by George and by him coming into the house with Caylee. Those details were the same.

The new detail was about the clothing. She told Dr. Weitz that Caylee went to bed wearing a nightgown, but when George brought her into the house in the morning she was wearing different clothes, striped shorts and a pink shirt, implying that George had changed her clothes. She explained in great detail that George's upper body was wet but that his lower body was not. The doctor took that as an indication that George held Caylee underwater while he himself was outside the pool. It seemed important to Casey to say that only her father's shirt was wet. She repeated her assertion that Caylee could not have died by accident and that George had murdered her.

She said that George yelled at her, "It's your fault. It's your fault. You're a bad mother." She said that she saw George carrying Caylee out of the house. She also told Dr. Weitz that she wasn't sure Caylee was dead, that in fact she thought Caylee might actually have been alive. From time to time during the thirty-one days, George would tell her that Caylee was okay.

She claimed that for the next thirty-one days, she was in a fog. She did not have a clear recollection of what she did or why she did it. She did tell him that she was not a "party girl." In explaining the "Bella Vita" tattoo, she said it was an ironic comment on the fact that her life hadn't been beautiful. Dr. Weitz could not elaborate further on what she meant by that statement. This was as far as we got in our first interview with him.

The goal of our initial interviews had been to gather the basic facts with the intention of conducting more probative examinations in the days ahead. But on the morning of our next scheduled appointment with Dr. Danziger, we received a call from Jose Baez saying that he wanted to withdraw him as a witness. There was no need for deposition, he said. No sooner had he dropped the eleventh-hour witness on our doorstep than he whisked him away.

I wanted to proceed, and when Jose and Danziger arrived at our office I insisted we continue the questioning. We questioned him briefly, but then Jose said he wanted to call Judge Perry to prevent me from asking another question. We did, and the judge said that just to be safe, if I wanted to continue, I'd have to file a motion, and we of course complied.

Dr. Weitz was also scheduled to give a deposition that day. When he arrived at the office, Jose did not interfere. Dr. Weitz told us that he had reviewed Dr. Dangizer's report. He brought to our attention Dr. Danziger's

MMPI results and agreed they were normal. Dr. Weitz had given her a battery of tests, including one designed to diagnose post-traumatic stress disorder brought on by trauma like sexual victimization. The test did not support the conclusion that she had been victimized. Weitz explained it this way to me: I am not diagnosing her as suffering from post-traumatic stress disorder, but all of these things that she did were as a result of the denial of having been sexually molested. You can understand all of this behavior by denial and suppression.

"So, when Casey said that Caylee was with the nanny, she believed it?" I asked him.

"Yes," Weitz said.

"When she was taking the cops through Universal, did she believe she worked there?"

"Yes."

"So what happened when she got to the end of the hall?" I questioned.

"Well, people can go in and out of denial" was his easy answer.

I didn't know denial could ebb and flow like that, but I was no psychologist.

After we took the doctors' depositions, both sides agreed in court that the transcript of the depositions should not be made public, because the allegations were so sensational. Until now their contents have never been discussed publicly. On the prosecution side, we wanted to spare George the weeks of pretrial discussions in the press. I could just see the *did he/ didn't he* debates all over HLN, and if there was any way to minimize that, I was all for it. As for the defense, we assumed that Baez wanted to keep the story under wraps so he'd get the "wow" headlines at the beginning of the trial.

Regardless of our motives, Judge Perry concurred with our assessments and the documents were sealed. In the end, though, Weitz did not testify either. Having completed the depositions of both therapists, we filed a motion to have Casey submit to an examination by a state-certified expert. This is a procedure that usually applies to insanity cases, and we felt it should apply in this odd circumstance as well. We argued that point in court, and Judge Perry agreed with us. If the defense was going to offer mental health testimony, we had the right to have Casey submit to an examination by our own expert.

After Judge Perry agreed, Cheney took Jose in the back. It was clear there were risks for them in giving our expert access to Casey. For one thing, our expert could get Casey talking and lead her in a direction that the defense had no control over. Then there was always a risk that she could reveal something she didn't mean to when our expert had her alone.

When they returned, we were informed that they were pulling both psychologists from their witness list. They might still have an expert testify on some hypotheticals about mental health, but they would spring that on us later during the trial.

I knew what Jose Baez had been up to. He had two possible objectives. The first, I think, was that he was trying to get Casey's story in front of the jury without having Casey actually testify. The two psychiatrists would have testified to everything Casey told them about what went down on June 16, as well as all her allegations about her father and brother. Meanwhile, she would be protected from having to take the stand because of the rules of self-incrimination. Baez's second motive was to present some explanation for why Casey would take thirty-one days to report that her daughter had disappeared or died. We were surprised that Baez had not anticipated the request for our own expert evaluation and considered that before showing his hand like he had. We appreciated the heads-up, nonetheless.

EVEN THOUGH THE WITNESSES HAD been withdrawn, Linda, Frank, and I all wondered how much of this George and Cindy knew. Just because the defense had dropped the witnesses didn't mean they were abandoning the argument completely. There was still a chance that George could be dragged into this.

One evening around the time that all this was happening, Mark Lippman, the attorney who by then was representing George and Cindy, filed a strange press release. It said something to the effect that George Anthony had nothing to do with the disappearance of Caylee. I thought it was an odd statement, and I figured it indicated that they knew about the allegations, so I contacted Mark. Linda was in the room when I asked him about his press release, assuming that the release had been somehow in response to these new inflammatory allegations from Casey. I wanted to know if in light of the allegations, we should expect George or Cindy to change any of their testimony. During the call, I sensed that Mark and I were not talking about the same sequence of events. "Mark, what is it that you think the new story is?" I asked.

Mark told me that a few days earlier, Baez had asked for a meeting with just Cindy. When she arrived at his office, Baez, Dorothy Sims, and Ann Finnell via the phone were waiting for her with important news. Baez proceeded to tell Cindy that Casey had authorized him to say that Caylee had died at the house and that her death had been an accident. Baez also told Cindy that the state was investigating George's involvement with Caylee's death. Baez claimed that the authorities had information from a witness who said that George's phone records held valuable clues.

I was speechless. Poor Mark only knew the tip of the iceberg. It was the cruelest thing I have ever seen an attorney do. Many times in defending a client a lawyer must do things that end up causing pain to innocent people. It happens, and I lay no blame on them. To tell this grieving woman, who for almost two years had held out hope that her daughter had nothing to do with the death of her little angel, that her own home was the place where it happened was bad enough. But to try and convince her that her husband was implicated and in jeopardy was beyond the pale. To me, there was no way to justify that kind of statement—no matter how "passionate" Baez may have been to defend his client. The only strategy I could see was that he was trying to get them to refuse to cooperate with us, fearing the prosecution of George.

"That is not the story that we have been given," I told Mark. I also informed him that Jose's claim that we were investigating George was a complete and utter lie. I believe my exact words were "That's a fucking lie."

I was outraged. Cindy and George hadn't been the most helpful people throughout our investigation, but no one deserved to be treated like this. I was appalled that Baez would dare to tell these anguished parents a fat, blatant lie, while simultaneously hiding from the real, horrifying accusation that he was likely to make in open court. It shouldn't have amazed me. From the moment I joined the case, I found myself saying over and over again, "I can't believe he did that." I kept trying to think the best of Jose and kept finding out how wrong I was.

I told Mark we weren't investigating George, although sadly there was more bad news. But I had to get back to him about it. Linda and I discussed the best way to handle the therapists' reports and we decided to invite Mark, Cindy, and George to our office. I gave Mark a call.

"We would like to speak with your clients," I told him. "Have them come to our office with you. What Jose is telling Cindy is not true. I understand that the Anthonys may not trust us, but if they would like to read the transcripts we now have in our possession, they can see exactly what Casey is saying about what happened." I didn't give Mark any indication of what I knew, beyond that the transcripts were from mental health experts.

Mark started guessing what it might be. "Are they saying that George disposed of the body?" he asked.

"No, it is worse than that. It is worse than you can imagine," I said.

Mark had a conversation with Cindy and George, telling them about Baez's fabrication. Cindy was furious. Mark later told us that she called Baez and cursed him out for lying to her, she then told him she was coming to see us to read the psychiatrists' transcripts for herself.

When Baez found out that Cindy was coming to our office to see what the doctors had said, he immediately shot off an e-mail to Judge Perry, essentially accusing us of violating Perry's order.

Linda said that Judge Perry's order indicated only that the transcripts would not be made public documents; it never restricted our ability to investigate the story, and there was no way we were going to let Jose's lies go unchallenged. Baez would later attack us on this point, but the judge agreed with us.

What we decided was that if the depositions were sealed, we would just discuss our notes and our recollections with the Anthonys. At this point, we felt we had to tell them. They needed to know the truth about what was going on. We were prepared for the defense to accuse us of all manner of witness tampering, but we were willing to take the risk. We felt a moral obligation to George and Cindy, even though we didn't know where their loyalties lay. We never deluded ourselves into thinking that anything we could do would bring Cindy out of her denial, but we figured that maybe if Cindy wasn't willing to come out of denial for Caylee, she might be for George.

George and Cindy were visibly upset when they arrived, polite but very apprehensive. They were not very talkative. We made the usual introductions, "How are you, nice to see you," that kind of thing.

I hadn't seen them in a while. The last time I had any conversation with either of them was with George at the Frye hearing. Generally, when we saw them at the hearings, there would be a polite nod exchange, though sometimes not even that.

Before the meeting, we'd told Mark that we would speak to him privately and share what we knew with him. Then it would be up to him to decide what to tell the Anthonys. We put Cindy and George in the conference room and took Mark into the office with us.

Linda and I carefully told him the story the shrinks had told us, as he jotted everything down on his legal pad to keep the story straight. He was in complete disbelief. He looked at us and said, "I cannot believe Jose lied to Cindy like that." Mark asked us a couple of questions for clarification, but not many.

"It's your decision what you tell your clients," Linda and I said. "We are going to give you privacy. You tell them that we will wait for them. When you are done, if they have any questions, we will speak to them, but we are not going to interrogate them or ask them any questions."

Mark left and went to the conference room to talk to the Anthonys for what seemed like twenty to thirty minutes. Linda and I were in a nearby conference room when Mark came to find us. Cindy and George had questions, and we accompanied him back to the conference room. Cindy was sitting at the table just looking down. George was next to her, his face bright red. Cindy looked angry. George looked like he had been crying, like someone had just killed Caylee all over again. He was just devastated.

"I just want you to know that none of this is true," George said to us.

Cindy patted him on the hand and said, "It's okay, George. Nobody believes this."

His words would catch in his throat as he assured us one more time, "I just want you to know that everything I told you is the truth and I am not changing any of it."

I remember Cindy saying something like, "I don't know what's wrong with her," referring to Casey. At least she was finally willing to admit that there was something not right about Casey. How it would affect her testimony at trial, though, was anyone's guess.

That said, I didn't get the sense of hostility I had in the past. I think the realization that Caylee had in fact died in Casey's custody, at the very least, changed their animosity toward us. While they didn't turn into supporters of the prosecution, they were not quite as obstinate.

Of course, the Anthonys weren't the only wild cards in the deck. By now, we also knew to expect some kind of a "surprise" witness from Baez in the middle of the trial; all we could do was hope that whatever it was, we'd be able to handle it on the fly. Over the years, we'd all become pretty good at that, since Baez was not the first defense attorney to practice the ambush tactic. Part of the frequency of these ambushes comes from an unfortunate flaw in Florida's discovery rule: it is extremely rare that discovery violations by the defense during the trial are punished by the exclusion of that evidence. Most defense attorneys know this, so the risk to the client is minor. A few years ago, the state added contempt against the attorney as one of the punishments in the judge's arsenal, but unfortunately it is rarely used. As prosecutors, all we could do was adjust and try to prepare for the unexpected.

Heading into the trial, there was no telling how it all would play out. We had confidence in our case. We knew what evidence we had on our side. We knew what evidence they had on theirs. We also now knew what their defense was going to be, and that without the therapists on the stand to be the mouthpiece for Casey's version of events, Casey herself was going to have to testify. Linda would be ready for the cross-examination.

It all came down to the jury now. Could we get a jury with a modicum of intelligence that would see through the bombast and the lies? Could we get a jury that would care enough about Caylee to put in the work necessary to see the truth, to see Casey for who and what she was? It was anyone's guess. As good as we felt about where we were, the jury was, and always is, a crapshoot—the one part we couldn't control.

PART III

CHAPTER NINETEEN

JURY SELECTION

Saying that Florida is familiar with high-profile legal cases is a gross understatement. In many ways, our state's laws regarding the media are tailor-made for precisely this kind of court case: our discovery laws release information to both the defense and the media simultaneously, and our court system allows cameras inside the courtroom. But even in a state that had seen its fair share of media trials, this was unlike anything we'd ever experienced.

The clamor for new information was unparalleled. Usually, in sensational cases, the media would request copies of discovery, but because of the overwhelming demand and the huge volume of documents (over twenty-five thousand by the end), we had to create a special website so that media outlets could easily access the latest batch of photos or documents that we'd provided to the defense. Even during the slower years when we were simply taking depositions and filing motions, it seemed like barely a night went by without some mention of Casey Anthony in the news.

Sometimes this extensive coverage of the case's minutiae would work to our advantage. While the defense was all too comfortable using the media to get their message out, we had determined in the beginning that we would not respond publicly to their comments. However, because the media would always cover the motions and responses that were filed by either side, we allowed ourselves to present a different kind of public response. I took personal delight at times in crafting lines in motions that I knew the media would pick up and run with. Ordinarily the motions would have gone by unnoticed, but in a case where literally every document was scoured, this was as close as we could come to putting out formal statements. In the end, it was the only way we had to respond.

It amazed me the way some people followed this case on the Internet. There were bloggers who read every single word of all twenty-five-thousand-plus documents. We would frequently get e-mails from people with suggestions for things to look into. Most of these were about as helpful as you'd expect, but occasionally there would be a gem that actually was of use. Likewise, there were regular blogs and websites that featured very well-considered commentary on the evidence, while others were just mean. The cycle of consuming new information and digesting it into analysis was incredibly fast. People came up with outrageous theories online one day and then moved on to something else the next. As a result, I think the defense actually used the blogs as sort of an informal focus group to test potential defenses. In my opinion, that may have made blaming George an appealing defense. It would have been fascinating to watch, if I hadn't been so busy living it.

Fairly early on, this overwhelming amount of pretrial publicity made it clear that we would need to face the issue of changing venues. When it appears to the court that a fair and impartial jury cannot be found in the county where the crime occurred, the law permits the court to move locations. There are some appellate opinions that suggest that the court should at least attempt to select a jury in the home venue before moving on, but most of the time that is a futile gesture.

In my career, I'd had five trials change venue to five different counties all over the state. In each of those instances, it was pretty obvious that the level of pretrial publicity was too high for a fair trial to take place. So when the issue first came up in this case, it was a no-brainer. There was a news report on this case almost every day; even the most trivial things would warrant mention in the news. Once they even ran a story on what items Casey was buying in the jail commissary. There was no way we were going to get a jury from Orlando, and anyone we would get, we wouldn't want.

So for almost two years we knew that we would be arguing this case before a jury from somewhere other than Orange County. At one point, the defense filed a motion for change of venue and Baez suggested, big surprise, Dade County, where he was from (the judge denied his request). Our laws give the judge some guidance in choosing the new venue, and demographic similarity is to be considered in the selection process. As a practical matter, though, the venue change is more about who will take us than where we want to go. A high-publicity trial from out of town can be a very disruptive affair. Judge Perry would have to schmooze his fellow chief judges from around the state to get one of them to help us out, but if anyone was up for the job, he was. Of the five out-of-town trials I'd done, four were with him. He knew what was involved in the process.

Wherever the trial took place, we knew that the jury would be sequestered, meaning that once the jury was selected, they would be shielded from any outside influence whatsoever. They would literally be prisoners in a gilded cage. There was no way we wanted to take the chance of a juror going home at night and seeing something on the news or overhearing someone talking about something they shouldn't hear and causing a mistrial. As discussion about the change of venue progressed, we had a thought: since we were going to have to sequester the jurors anyway, we argued and the judge agreed, we might as well have the trial in Orlando and avoid the expense of putting all of us up in hotels in another city, too. So it was decided: we would pick a jury somewhere else and bring them to Orlando. That way, I would only be away from Rita and the kids for a week or so for the jury selection, as opposed to six weeks or so for the trial.

SHORTLY AFTER HE'D JOINED THE case, Judge Perry had told us he was going to keep our eventual location a secret until right before the trial. His main concern was that if the media got hold of the location, they would be on the streets days before jury selection began, doing man-on-the-street interviews and further tainting any prospective jury pool. As we got closer to the trial, the lead time the judge said he would give us to make arrangements at the new location kept getting shorter. First he said we would find out two weeks before the trial, then one week, then finally it was the Thursday before the start of the trial. From time to time, Judge Perry would drop little clues, and then smile that mischievous smile of his. I was pretty sure he was messing with everyone, but he really enjoyed pulling your leg sometimes.

Judge Perry also created a process whereby the media could, by signing a confidentiality agreement, get the location a day in advance. This would allow them to get their equipment in place but prevent them from publicizing the location. It was a nice thought, but some of the news outlets appealed the order, and the district court agreed with them that the court couldn't force them to sign an agreement as a condition to finding out where we were going. Instead the ruling stated that the judge didn't have to tell them where we were going at all. So he didn't.

Finally, the Thursday morning before the start of the trial, Linda was called to the judge's chambers with Baez to get the news. First Judge Perry made them sign copies of his order specifically naming those involved in the case or those who would need to make the travel arrangements and ordering us all under pain of contempt not to reveal the location. Linda came back to her office where Frank and I were waiting. She smiled like the Cheshire Cat as she entered.

"Where is the best place you can imagine we'd go?" she asked.

"Tampa," I said.

She looked at me and said, "Pinellas County."

So for all of Baez's efforts to get this jury from his old stomping grounds, we were going to get them from mine. I was going home.

Though the criminal courts complex had been built since I moved away, one of the trials I had done with Judge Perry in the past was there, so I knew the layout. The courthouse was out near a little regional airport halfway between the two largest cities in the county, Saint Petersburg, where I grew up, to the south and Clearwater to the north. We went up and told Lawson and, authorized by the order, he immediately called the state attorney in that circuit, Bernie McCabe. It turned out that he had known about it for months from his chief judge. He was most gracious and offered the use of his office and any assistance we would need.

The next day the defense filed an objection to the chosen venue, and I liked the way Judge Perry handled it. We had a hurriedly called hearing in chambers with all the attorneys present and a court reporter. When the defense began to complain about the demographics issue—apparently Pinellas has a smaller percentage of Hispanic residents than Orange does—Perry looked at them and said, "Well, the only other place I can think of that can accommodate us on such short notice is Jacksonville. You want to go there?" Located in the northeastern corner of Florida, Jacksonville is thought to be a more conservative area politically, and thus was not the first choice of the defense. They withdrew their objections, and we left to pack.

On that Friday the *St. Petersburg Times* was reporting unusual activity at their courthouse: extra deputies being brought in, additional food for the courthouse cafeteria, and parking spaces being roped off. The logistics alone had tipped them off, and while no one was confirming it, the media pretty much knew. My sister Judy, who had followed the case, sent me a text when the article came out asking if it was true. I told her I couldn't answer till Monday.

In a way I was kind of relieved that they had a clue where we were going. We had nightmares of the media camped outside our homes waiting to follow us to the location. I had decided not to drive, so Linda agreed to pick me up in her car. She showed up Sunday morning dressed casually for the drive over. It's always weird seeing people that you encounter every day in a business suit suddenly dressed differently. She was wearing an odd-looking shirt with a number on it, white pants, and white sunglasses. I packed up the car and off we went. The drive to Pinellas is about two hours, so we talked about the case a bit on the way but mostly just chitchatted.

We arrived at our hotel after Frank, who had already checked in. He met us in the parking lot. When Linda got out of the car, Frank laughed and said, "Nice outfit."

"Finally," Linda responded. "Someone who is observant. I've been riding with this dummy for two hours and he hasn't noticed a thing."

What had escaped my attention was this: When Casey was arrested, a photo of her being escorted in handcuffs by the police had been taken that had been shown a thousand times. In it, she is wearing a blue hooded short-sleeved shirt with the number 82 on the front. It was one of the items she bought with her friend Amy's forged checks, along with a pair of white sunglasses. I had forgotten that early in the case Linda had gone out and bought the identical shirt and glasses. So the entire drive, she'd been in her Casey costume. I totally missed it. They had a good laugh at my expense, and at that point I think we all needed a good laugh.

Once we were all assembled, Linda had an interesting suggestion. We were still trying to keep a low profile since the word wasn't out officially that we were in town. Linda wanted us to sneak over to the courthouse and get a group picture to commemorate the occasion. Frank and I thought it was a great idea. After dinner, we went over to the courthouse and scouted out a place for our picture. There were too many news trucks already near the building itself, so we cruised through but didn't stop. I kept thinking we were going to get stopped by some cop thinking we were up to no good. Finally we settled on a sign on the road at the other end of the parking lot. Linda pulled off on the shoulder, and we all got out and posed—Linda in her Casey costume, Frank in jeans and a T-shirt, and me in my favorite flowered Hawaiian shirt—next to a sign that said Pinellas County Criminal Justice Center. (And in case you were about to flip to the photo insert, no, that picture is not in this book. Some things are just for us.)

The next morning we arrived early for the first day of jury selection. We were warmly greeted by Beverly Andringa, the chief assistant state attorney and sort of second in command at the office, who then introduced us to Tom Diebold, the lead investigator in the office. Both Beverly and Tom were extremely helpful and offered us a conference room to use. Throughout the selection, Tom continued to assist us during the times when it became necessary for us to investigate what jurors told us about their backgrounds. In addition to offering us the use of their helpful staff, the state attorney's offices were quite convenient, as they were located in the same building and on the same floor as the courtroom. It was just a matter of going out a door, and we were just down the hall.

The chief judge of the circuit allowed us to use their largest courtroom for the public proceedings and an adjacent room normally used by their grand jury as a waiting area for the potential jurors. The courtroom was huge. It could easily seat a hundred and fifty spectators.

During the lead-up to the trial, Judge Perry had frequently said that we would be using an unusual method for jury selection. To understand the importance of the change he was referring to, you must understand a little about the usual method of jury selection. First, the name is a little misleading. It makes it sound as if you get to look at a list of available options and choose the ones you like, like picking from a menu. The more proper name would probably be jury exclusion. Instead of being able to choose people you like, you actually can only exclude people you don't. The normal procedure begins by questioning the jurors as a group all seated in one room. When all the jurors have been questioned, they are then individually offered to each side according to their order on a seating chart until the required number has been selected. This process gives the attorneys the advantage of knowing who the next juror will be, should they choose to exclude someone presently on the panel.

While this is the system that's commonly employed, Florida law does not mandate this exact system. The judge has the ability to use alternate systems for selection, so long as the process does not unduly restrict the ability of both sides to ask relevant questions and does not prevent either side from excluding jurors up until the time the jury is sworn to hear the case. Sometimes judges get frustrated with attorneys using these rules in a tactical way to get a better jury. Throughout the jury selection Judge Perry kept changing the way he was doing it. We started with a group of one hundred potential jurors, and he began by discussing hardship, trying to weed out those who, because of economic or other personal issues, just could not serve for six to eight weeks. We lost about half the panel on that. With the pool that was left, he then brought them in individually to discuss publicity, the death penalty, and then any other topic that seemed fitting.

For the next day and a half we repeated that process over and over again. It was incredibly tedious. I must confess I hate jury selection, especially in a capital case where you hear the same questions over and over again. Ann Finnell, who would be handling that portion of the case for the defense, had a series of eleven questions that she asked of every single juror, and as you can imagine, by the fiftieth juror I could recite the questions from memory. By the two hundredth juror, I wanted to pull my hair out. To her credit, she accomplished all these questions with a terrible cold. I felt sorry for her; then I caught it from her. I was coughing for a month, while she was better in a few days.

When we got through the first hundred jurors on the hardship issue, the judge called up another group of fifty to question. As Linda passed some of the jurors in the hallway she took a long look at one small-framed older woman. Then she came up to me and told me that she thought she recognized her from the case. Linda had done many of the depositions of the EquuSearch searchers by herself. She asked me if I remembered a story of two older ladies who had come over from Pinellas County to volunteer in the search, one of whom was a real gabby character—the kind of person who if you ask her what time it is, she'll tell you how to make a watch. I had a vague recollection of the story, and Linda then said she thought one of those women was on the jury panel. If this was the lady she described, we were in trouble. Our fear was that, being the gabby type, she would have discussed her involvement in the case with other jurors.

Linda told the defense and the judge. We brought the potential juror into court and confirmed that Linda was correct, this woman had indeed volunteered for EquuSearch. We began to speak to the other jurors and our fears were confirmed: she had told anyone that would listen about her involvement. Just to be safe, the judge struck the whole group. Since we had no other jurors to question, we lost the remainder of that day. What are the odds that of the almost nine hundred thousand residents of Pinellas County, the one person who was involved in our case was called in for jury duty on that particular day? Like so much else in this case, it was the strangest of coincidences.

The questioning dragged on through the first week with little progress. We'd get to court early, eat lunch in the cafeteria, work until six, and return to the hotel for dinner and sleep. It is a grueling schedule. Judge Perry, who thought we would be able to pick the jury in a week, was getting visibly frustrated with our lack of progress and made us work on Saturday.

On Saturday afternoon Rita and the kids came over, and I sure needed the break. It was such a relief to see them. We took the kids to the beach on Sunday morning, and they left by midafternoon. By three that afternoon I crashed—we were all exhausted, and eventually the process got to everyone. On Wednesday of the second week, we had to break at midday because Baez was throwing up in the bathroom. The way he was sucking down Red Bulls and energy drinks, I'm not surprised he got sick.

Tedious as it was, this was the most technologically advanced jury selection I had been involved in. We used the Internet extensively. Our greatest concern was having a juror who was looking to cash in. We actually smoked out a couple of potential jurors through Facebook and Twitter postings.

As the days of jury selection wore on, we came to the realization that the amount of publicity here was almost as bad as back home. Almost everyone had heard about it. As if the rigors of six to eight weeks away from home weren't bad enough, the publicity eliminated most of the jurors that we felt we wanted. It wasn't just that they'd heard about it; many had formed strong opinions about it. The problem was that the prosecution needed people who formed strong opinions.

This was still a circumstantial case where the defendant's guilt would be proved by connecting pieces of evidence that told a story. Most murder cases are circumstantial. Murders are rarely committed in front of witnesses; most are secret crimes. Sometimes circumstantial evidence is the only way to answer the question of the whos, whys, or hows of a crime.

Though some in the media speak derisively about a case by referring to it as circumstantial, a well-connected chain of circumstantial evidence is often stronger than an eyewitness case. The downside to circumstantial cases, however, is that they require more of the jury—more thought, more attention, and often more intelligence. Of the seventy murder cases I have brought in my career, the vast majority of them were circumstantial. Most of the people who sit on death row today were convicted on circumstantial evidence.

Think of it this way: In this case we needed jurors who cared about what goes on in the world and were willing to do something about it. Not necessarily activists who go out and protest, but people who would give a damn about what happened to a little girl. We needed jurors of intelligence who could comprehend the evidence we were going to be giving them—not just the scientific evidence, but the evidence as a whole. No one was going to give them this case on a silver platter; we didn't have the evidence to serve anything up nice and easy. The jurors were going to have to put the pieces together and apply some commonsense understanding of how people act and don't act. It wouldn't require a formal education, but it would take intelligence. Last, we needed jurors who believed in following the law and were willing to take on the responsibility of making important decisions.

The difficulty we found was that the people who cared about what was going on in the world around them were the very people who had watched the case in the media. And because they were moved by what had happened to Caylee, they'd followed it even more. As intelligent people who'd listened to the evidence as it had been revealed in the media, they'd followed that evidence to its logical conclusion. As people who believed in the law, they were honest about their previously formed conclusions when they were asked about them. The end result was that anyone who would see the evidence the way we wanted them to had already seen the evidence and drawn the conclusions we drew. Those conclusions reflected the attitude in the court of public opinion, but in the real court they had to be disqualified.

In the end, it took us eleven days to get the jury selected. We struck down many, and the defense did as well. When all was said and done, the jury was made up of five men and seven women, with one African-American woman and one African-American man. Their backgrounds were as follows:

JUROR 1: An older woman who was married, as I recall. She had been trained and worked as a nurse for many years, but now she was in retirement, working as a counselor. She seemed nice, but not a take-charge kind of person. When it comes to juries, older folks tend to be judgmental, but people involved in counseling generally are not, so that combination made her hard to read. She had no major minuses for us, but gave us no great enthusiasm.

JUROR 2: An African-American gentleman who I believe had heard about the case and candidly admitted that he thought Casey was guilty. However, he said he could keep an open mind. I liked him. He seemed levelheaded. I didn't think he'd be the foreman, but I thought he'd listen to us. I was surprised the defense didn't strike him after his admission that he believed Casey guilty.

JUROR 3: Jennifer Ford. I use her name because she has been interviewed publicly since the trial. A nursing student in her thirties, Jennifer appeared to be starting her career a little late, so I sensed that she had a change of career path at some point. Working and going to school is tough, so I thought she would judge Casey's apparent laziness harshly. I don't recall that she had kids, which was a minus in my mind. The way I remember it, Frank didn't care for her, saying he didn't like her attitude. I guess his instincts were good after all.

JUROR 4: An African-American woman in her forties. One of the first things she volunteered was that she didn't feel she could judge other people. Usually when someone brings something like that up, it's a sure sign that they either really mean it or just don't want to be there. Later she would modify that somewhat to claim that she thought she could serve in spite of that belief. We tried to strike her, but the defense objected, claiming we were striking her based on her race. I thought it was an obvious call, since by her own admission she was going to have trouble judging anyone and judgment is the sole purpose of the jury. My jaw dropped when Judge Perry wouldn't let us excuse her. I thought that legally we were acting reasonably and within the law. I only hoped that the judge saw something in her I had missed, but her views on judgment made her seem like a sure vote for the defense.

JUROR 5: The "roach coach lady." Her job was working on one of those mobile lunch wagons, thus the nickname. An older woman with very little education. We would have struck her if we'd had anyone better. She had grown kids and had worked hard all her life. I hoped she would bring that life experience to bear when listening to Casey 4.0.

JUROR 6: The baker. A married father, he clearly did not want to serve, but he didn't have a good reason not to. His kids were young, as I recall, and I thought he would not buy into any excuse for a mother partying shortly after her daughter died. He was okay but still not the leader that we needed.

JUROR 7: A white female in her early forties. I believe she worked in some occupation related to children or child welfare. I liked her, as she seemed fairly well-educated and levelheaded. She was the only juror I recall who showed much emotion throughout the trial, and at the end of it all, when the clerk read the verdict, she was the only one who shed a tear.

JUROR 8: A white female in her fifties. She worked for AT&T in a job she'd had for many years. She also did not have too much formal education, but we hoped life experience would play a role.

JUROR 9: A white male in his fifties. He had never married, but he spoke with great affection about some nieces and nephews. Originally from Indiana, where he'd managed a sawmill, he referred to himself as "semiretired." Rather mild-mannered and not forceful, he was a very thin fellow, who actually looked rather frail. I knew he was not going to lead anyone and would probably follow the majority.

JUROR 10: A white male in his forties who'd never married, lived alone, and also worked at the phone company. He was fairly tall, very friendly, but a definite follower. He was the guy who sits in the cubicle next to you for years and never makes waves. He's always pleasant and easy to manage—every supervisor's dream.

JUROR 11: The one we referred to as "the coach." He was a high school sports coach who was working in special education. He was from Pittsburgh—same hometown as Linda, so she liked him—and he seemed like a good-looking, stand-up guy. He hadn't heard much about the case. I figured that as a high school teacher he probably had experience of being lied to. I also thought that as a high school teacher, especially as an attractive male, he must always have had in the back of his mind the possibility of a false allegation of a sexual nature by a female student. If they made the allegation against George, that might help us. Linda pushed hard for this guy. She thought he would be the leader we were looking for.

JUROR 12: My favorite. The defense had exhausted all of their challenges. She was pro death penalty, which in itself was not that big a deal, but I thought it showed she was strong in her opinions. She was in her sixties. Retired but working at a local supermarket chain. I wasn't sure that she had a lot of formal education, but I hoped she'd have a lot of common sense.

When we got to the end, we had these twelve jurors as well as five alternates. We could have struck four more of the existing jurors and replaced them with alternates, but when it came to the five we had remaining, I just didn't see that any of them was an upgrade over what we had. In fact, a few were much worse, and going to them would also have resulted in bringing in a new panel and extending our stay another few days.

I wouldn't say we were happy with the jury. They were very bland and not all that impressive. They were not the jury we'd wanted when we set out to do this, but they were the jury that would ultimately decide the fate of Casey Anthony.

CHAPTER TWENTY

―――

SEARCHING FOR TRUTH

The day before the trial began, Monday, May 22, 2011, I met with George Anthony for the final time. He came to my office with his attorney, Mark Lippman, looking as worn down as I'd ever seen him. I just wanted to meet with him to go over what I was going to ask him in testimony. As we spoke, he seemed to have come back to the place that he was the first time we met him. He seemed to be accepting his daughter's involvement in all this. That day, right before the trial began, he actually said something that I hadn't heard from him before—ever.

"I know that Casey did something to Caylee," he told me. "I just don't know what."

Hearing him utter those words was actually heartbreaking because he seemed very torn between the real affection he still felt for his daughter and the greater affection he had for his granddaughter.

"We don't expect you not to love your daughter," I told him. "Or have any of this affect your feelings for her."

"This case has been about Casey for far too long, and not enough about Caylee," he replied.

I couldn't have agreed with him more and I told him so, which seemed to please him.

I shared a few things with him that we were planning on doing at the trial, and he seemed comfortable with all of it. George lit up when I told him the first part of his testimony would be about Caylee. He really seemed to miss talking about her. For so long, everybody had been talking so much about Casey that Caylee was often forgotten.

I told him how we had to prepare for the worst, even though the defense had withdrawn the names of Dr. Danziger and Dr. Weitz from its witness list. Now that we knew they had the molestation card in their hand, we didn't know how or when they would play it. I told George how we would handle these accusations of sexual abuse, if they were made. That we were going to allow him to immediately deny and refute them. We were going to address them head-on if they were brought up. I took him through the various stages of his testimony, and what he should expect. All he needed to do was be truthful.

George definitely seemed like he wanted to tell his story and tell it for the last time. He just wanted it done. The hardest part of our conversation was when I had to bring up his suicide attempt. I told him that if the defense was going to accuse him of killing Caylee, the strongest piece of evidence refuting that was the suicide note, and that really seemed to hit him hard.

He made a comment along the lines of "Whatever doesn't kill you makes you stronger," that kind of thing. I think he was prepared to deal with it. It was best for both of us that he was prepared to talk about it, if it came up.

As we were wrapping up, George turned to me and said, "I'm happy this trial is finally happening. This way I can finally know the truth."

I looked at him, and spent a brief moment looking into the eyes of a man that I'd spent nearly three years grappling with. In that time, I'd found him both maddeningly frustrating and tragically relatable. He didn't deserve what he'd been put through—no one did. But still it was hard to ignore how even now, he could not totally confront what I felt was the plain, undisputable truth: that Casey killed Caylee. Still, even if Casey was found guilty, even if the jury believed our version of the truth, that didn't mean he'd be able to completely embrace the idea that his daughter was a killer, and it didn't mean all his questions would be answered. That's the tricky thing about justice. As much as I wanted to assure him that everything was going to be okay, I knew from every trial I'd ever worked on—from the traffic division to homicide—that justice rarely feels like you expect it to. I wanted to tell him that we'd finally know the facts, but I also had a responsibility to be brutally honest with this man, who'd spent too much time being lied to and lying to himself.

"We probably will never really know the truth. The truth was buried inside Casey, and we just have to accept that we may never get to the bottom of it."

BUT WHAT OF OUR TRUTH? What about the truth that we on the prosecution had come to believe in? What was our version of the events? The evidence in the case told us that Casey had murdered her daughter, and the State had committed to allowing the jury to decide if it wanted to sentence her to death. As such, we'd spent nearly three years working a theory about how Caylee died. It wasn't necessarily something we'd present to the court all in one place, it might not even be something that we would acknowledge altogether, but it was something we had to have for the broad outlines of the narrative we were presenting.

As with all criminal cases, we the prosecution got our facts from the investigators and experts who have worked the case, and we had to build these facts into the best case we could at trial. After we had gotten the evidence from the Orange County Sheriff's Department, we knew our strong points and began to develop them. We knew Caylee's skull had three pieces of duct tape across the nose and mouth. We had Casey's tattoo, "Bella Vita," so we had a strong motive that Casey desired a life not burdened by having a child. We had lots of evidence tying Casey to the homicide, the Winnie-the-Pooh blanket, the laundry bag, and of course, the duct tape. Furthermore, we had forensic evidence in the form of the odor and the hair analysis which demonstrated that Caylee had been in the trunk of the Pontiac.

Casey had not reported her daughter missing for thirty-one days, a crime in itself in my mind. She had spun lies until they dead-ended and could go no further, about everything from a phantom nanny to where she worked to where she had been those four and a half weeks. In our opinion, none of this was the behavior of a grieving mother. Even though police had not given Casey a polygraph, I believe she was such a good liar she would have likely passed it anyway. A lie detector would only prove just how convinced she was of her own fictions.

As happy as we were with our strong points, we had to consider our weak points as well. After all, absent a cause of death, this was a circumstantial case. To us, the presence of chloroform in the trunk pointed to Casey using it on Caylee, probably to knock her out. However, no chloroform was found in the Anthonys' home when it had been searched. Similarly, there had been a "how to make chloroform" search performed on Casey's computer in March of 2008, but three months had gone by before Caylee died, which left a gap between when she conducted the search and when the child was last seen.

It would be harder to argue that Casey had used chloroform on Caylee when she had not made a more recent search, however, we had the evidence of chloroform in the trunk and we had discovered something interesting on Ricardo Morales's MySpace page. An advertisement-style photo of a man and a woman on an upscale date in a restaurant mentions the powerful anesthetic. The man is leaning over the woman to kiss her neck, and in the hand obscured from her view is a man's handkerchief. The caption states, "Win her over with chloroform."

This posting may have aroused Casey's curiosity about the knockout potential of chloroform, and gotten her to thinking of using it. But we really weren't sure how our chloroform theory would hold up in court. At the time, our computer forensics person had reported that there had been searches performed on the Anthonys' home computer that included the word "chloroform," "how to make chloroform," and one search for "how to break a neck."

Another challenge was overcoming the fact that everyone said Casey was a good mother. Caylee never showed evidence of abuse or neglect. Friends of Casey said she was fond of her daughter, nobody had seen her become annoyed or short-tempered with her daughter. Caylee's room was neat and tidy and filled with toys.

This was an area where more candid testimony from Cindy Anthony would have been helpful. We knew from Cindy's coworkers that Cindy had her own doubts about Casey's parenting of Caylee and that Cindy felt Casey wanted to party too much rather than take care of her daughter. We also knew that some had even gone so far as to suggest to Cindy that she seek custody of Caylee, a drastic move to be sure, but also one that Cindy seemed to have considered. If Cindy had owned up to those conflicts with Casey—in police interviews, in depositions, and on the stand—we would have had a powerful rebuttal to defense claims of Casey as the perfect young mother. It wouldn't have explained Casey's jump to violence, but it certainly could have gone a long way to showing the jury where Casey's priorities lay. Unfortunately we never got that level of cooperation from Cindy.

Another hurdle was how the law severely restricted our ability to persuade the jury to focus on the victim. The appellate courts are very sensitive to attempts to evoke naked sympathy for the victim that may affect the jury. However, the courts rarely restrict the ability of the defendant to play the sympathy card under the guise of a legitimate defense. Even the best judge will often err on the side of excluding evidence about the victim that does not relate to an issue in the case.

Ultimately, though, we thought the weak points of our case were minor, and easily surmountable with the right jury. We knew that in the opening remarks we would be safe introducing Caylee to the jury in a general way, but that eventually she would be reduced to a mere piece of evidence in the case. We could only hope the seed we planted early would be enough to make the jurors care enough about Caylee to sustain her image throughout the weeks. After that, it would be up to the jurors to keep her at the forefront.

There is this common belief that jurors' hearts go out to children who are the victims of homicide, but in my experience that is less the case when a parent is accused of the crime. They have a much easier time accepting the homicide when it has been committed by a stranger. It is too horrible to comprehend that a parent could kill his or her own child, especially one so young and defenseless. For a jury, maternal filicide was the most difficult crime of all.

Our theory was as follows:

What we knew of Casey was that the primary motivating force in her life was herself. There is a self-centeredness that comes with adolescence, and while most teens outgrow it, Casey never did. We knew we would never fully understand the real relationship between Casey and her mother. Cindy's denial prevented that. But from everyone we'd talked to and from what we'd witnessed ourselves, we did know that there was conflict.

George and Cindy had expectations of Casey, seeing that she was living in their home. They expected her to work and contribute to the household. Exactly why Casey didn't work, we don't really know. Maybe she was just lazy, maybe she wanted to spend more time with Caylee, or maybe she felt entitled and didn't want to work. Eventually, lying about what she did during the day was easier than explaining to her parents why she was unemployed. But not working meant she had no money. Because she had created the illusion that she was employed, she couldn't pretend she needed money, because supposedly she was making her own. Therefore, she started stealing from her parents, which soon became as easy as spinning her lies.

Casey now had two things in her favor: she had her parents off her back because they thought she was working, and she had money skimmed from wherever she didn't think it would be noticed. The problem remained that she was with Caylee 24/7. After spending the entire day with her toddler, she wanted to get out in the evening to socialize, as any young adult would. However, based on our conversations with Cindy's coworkers, we speculated that Cindy was hard on Casey about that. After all, Cindy thought Casey had already been out all day at her job, so to her, Casey going out at night meant she was shirking her responsibility as a mother. And of course, Casey couldn't explain that she'd just been with Caylee for eight hours straight, because doing so would reveal the lie about her job.

When she started a relationship with Ricardo Morales at the beginning of 2008 and wanted to be out late, she told her parents she had been promoted to event planner at Universal with flexible hours. It was brilliant. Now, any time she wanted, she could say she had to work in the evenings. When she wanted to spend the night at Ricardo's, she used a made-up babysitter, Zanny, who had enough room in her apartment to have Caylee, or even both Casey and Caylee, spend the night. The plan was so well thought out that Casey came out looking incredibly responsible. If she "worked late," she didn't have to wake Caylee when she got off. In reality, she and Caylee would spend the night at Ricardo's.

In Casey's eyes, Ricardo was a potential dad to Caylee. He wasn't much of a party guy, preferring to stay home in the evenings. Casey, Caylee, and Ricardo were like a little family unit. Caylee fit right into this lifestyle. The next problem started when Casey started dating Tony Lazzaro.

Tony was different from Ricardo. He was a night owl and a nightclub promoter. He had a totally different lifestyle that had no room for a little kid. Why not just leave Caylee with Cindy in that case? We thought it was probably because Casey didn't want her mother all over her about ignoring Caylee, but we also knew that Cindy was growing frustrated with Casey's entitled behavior. For a while, Casey had been dropping Caylee off at Gentiva, where Cindy worked, and basically taking advantage of Cindy as a babysitter whenever she wanted. We knew this from the depositions of Cindy's coworkers, but Cindy herself always stonewalled inquiries about any conflict in the relationship, so we were left with just hearsay. However, something happened the night of June 15 that triggered a blowout.

Cindy had become increasingly exasperated as one thing piled on another: missing money; unauthorized charges on her credit card; either dumping Caylee on her or withholding Caylee from her, whatever suited Casey's fancy; and generally irresponsible behavior. The only specific rumor that we had heard about that meltdown on the fifteenth was that Cindy had found pictures of Casey at an "anything but clothes" party on Facebook and had lost her last bit of patience. In the photos, Casey was wrapped in an American flag and holding a beer. Cindy was enraged. Our theory held that Casey decided that night of June 15 that she was going to take Caylee from the household for good.

I imagine Casey told herself some lie to rationalize that murdering her baby was best for Caylee. Maybe she told herself that she didn't want Caylee to grow up with Cindy, as she had. Or maybe she knew that it wouldn't be long before Caylee began to really talk, and once that happened, the made-up babysitter, the fake job, the whole world would come crashing down. When you are that good at lying to other people, you get really good at lying to yourself. This was all guesswork on our part. What Casey was actually thinking, we will never know.

I would tell the jury that Casey used chloroform to put Caylee to sleep so she wouldn't suffer, put duct tape over her nose and mouth, wrapped her in her favorite Winnie-the-Pooh blanket, and put her in the trunk to die. She went off to Tony's and went on with her life with Caylee dead in the trunk. The next day, she went back to her house after George and Cindy had left for work and backed the Pontiac into the garage. She got the laundry bag and garbage bags off the shelves where they were kept, and took Caylee into the backyard to bury her. The shed was locked, so she couldn't access the tools. She went next door to borrow a shovel from their neighbor, Brian Burner, telling him she was transplanting bamboo.

Back in her own yard, which was protected from view by a six-foot high stockade fence, she laid Caylee's lifeless body on the grass. It appeared to us that she started a grave, based on the cadaver dog alert, but she got lazy or scared and decided against burial there. She put Caylee back in the trunk, and either that day or the next, snuck out to the woods, walked twenty feet in, and dumped her body.

I don't think that Casey thought through how she would get away with this in the long run. Her ability to adapt and lie had always gotten her through to this point, so why should it fail her now? It always reminded me of Scarlett O'Hara—"I'll think about that tomorrow."

A lot of denial kept Caylee's disappearance from being known for thirty-one days. A lot of good luck for Casey kept anyone from finding the child for six months. Three pieces of evidence found in the trunk of the Pontiac—the odor of decomposition, the hair with the band of death, and the high level of chloroform—were the keystones of our forensic case. The duct tape over the mouth and nose of the little angel's skull was our smoking gun. Casey's lies would fill in the motive: that her new lifestyle had no room for a child.

We were fully prepared for anything the defense wanted to throw our way.

CHAPTER TWENTY-ONE

OPENINGS

On Tuesday, May 23, at precisely 8:13 A.M., I pulled in front of the Orange County Courthouse like I had so many times before. This morning was different, though. The level of excitement and commotion had reached a fever pitch. One of our investigators was waiting to escort me in. Walking past a line of people waiting to get into the trial, I heard some of them calling my name, which was kind of creepy. Of course the press was all over us, taking camera shots of us walking. I didn't know why they were so obsessed with capturing that shot, but they were.

Across the street from the courthouse was a five-acre vacant lot owned by a development company. For years it had been slotted as the site of an office building, but for now it was Camp Casey, our nickname for the media zoo. It had been rented by TruTV, which then divided it and rented it out as smaller lots assigned to all the other media outlets, Headline News (HLN), CNN, etc. There was a sprawling overflow of media trucks with satellite dishes attached from all over the country. Stages, tents, and backdrops were built to accommodate the daily bulletins and nightly newscasts of the networks. A second, smaller lot just to the north of our office was converted into Little Camp Casey and rented by two local media outlets.

I had been involved in many cases before that were high-publicity, with a high level of local interest. Once in a while in the past, someone would approach and congratulate me or thank me for my work during or right after a trial. It was very flattering but not intrusive. This case was different. The cameras were on us every time we walked in and out of the courthouse, even for little hearings. There must be a hundred hours of tape of us doing nothing but walking, just walking.

The first time someone asked to take a picture with me outside the courthouse, it freaked me out and I politely declined. The next time it happened I was walking back from lunch and a woman with a small group of teenage girls stopped me. Moments before, they had poked their heads into the restaurant where I was eating, and when I stepped outside, they followed me like I was a sports legend. Finally, they made their move and asked me to pose with them for a photograph.

I realized in that moment that for them this was a thrill, something to tell their friends about. It wasn't that I was someone special, it was that I was *connected* to something special. Somehow this made me a minor celebrity.

Nothing about me was different. I was doing the same work in this case that I'd done dozens of times before. From that point on, I took it in stride and just accepted the fact that, as bizarre as it was, I had fans. There were times during the trial when the admiration became difficult. When Linda, Frank, and I would walk to court, we would be cheered, as if we were entering the ring at a sporting event. That never sat right with me. This was a trial for the murder of a little girl, and the celebrity aspect made it seem like a spectacle.

When we got inside the courthouse, Linda, Frank, and I didn't have to go through the same security checkpoints as the public. Since we were employees with ID, we could enter through a turnstile with a number pad for our PINs, so at least we could skip the metal detectors. The three of us were dressed for the occasion. Linda was wearing the big hardware. She had told us she was going to surprise us with a new addition to her

wardrobe. As a rule, she dressed in black, brown, or gray suits—very con-
servatively. Today, she showed up in a bright chrysanthemum-pink jacket.
It looked very nice, and we were all very impressed that she had made
herself visible for the beginning of *State of Florida v. Casey Anthony*. Frank
and I were in our regular suits. I, of course, had on one of my signature
Jerry Garcia neckties. I was not a Grateful Dead fan, but I liked the ties.
We took the elevator to the twenty-third floor of the courthouse. The trial
was taking place in the Roger A. Barker ceremonial courtroom, which was
also a functional courtroom reserved for grand jury proceedings and special
high-profile trials or trials with multiple defendants.

The courtroom was impressive, with a ceiling two stories high and a
balcony that accommodated a hundred spectators. It faced south with two
big windows looking out on Orlando behind the judge's bench. It had been
built as a largely ceremonial center with little attention paid to acoustics,
but over the past ten years, the sound system had undergone some improve-
ments. Judge Perry had just authorized the most recent round, and we were
assured that the sound had improved considerably. Even so, it took three or
four days before everyone could be heard without strange echoes or feed-
back. They did a great job of fine-tuning the system, and by the fourth day,
we finally got to the point where everybody could hear us.

Along with us were Mario Perez and Arlene Zayas, who were the primary nonlawyers working with us on the case. Both people stayed with us
throughout the trial, each with his or her own carved-out role. Mario would
be our computer operator during the entire trial. Linda had wanted to hire
a professional trial presentation company to come in and help us with the
graphics and trial exhibits. Sadly, juries today expect dazzle and high-tech
presentations, and Linda thought we really needed the extra polish. She had
lobbied hard for it, but in the end the office wouldn't go for it. Instead, we
bought some presentation software that Mario, an invaluable though silent
member of the team, learned to use. The software was far above and beyond
what we had ever used in the past but still fell short of what Linda wanted.

Arlene, meanwhile, served as our witness manager and secretary,
which meant that she was in the unfortunate position of being the one
we would yell at for things that were not her fault. Needlessly stressful for

her, but that's the role of the witness manager, to take the grief. She knew we weren't criticizing her personally. It was her responsibility to have all seventy-five witnesses there when we needed them, which was no small job. Linda, Frank, Mario, Arlene, and I left the office that Monday afternoon knowing everything was in place, but not really knowing just how crazy the trial would be.

Linda, Frank, and I each had our own role to play, too. I was going to be the forensics man and the one who took on George Anthony. Frank was assigned to the "friends of Casey," plus Lee Anthony. Linda was going to handle all the law enforcement witnesses, Cindy Anthony, and Casey herself, if and when Casey took the stand. We had to anticipate that Casey was going to testify, based on the posturing of the defense and the allegations they we knew they were about to dive-bomb us with. Linda was exceptional at cross-examination and was really looking forward to her marquis moment with Casey.

The courtroom felt different now that it was filled with people. Our team had prepared for this day for three years, and now that it was curtain time, I was feeling the rush. The gallery had filled in a half hour earlier with journalists and citizens who had waited all night for tickets. The court stenographer was at her post, the bailiff was by the jury box, and the clerk was positioned in front of Judge Perry's bench. The jury was in place, all seven women, five men, and three alternates.

The prosecution team sat at the table on the right, directly facing Judge Perry. I was in the center, flanked by Linda and Frank. Frank sat to my left and Linda to my right, closest to the defense table. The defense had a long table along the right wall; starting from the side closest to the bench, the order was Cheney Mason, then Jose Baez, Casey Anthony, and Dorothy Sims. There were various unnamed assisting attorneys sitting at the table as well. Ann Finnell made an appearance on only one day, when she came to argue that the death penalty was unconstitutional based on a recent ruling by a federal judge. Casey was dressed in a white three-quarter-sleeve button-down shirt, her long brown hair tied back in a high ponytail. She wasn't wearing any makeup, and she had her puss on, lips pursed like she was annoyed and ready to rail into somebody.

The trial started right on time, with the Honorable Judge Belvin Perry presiding. We promptly went into the opening arguments. As we had planned, Linda started off by saying that it was time to tell the story of a little girl named Caylee. We had previously discussed a way to get the jury thinking about Caylee whenever they thought about the case. It was our hope to bring the jury back to the toddler by humanizing her, to get them to see her as someone they would ultimately care about. They had already been sitting in the courtroom for two weeks during jury selection, and all they had seen was Casey, Casey, and more Casey. Throughout the case's history, Caylee had largely been a footnote. But she was a real person, a little girl, and hopefully, she would take center stage long enough to make an impact and capture some hearts. Knowing Caylee would help the jury truly understand the case.

We came up with what I thought was a great plan. Linda would show the jury the last photo of Caylee when she was alive, taken on Father's Day during the visit to her great-grandfather at the nursing home where he lived. She would then display the photo of her remains as they were found off Suburban Drive, a photo that no one in the public had seen before, and describe it as the last photo ever taken of Caylee Anthony. She would say that the story of this case was what happened between those two photographs.

Linda delivered it perfectly. I looked at the jury and expected to see from them in the same shock I had felt the first time I had seen the photo. But, I saw nothing in their faces. They were unmoved. How was this possible? I thought to myself. How could anyone look at that and be unmoved? I shrugged it off. Maybe the jurors were just good at hiding their emotions.

Our plan was to lay out the rest of the case chronologically, as Linda had suggested, giving the jury the story of that six months between when Caylee died and when she was discovered. Linda did a great job of reviewing the history of the crime and very methodically telling the jury about the pattern of lying that Casey had demonstrated. Linda showed how Casey twisted her stories to accommodate new challenges whenever they arose. Our goal was not only to put our case out there, but to convince the jury from the start that Casey's lying was not merely habitual, it was purposeful. Linda went day by day showing how Casey built her fabrications, laying out each and every one consistently. Their minute, complex details would change only when they reached a dead end, but at that point, Casey would still try to morph and adapt them again to give them the longest life possible. We knew the nuclear lie was coming from the defense in this trial. We wanted the jury to expect it, and we wanted to drill home that the "big one" was going to be just the next step. We couldn't tell them that they were about to hear a big lie, but we could hope we had prepared them well enough to see it that way.

At one point in the opening I began to think to myself, we need to skip over some of this stuff. A moment later, Linda seemed to sense the same thing, so we left out some of the details in the early July period. We wanted our opening to be full impact, all the way. We didn't want to lose anyone's undivided attention. We had originally planned to mention the tattoo, but Linda wisely saved the exact wording for later.

Linda did give a brief overview of the forensic evidence from the Pontiac, but she did not really feature that in her opening. She discussed finding the body, but she skipped over Kronk, since she we knew we would not be calling him. She did a great job connecting the remains to the house. She closed with the observation that Caylee's death allowed Casey to live the good life for those thirty-one days and that she, Casey, was guilty of murder in the first degree.

Linda was phenomenal. We had talked a lot about the organization of the argument and different things that she should say the months before the trial, and she did it brilliantly. It was just fantastic. In about two hours and fifteen minutes, she laid out everything we'd talked about. She showed the pattern of Casey's lies and the facts that led to the lie that they were about to hear.

After Linda's opening, we broke for lunch. Everyone just raved about Linda. She doesn't like to be the center of attention on a personal level, but when she is performing as an attorney, she really appreciates the adulation and kind words. At lunch, she felt really good. We all did.

When we came back to the courtroom, it was time for the defense's opening remarks. Jose Baez was to deliver them. The only word to describe his opening is . . . odd. I have never seen a defense that was so scattered. As we suspected, they brought up Casey's nuclear lie, but it wasn't as though they centered on that single counternarrative. It was like they couldn't decide on one defense, so they were throwing out everything, alleging that it was an accident, blaming George for disposing of the body, blaming Roy Kronk for moving the body, throwing in some nasty attacks on the investigation.

Baez opened the defense's case by saying that he was going to tell the jury exactly what happened to Caylee Marie Anthony. Generally that is considered a pact, if you will, that exists between the defendant and the jury. The defense is going to produce the evidence to tell the jury what actually happened. It is generally thought that specificity is dangerous because juries expect attorneys to come through on their promises, and when they don't, jurors may hold that against the attorney or the client.

Baez did a good job trying to separate the evidence from the issue of how Caylee actually died. It's hard to turn the fact that your client is a habitual liar into evidence helpful to that client. He made it seem plausible, even if superficially so, by arguing passionately that his client's inappropriate actions had nothing to do with how Caylee actually died.

Baez talked about the incredible dysfunction of the Anthony family. I was sure he left the jury expecting to hear psychological testimony describing a complex family history, which, of course, I knew he could not produce, since the two therapists were off the witness list. At the root, I think Jose was relying on the belief that it is almost impossible for people to believe that a mother could just kill her child. They are willing to accept almost any other explanation, no matter how ridiculous. But wouldn't the jury actually require him to prove the truth of what he was claiming? I must credit Casey; she came up with an explanation that would blame someone else, George Anthony, and make it look like she was the victim—classic Casey. Would the jurors buy it? We knew Baez couldn't prove it unless Casey testified, and even then it would be about whether the jury would believe her lie.

I noticed that the defense team had lowered Casey's adjustable chair more than was normal for a person of Casey's height. Only her head and shoulders were visible above the table. I was sure it was deliberately staged to make her appear smaller and meeker than she was. But wouldn't the jury see through those ploys? How smart do you have to be to know you are being played?

When Jose talked about Casey's supposed molestation, Casey was crying at the defense table. I found myself thinking of something that both therapists had mentioned in their depositions with us: when Casey talked about the molestation to them, she had been angry, but she wasn't crying. Apparently she'd refined her performance since then, so Casey really played it up during this whole trial. She appeared to have been very well coached.

It's interesting that Casey actually did a very good job of concocting a new lie that incorporated small bits of fact. That was the beauty of being able to wait until all the evidence was in and make up a story. That way you could make sure it all fit. One example: the defense had one tiny discreet fact, the fact that when Casey went to a wedding looking like she had been gaining a lot of weight, and the family hadn't acknowledged she was pregnant yet. That one fact was all Jose needed to sell the entire broad idea of a dysfunctional family to the jury.

If you look at Casey's background, this was her greatest gift, her ability to concoct believable lies that had just enough truth in them to fool the gullible. This defense was classic Casey, and from everything I saw in the case and heard from that side, I had no doubt that the meek, mild little waif the jury was seeing was running the show in the back room. Jose was the mouthpiece, but Casey was the architect. We had hoped the jury would have seen that through all the presentation of evidence, this was Casey 4.0, the next lie.

Baez was actually arguing that the fact that George and Cindy would be testifying at their daughter's trial about facts in the case was akin to throwing her under the bus and evidence of family dysfunction. I didn't know if the jury specifically bought that part, but arguing that George and Cindy testifying meant there was something amiss with the family offended me. It was as if the love of Cindy and George for Caylee and their desire to know the truth were strikes against them. Casey was so egocentric, all that was supposed to matter to them was Casey, they should basically do anything for her. Jose was insinuating that a good father would have kept his mouth shut and that only Casey should matter. But surely Caylee would matter to the jury.

Baez acknowledged that the Anthonys were religious about removing the ladder to the family's aboveground pool so that Caylee could not get into it. He then proceeded to suggest to the jury that on June 16, they left the pool ladder up. He didn't give a reason why they left the ladder like that; he just wanted the jury to believe it because he said so. Would jurors prefer to accept Jose's completely unprovable speculations than what the witnesses actually said?

Moving confusingly to more speculations, Jose argued that George, by reporting the gas cans missing on June 24, was somehow trying to implicate Casey. However, Baez never suggested why George would want to implicate her, or why, having been allegedly involved himself, he would want the police alerted at all. Like so many of Baez's arguments, this was one that, if you truly thought it through, didn't make any sense.

In the end, though, maybe it didn't matter what held up under the scrutiny of daylight. Perhaps I may have been giving the jury too much credit. I think he may have had a better understanding than I did of the level of analysis that this jury would take part in, and maybe his philosophy was "let's just throw everything up against a wall and see what sticks." If you throw one hundred red herrings out there, maybe you can get each juror to pick a different one. But the gas can argument, in particular, just never made any sense to me.

Similarly, the line "Follow the duct tape and it will show you who put Caylee's remains where they were found" was another of Jose's arguments, which implied that it was George. However, Baez then backtracked strangely, saying, "Maybe not."

Baez's next alternative was the meter reader theory. Roy Kronk was a morally bankrupt person who took Caylee's body and hid it at the Suburban Drive location, Baez said, another argument for which he would present not one bit of evidence. He went on to say that the sheriff's office had searched the area where the body was found before December and found nothing, another "fact" that was not a fact at all. I was surprised that the defense didn't abandon the Roy Kronk argument. It didn't fit with the overall "blame George" defense, and not even Baez had claimed a connection between George and Kronk.

It also tickled us that Jose got up in front of the jury and argued how disreputable and morally bankrupt Kronk was for selling a photograph of his snake carcass, with interview, for $20,000, when Baez had engineered

Casey's sale of Caylee's pictures to ABC for $200,000. Indeed the irony, once again, was rich.

Kronk had always been a difficult part of this case for us. He clearly had not been completely forthcoming about finding the body in December, why he went there, and why he was embellishing his story. As difficult as Roy Kronk was, clearly he did not place the skull there. There was no question about that. So that was an interesting choice on Baez's part, to go with that argument. He did a good job with it, though once again it was only effective so long as you didn't think too hard about it.

It was Jose's strategy of arguing both sides, "maybe he did it, maybe he didn't," that he put forth about both George Anthony and Roy Kronk. It was also so ludicrous to accuse two different people, completely unconnected to each other, of putting the duct tape on the child. I thought surely the jury would see this. According to Jose, either George put the tape on Caylee and it was there from the day she died, or Kronk put the tape on Caylee later, after she died. Jose had no logical motive for either man to do so. Connecting George to the duct tape on the gas cans was meaningless. Hearing this argument was probably the time when I first began smile-smirking as I sat at the prosecution table. I am not proud of that behavior, but at least I was not breaking out in laughter at the ridiculousness of the paradox. It's all relative.

Baez also asserted that the only evidence connecting anyone in the home to the remains was the duct tape, which is absolutely false. There were a number of other things that connected the remains to the house; they'd see that in the evidence.

As the opening drew to a close, Baez raised the idea that George's suicide attempt was an indicator that he was somehow complicit. He implied that there was information in the suicide note, although he did not elaborate. I decided at that moment to have Yuri Melich get the letter and find some way to get it into evidence.

My ears perked up when Baez twisted the story, saying that the defense was not saying that George killed Caylee. I knew Casey had told both of the shrinks that that her father had drowned her daughter. I thought we might be witnessing the birth of Casey 5.0. Would she really change the story again, in the middle of the trial?

As an attorney, it's mind-blowing how effective you can be when you are not limited by the truth. Attorneys are immune from libel or defamation in court. An attorney can say anything during his opening remarks and not be sued, so that he doesn't have to do his opening looking over his shoulder. On the other hand, to me, it is unethical for a lawyer to spout whatever he wants in an opening statement without a good-faith belief that he will be able to prove it at trial. It did not appear that Baez shared my convictions on that matter.

If Baez knew that Casey was not going to testify, then it would be considered unethical to float such inflammatory accusations against George without qualifying them. Of course, Baez could always justify introducing statements like this by saying "Well, I thought she was going to testify."

But that's again one of the mysteries of this case. Baez planted the idea that there was some deeper psychological issue with Casey knowing that he couldn't prove it. I'm still dumbfounded that he was able to get this jury to assume things without proving them. I don't think I have ever had a trial before where a jury was so eager to assume facts favorable to the defendant without actually making the defense prove them. But, hey, I give Baez credit, he got them to do it.

The prosecution team hoped that by hearing about the progression and tweaking of her lies, the discovery of Caylee's body, and the connection of that crime scene with the Anthonys' home, the jurors could interpret the defense's opening, filled with unsupportable allegations, as just another of Casey's lies. But of course that would require some intellectual effort and some actual thought on the part of the jurors.

The jury is instructed that what the attorneys say is not evidence. Their job is to express some skepticism toward both sides and say, "Okay, now prove it." We knew we could prove Linda's claims in opening, and we knew Baez couldn't prove most of his. We could only hope the jury would do its job.

CHAPTER TWENTY-TWO

———

THE BIG SHOW

Planning the order in which we would call the witnesses was the part of the case preparation I really enjoyed. The order can be complex, especially in a case of this magnitude. Sometimes it is driven by consideration of legal requirements for the admission of evidence. You have to connect a piece of evidence to the case before the jury can see it. Sometimes that may require testimony from multiple witnesses. You may have to call a few cops who had casual contact with a suspect before you can get to the one who took the confession. Sometimes decisions are driven by what your choices allow the other side to do. A delay in presenting a certain part of a witness's testimony, or leaving it out entirely, may affect the ability of the other side to effectively contradict him. You must consider the emotional impact the testimony will have and how it will affect the jury's view of what comes next. Lastly, there is the attention span of the jurors to consider; you can't expect them to stay awake through too much complex testimony back-to-back.

In total we were planning on calling approximately seventy witnesses. Of those, ten or so were going to be particularly important, including George and Cindy, Dr. Vass, and our medical examiner, Dr. G. The key pieces of evidence would be the findings of smell and chloroform in the trunk, the testimony of the cadaver dog's handler, and the hair from the trunk.

Linda, Frank, and I set up a dry-erase board in one of the offices and started mapping out our witness chart. Linda is a fan of color-coding. I would often tease her about her affinity for colored-dot stickers on everything. She marked Frank's witnesses in red, my witnesses in blue, and her witnesses in green. This way, we would know at a glance which witness was assigned to whom. The order of the witnesses was largely mine to plan, with tweaks from Frank and Linda. I think I just enjoyed this stuff more than they did, so they deferred to me. My plan was to play the case out in a mostly chronological order. We'd start with George and the events of June 16. From there, we'd move into the thirty-one days through testimony from the friends of Casey, plugging George, Cindy, and Lee in for those portions of testimony where they belonged. After that, we'd look at the Pontiac—how it was towed, George's discovery of the smell, and retrieving the car. The plan was that this would involve the jury in the mystery, leaving them wondering for days of testimony, What the hell happened to Caylee?

That led us naturally into all the events of July 15, the day Caylee's disappearance was confirmed. We'd tap Cindy and Casey's behavior, the involvement of the police, Yuri Melich's entrance as lead investigator, the Universal wild-goose chase, and then the arrest. The jury should be ready for something a little drier now, so we would then move to the forensics of the car, the dog alerts, the odor evidence, the hair evidence, and tying the chloroform to the searches on the computer. This evidence would give the jury a peek at the answer they'd been seeking for a week: What happened to Caylee?

After all that, we'd give their intellects a rest and hit them emotionally with the calls Casey made to her family from jail and the jail visitation videos, showing the jury her true colors. Then we'd drop Casey 3.0, the "Caylee kidnapped by Zanny at Blanchard Park story" we'd heard from Lee, on them. Lee had heard that story from Casey in the fall of 2008, so going chronologically we would next move to December 11, 2008, the discovery of Caylee's body. All the evidence that flowed from that event would produce our next chunk of witnesses.

The tattoo was the one thing I wanted to take out of order. I wanted to save that for last. I felt it was a verification of our theory and Casey's most vivid expression of life without Caylee.

After we had learned about Casey's newest accusations and Baez's newest plan of attack, we'd debated changing the order of our witnesses, but ultimately we decided to still call George first. Our thinking was, if the defense was going to accuse George of molestation and covering up Caylee's death, then opening with George was a perfect plan. It would allow him to refute the accusations right off. Although we would lose the mystery of Caylee's whereabouts, we'd gain the jury's savvy that everything it was hearing was thirty-one days of lies. They'd know for certain that these were lies, because they'd know Caylee was dead.

The trial was still in Day One when George, tense but ready, neatly dressed in a white button-down shirt, sat down in the witness box. I asked him a series of questions about the events leading up to June 16, and he did well. George said everything he'd said all along, and he said it with a great deal of feeling. His emotions were real—both his joy when he talked about Caylee and his sadness when he talked about never seeing her again. Now I had to address the defense's bombshell, the alleged molestation of Casey.

Whereas my initial questions were asked in a conversational tone with appropriate pauses for the emotional moments, the next questions were very deliberate and emphasized every word. I asked him if Caylee had drowned, and he had gotten rid of the body. He choked up when he answered that he would never do such a thing. Meanwhile, Casey was shaking her head and rolling her eyes, directing her theatrics at the jury. She glanced at her father only long enough to cast him a glare, although he never made eye contact with her.

Painful as it was, I next had to bring up the allegations of sexual abuse. If Baez's opening was any indication, the defense was going to use this claim to justify Casey's thirty-one days of silence. They'd say she hadn't told anyone about her daughter's death or her father's role in its cover-up because she was a master secret-keeper; she'd been keeping them since the age of eight, when her father supposedly began to molest her.

I asked George right out, "Have you ever molested your daughter?" He got kind of quiet. I could tell it hurt him, but he emphatically said no. As for all the other allegations, he very, very adamantly denied them all.

Day One was over, and George had done a great job under fire. He hadn't lost his cool, which was sometimes a problem, and he'd been honest and believable. Linda, Frank, and I left the courthouse feeling very good about the first day of what would certainly be a long trial.

DAY TWO WAS FRANK'S TURN to take the floor. He was our "friends of Casey" prosecutor, and the day was filled with them. He had the unenviable job of trying to coordinate all the twentysomethings who, by this time, had scattered all over the country. Many weren't happy to be connected to Casey, so in terms of witness management, Frank's list was the most challenging.

His medley of witnesses started out with testimony from Tony Lazzaro's roommates: Cameron Campana, Nathan Lezniewicz, and Roy "Clint" House. Frank did a terrific job of showing how freely Casey's lies flowed by using these three young men to confirm the stories she'd been telling to justify Caylee's absence.

Next on the stand was Brian Burner, the Anthonys' next-door neighbor. Casey had borrowed a shovel from him on June 17, 2008, and we considered his testimony additional evidence that Casey had tried to dispose of Caylee's body. Two shot girls from Fusian, Jamie Realander and Erica Gonzalez, followed Burner. All told, there would be twenty-one "friends of Casey" called to testify. We were trying to impress by sheer numbers how many people Casey had partied with, duped, or lied to. We wanted to show that no one, not a casual friend or a best bud, was immune from her deceptions.

We did make a misstep with one of these early "friends of Casey's," a woman named Maria Kissh. She was an acquaintance of Casey's and the girlfriend of one of Tony's roommates. She testified that she had been in the Pontiac at some point following Caylee's disappearance, and that there had been no odor in the car. In her original statement, Maria had said that she had been in the car; however, she had not specified *when*. During her testimony, Frank asked her when she had been in the car anyway, and her response was June 16, which surprised us all. This left the door open for Jose to promote his theory that the body was never in the car.

Thankfully, her testimony was repaired through the testimony of Tony Lazzaro, who explained that Maria had been in the car *before* Caylee disappeared, not after. Problem solved, but it gave us all a bit of heartburn.

Tony's testimony introduced another issue bigger than that of Maria Kissh, however. During the early investigation, we'd learned that before her arrest Casey had told Tony she'd been molested—although not by George, but by Lee. When Baez cross-examined Tony, he asked him questions about the confidences he'd shared with Casey. We knew exactly where he was going, and we also knew the dangers. By sharing the conversation that had passed between Tony and Casey, Baez was introducing hearsay by Casey. Doing so would mean that Casey's past character was an addressable issue, and as a result, the prosecution would be able to bring up Casey's criminal past—her prior convictions for check fraud against her friend Amy Huizenga.

For the time being, we stuck with our objection to Baez's line of questioning as hearsay. Judge Perry sent the jury back to their hotel and met with us and the defense together. He wanted to decide for himself if what Tony had to say about Casey's confidences was admissible to the jury. He began by asking him when Casey first told him about her brother's alleged misconduct.

"It was either around June 30, 2008, or July 5, 2008," Tony recalled.

Judge Perry asked him if he knew what Lee had done. Tony said Lee had tried to feel his sister's breasts, but Casey said he was unsuccessful. Next, Judge Perry wanted to know if Casey mentioned anything inappropriate on her father's part. "Could you relate to us what she said occurred in terms of abuse with Mr. Anthony, as in much detail as you can recall?"

"Hitting. That's all I can remember," Tony replied.

"What did you take that to mean or did she give you a more specific description of hitting?"

"I took it as discipline." Tony answered.

Judge Perry continued, "Did she tell you . . . besides using the word 'hitting,' did she say anything else?"

"Not to my knowledge."

The judge ultimately agreed that Tony's information was hearsay and the jury was not allowed to hear the testimony.

ON DAY FOUR, GEORGE ANTHONY returned to the stand. His testimony this time had to do with the duct tape on the gas cans. Based on the unfortunate way that George had chosen to frame this story at the deposition, I knew this area would be problematic, but I was prepared.

At the time of his deposition, way back in the summer of 2009, George had been evasive about the duct tape. He'd claimed that some of the tape had been on the gas can for years, but that he hadn't put that particular piece of tape over the vent hole, seemingly implying it must have been placed there by the police. In this statement, he had put his support behind Casey at great risk to his integrity as a witness.

Now, with Casey's allegations against him fresh in everyone's minds, he told a different story. On the stand, he said that when Casey brought the gas can back to him, it didn't have a cap on the vent hole, the implication being that Casey had lost it. George then said he'd put a piece of duct tape on the hole, then and there on June 24, 2008. The whole story was completely inconsistent with his deposition. I'd long known that his attempt to help Casey back then would come back to haunt him, and sure enough it had.

Understandably, Baez picked up on the discrepancy between whether there had been tape on the gas can during his cross-examination of George. He ended up asking the same question that I had asked during the deposition: "When the gas was returned, did it have duct tape on it?"

Rather than saying, "No, it didn't," and staying consistent with what he'd said to me only an hour or so before, George started to be difficult with Baez, answering his questions with questions for the sole purpose of frustrating him.

This was not helpful to our case. George must have hated Jose, particularly because of the latest allegations. I think George may have believed that it had been Baez's idea to accuse him of molesting his daughter. In George's mind, Casey had only submissively gone along with her lawyer's plan. None of us on the prosecution saw it that way. To us, the molestation accusation had "Casey" written all over it. Regardless, one thing I was sure of was that Baez knew how much George disliked him and used it to his advantage. Baez probably wanted the jury to see George's hostility, and George took the bait. He was not bright enough to read what was happening. I wanted to say, "George, just stop playing games, just answer the question," but I couldn't. I've always wondered if on some subconscious level George was trying to look guilty. Maybe this was his way of helping Casey. I didn't really think so, but I wondered. For someone who was innocent, he had a way of making himself appear suspect. I didn't think it would seriously hurt our case, or lend any real credence to the defense's baseless accusations, but I knew this was not the face of George that we on the prosecution team wanted to project.

Baez knew that George would continue to try and dance around the connection between the tape and his house. By now, we also had a video in which the same duct tape was being used at the "Find Caylee" command center. This further made George look like he was lying. If initially he had been trying to protect Casey, now he was looking as though he was trying to protect himself, something not lost on Baez.

Ultimately, George said that the gas can didn't have duct tape on it when Casey brought it back. So why the game? He was playing right into Baez's hands. I just wanted to slap him, and this wasn't even the end of it. The next thing I knew, George was arguing with Baez about how often he mowed his lawn.

"You cut your grass every week?" Baez asked.

"Well, every week, two weeks, ten days," George answered instead of just simply saying, "Yeah, I cut my grass every week in the summer." Baez then brought up George's call to the police to report that his shed had been broken into, implying that his call was an attempt to set Casey up.

I could tell that George wanted to spar with Baez about anything. But not only was he not as practiced at the dance as Casey, he didn't have a motivation to stop. Normally, a lawyer can appeal to a witness's better judgment by saying, "You're at risk of allowing the accused murderer to go free by the way you are acting." But George didn't have that motivation because the accused murderer was his daughter. Instead, he was exercising his private outrage at Baez, and ended up looking like he was trying to hide something. He was only shooting himself in the foot. All we could hope was that the jury would understand that George's anger was justified, that it was directed at Jose, and it was not indicative of complicity.

As much as George wasn't doing himself any favors, I thought some clear questions with concise answers could help dispel any doubts about George that surrounded him. On redirect, I tried to make the point that in June 2008, there was no way George could have known that the gas can or the tape on it had anything to do with Caylee's death. I asked George what he had done with the gas cans in the four months between the fight with Casey and the discovery of Caylee's body. When he said he had stuck them in the shed for four months, I made my point that it would be pretty stupid for someone who was involved in a crime to deliberately keep the evidence around. I wasn't sure if it had undone George's struggles with Baez, but hopefully it had helped.

After George was dismissed, the jury had two questions of its own for Judge Perry. They wanted to know which twelve of the fifteen jurors would deliberate the case and which three were alternates. Would it be the first twelve and the alternates were the last three, or would the order be mixed up? The other question was, Did the alternates get to go home when the jury deliberated? Day Three of the trial and they were already talking about wanting to go home—not a good sign.

That night, they started sending out requests for DVDs that they wanted to watch. Some of them were kids' movies, which was kind of weird. Judge Perry pointed out that they had already agreed on a list of movies, two hundred in all, but there apparently were some additional ones that they wanted. As I look back on it, I understand that the jury was sequestered and it was a long trial, but they were a rather high-maintenance bunch. There seemed to be a lot of thought and discussion about what entertainment they wanted, which movies they wanted to watch, and which restaurants they wanted to go to. Yet, as we would learn later, when it came time to deliberate, they never asked a single question about the evidence.

There was another mentionable high-maintenance incident when one of the jurors ran out of water during testimony. He looked at the court deputy, held up his empty water bottle, and shook it, like the court deputy was his personal butler and should fetch him a new one. The court deputy was annoyed at being treated like a servant.

Throughout the trial, Judge Perry was very accommodating of the jury, really wanting to keep them happy, satisfied, and reasonably entertained. They wanted to watch the finals of the Tampa Bay Lightning hockey game on television, so Judge Perry was going to get somebody from the cable company to acquire a tape of the game for them to watch. In the end, the local cable company hooked them up so they could watch the game live and on national television. Judge Perry gave the company a nice nod for their kindness. When the jurors wanted pretzels in the break room, he provided them. He spent a lot of time on their comfort. I now wonder if the judge made it too comfortable for them.

WHEN THE TRIAL RESUMED, FRANK called more "friends of Casey" to the stand. One of them was her ex-boyfriend Ricardo Morales. Frank asked him general questions about the Anthony family and the relationship between Casey and Caylee. He said he had last seen the toddler on June 10, the day he and Casey broke up. During the cross, I thought Baez behaved inappropriately toward Morales, drilling him about selling a photo he had taken of Caylee wearing the pink "Big Trouble Comes in Small Packages" shirt and others of Caylee to a magazine. He acted all indignant that this man would sell photographs of this poor dead child for $4,000. It was so hypocritical, when Jose had brokered the sale of photos of Caylee for $200,000 on Casey's behalf. You wonder, how does he live with that?

Ricardo's friend Troy Brown, Troy's ex-girlfriend Melissa England, and four friends of Casey's—Iassen Donov, Dante Salati, Christopher Stutz, and Matthew Crisp—followed Ricardo Morales. All of them testified to Casey's lies. On cross-examination, Jose did manage to get the majority of them to say that Casey was a good mother.

In retrospect, I think the sheer quantity of lies might have taken away some of the impact of the individual lies. Almost like in aversion therapy, exposing someone to something that bothers him enough makes it seem not quite as bad. After about a dozen of these witnesses, I thought it got little boring to keep going over and over the same questions and the same points. We stressed to the jury that Casey was a woman who went on as if nothing had happened after Caylee disappeared; in fact, her life got better. Looking back on it, though, it was probably overkill. I thought we had made the point and I suggested we could cut out a few. Linda decided we should stick to the plan, and she was the boss. I did suggest to Frank that he tighten it up, which he did.

This was around the time I began to tell Linda and Frank that I thought Casey was not going to testify. I was feeling stronger and stronger in my conviction that she wasn't going to take the stand. I thought Jose's whole opening statement was probably something that he was going to put out there and never prove. They both thought I was crazy, and that based on what Baez said in opening, she had to back it up on the stand. I completely agreed with the logic of what they were saying. But I pointed out that in the three years we had been dealing with this guy, he had filed motions or made statements time and time again, and got indignant when we made him back them up. I had this gut feeling that he thought he could just say anything, and people would believe him.

On May 27, Simon Birch took the stand. He was the manager of Johnson's Wrecker, the place where George and Cindy came to retrieve the Pontiac. He testified that the smell from the Sunfire to him was foul and potent, like that of decomposition. He said he had been in the towing business for more than twenty years, with a two-year stint in waste management, and had smelled everything you could imagine in a car. He was firm in his belief that the odor in the Pontiac was from a dead body. He related that when he and George Anthony opened the trunk, lots of flies flew out. There was a bag of garbage in the trunk, which they tossed into the Dumpster. It did not help the smell in the trunk at all.

MAY 28, THE DAY CINDY Anthony took the stand, was emotional for everybody. Linda was leading the questioning, which began with extremely personal treasures. It was necessary for the prosecution to have Cindy identify certain items taken from the house that were related to items found with Caylee's remains. That meant Cindy needed to look at pictures of Caylee's room, which brought her to tears. About an hour into testimony, she became so emotional that we took a break to allow her to compose herself.

Cindy remembered her last day with Caylee, Father's Day, June 15, 2008. She talked about Zanny, saying that Casey had been referencing the invented nanny as far back as 2006. Cindy did her best to recount the thirty-one days Caylee was missing. When Linda started to ask her about a MySpace page she had created on July 3, 2008, just to be able to reach out to Casey, the defense objected on the grounds of hearsay and the objection was sustained.

Linda was only allowed to go into those areas of the MySpace page that had been written by Cindy on her own page. She was limited as to what she could ask Cindy about her and Casey's communication, because Casey had not posted responses on Cindy's page. Casey's own MySpace had postings under the subject line "Diary of Days," which appeared to be direct responses. Her page had such things as "On the worst of days, trust no one, only yourself," "What is given can be taken away," and "Everyone lies. Everyone dies. Life will never be easy." But Cindy was not allowed to testify to any of that.

These constraints compromised Linda's ability to bring out a fuller understanding of the mother-daughter relationship. Cindy said the exchange between herself and Casey on MySpace was the first time they had "talked" since Cindy's attempt to intercept Casey and Caylee at Universal Studios. Cindy's subject line on her MySpace plea to Casey was "My Caylee is missing," and Linda asked if she could clarify what she meant by "missing," if she thought Caylee was safe somewhere with her mother. Cindy said that "missing" meant "missing in my heart," not "missing" as in disappeared from the face of the earth.

Cindy did say that she had felt betrayed by Casey, which for her seemed like a big leap over positions she'd taken in the past. Linda went through the MySpace posting line by line in an attempt to get Casey's responses to Cindy's comments, but presenting the interchange this way was not nearly as effective as having the jury read it. Linda continued asking Cindy about her communication with Casey during the thirty-one days. Cindy said she eventually gave up trying to call her daughter, so started texting her to see if she could talk to Caylee. Casey always had an excuse, any reason why Caylee wasn't there.

I couldn't make sense of Cindy's just accepting Casey's excuses. I think she feared that if she pushed Casey, then Casey would take Caylee away for good and she would never see her again. After all, Casey had the leverage, she had what Cindy wanted. I just couldn't understand why Cindy couldn't be right up front instead of making excuses for Casey.

Linda asked Cindy about the odor in the trunk of the Pontiac, once described to a 911 operator as being like the odor of "a dead body in the damn car." But Cindy had watered down that strong opinion about the smell considerably over the years. Now she told Linda she accepted George's explanation that there was garbage in the trunk. She acknowledged that she had some experience with rotting flesh, being in a medical field.

The 911 calls Cindy had made on July 15, 2008, were introduced next. The tapes of these conversations created the most emotional moment in the trial to date. Jurors, who had not shown much emotion before this, seemed to perk up as the first call started to play. Cindy looked uncomfortable as she heard her own voice. There was something about hearing the calls now, knowing that her granddaughter was dead, that was heart-wrenching. She listened with her hand covering her mouth, looking like she was wishing she could retroactively silence herself. Her recorded voice reverberated in the courtroom, becoming increasingly distraught with each additional call. Everyone could hear the voices of Cindy and the different operators as the text of conversations scrolled on a screen. Her first call had reported the stolen car, and she sounded annoyed at her daughter, who was sitting next to her in the car. The second call was from her house. She was quite upset, and mentioned that her granddaughter was missing. In the third call she was frantic, saying Caylee had been kidnapped by the babysitter.

By the time the third 911 call was played, Cindy was a mess. Looking down at her hands through her tears, she related the first time she had heard that Caylee was missing. With her head nodded down toward her chest and her face red from sobbing, she put one hand over her eyes and her mouth, her entire face, really and hung her head completely below the bar of the witness stand. She looked like she was trying to hide from her own words.

The taped conversation reached the point where Casey took the phone from her mother to tell the 911 operator what was going on with Caylee. Anyone who knows the tapes knows how calm Casey is when she tells the operator that Caylee has been missing for thirty-one days, but she's been looking for her herself. Meanwhile, in the courtroom, Casey's calm voice on the tape, juxtaposed against the sight of her mother sobbing and doubled over in emotional pain on the witness stand, was wrenching indeed. When the tapes were finally over, Cindy popped her head back up and sat up straight, trying to regain her composure as Judge Perry called a quick recess.

I thought Cindy's reaction to the tapes was telling. She was so willing to go after Casey when she had thought her daughter was withholding Caylee from her. When it turned out Casey was keeping Caylee away from everybody, she was not quite as overcharged and frantic.

Next Linda played back the jailhouse calls between Casey and her parents and friends when she had first been arrested for child neglect and lying to the police, right after the lies had unraveled. To me, these conversations show the true, unvarnished Casey, Casey at the core. They show how thoroughly selfish she is, turning talk about Caylee back to her and her own plight. Cindy was better prepared to listen to these tapes. She sat stoically, not covering her mouth like before. Her expression was blanker than before, though; she looked exhausted.

The phone conversation between Kristina Chester, a friend of hers, and Casey provided me with one of the quotes I found most telling about the young mother at the defense table. Kristina had been trying to get Casey to talk about Caylee, but Casey only wanted to talk to Tony and was desperate for somebody to give her his phone number. Kristina kept asking if Tony was involved in Caylee's disappearance, and Casey kept answering in the negative. Finally, after Casey asked for Tony's number for the umpteenth time, Kristina asked, "So why do you want to talk to him?" and Casey answered narcissistically, "Because he's myyyyy boyfriend."

Kristina said, "If anything happens to Caylee, I'll die," and started to cry. Casey seemed quite annoyed by her friend's tears. "Oh my God, calling you guys? A waste, a huge waste," she said in reply.

Cindy began to sob again on the witness stand, head hung low, when she heard her daughter so callously dismissing her friend's emotional state. She also sobbed when Casey talked about how her family had let her down. Casey, sitting at the defense table only a few feet from her mother, made no response or reaction at all to the tape or her mother.

During cross-examination, Cindy's ambivalence that we'd been witnessing for the last three years came roaring back. She spent some time painting an idealistic picture of Casey as a mother, and even when talking about why she thought Casey's long-term lies were so elaborate and detailed, she couldn't help but excuse Casey. To her, the scope and intricacy of the lies implied that they were illusions, not lies. Cindy equated them to a situation where children create imaginary people.

Once again, Cindy appeared to be whitewashing every bad behavior her daughter demonstrated. The codependency between Cindy and her daughter was striking. She was finding it impossible to make Casey accountable for anything. Maybe she was putting a lot of the blame for Caylee's death on herself: if only she had not pushed Casey so hard, if only she had been more generous with her time, then maybe no one would be here. I was finding it hard to stomach the fact that Casey was sitting so close to her mother, who was falling on the sword for her, with a derisive sneer on her face.

Even Cindy's testimony about the pool ladder was suspect. When Cindy had originally told coworkers about coming home to find the ladder on the pool, she had not pinpointed an exact date. But now, in response to questions from Linda, she was claiming that it was the evening of June 16, when she arrived home from work, that she found the ladder on the pool and the access gate to the backyard open. Cindy said she was absolutely certain she had put the ladder down, therefore making it inaccessible, the night before.

One point she remained steadfast on was the smell. Baez tried to get Cindy to say that the odor in the trunk didn't smell like rotting flesh. He asked her to choose which it resembled more—garbage or rotting flesh. "The closest thing I could resemble it to was rotting flesh," she honestly answered. That was her strongest statement on the issue. It shows why sometimes it's better to quit while you're ahead.

Frank was the man to examine the next witness, Amy Huizenga. Amy had been the person who took Cindy to Tony Lazzaro's apartment to get Casey on July 15. After Casey came out and saw her mother waiting for her, Amy said there was a massive mother-daughter explosion. She described Casey's demeanor in the car with Cindy after the three of them left Tony's together. She said Casey sat in the front seat with her arms crossed, giving glaring looks, "like a sixteen-year-old who'd been caught doing something bad." The conversation between the two in the car was either one-way or circuitous, Casey only speaking when her mother demanded to know where Caylee was. Her responses contained very few words, saying things like, "She's with the nanny."

Lee Anthony, Casey's brother, was another of Frank's witnesses. Casey briefly broke down in tears as he settled himself into the box. He was a very different Lee Anthony from the one we had seen at his deposition during the summer of 2009. He had refused to meet with Frank before the trial, so we knew something was up. We had to consider him a somewhat hostile witness.

In deposition nearly two years prior, Lee had been cooperative and relatively neutral in tone. He gave testimony consistent with his prior statements to investigators. But now in trial, Frank found it much more of a chore pulling the facts out of him. In deposition, Lee had told his story in a conversational, informative narrative. Very early in his trial testimony, however, it became clear from his four-word-or-fewer answers that he was less willing to volunteer information. Lee gave the facts without the same emotional tone he had shown in deposition. Then, he had demonstrated a frustration with his sister. Anything resembling that emotion was gone from his testimony at trial. Right off the bat, Frank's questions received a response of "I don't remember," and Frank had to refresh his memory. In fact, he acted like he was having trouble remembering a lot of things. Frank finally decided to give him his deposition to refer to in an effort to help him along.

As a prosecutor, these kinds of situations were never easy to deal with, but Lee's attitude surprised us. Perhaps, in some way we were so focused on

George and Cindy, on their record of standoffishness, that we simply took Lee for granted. It wasn't clear to me what had changed in his attitude, but something was decidedly different, and his testimony was not producing the effect that we'd hoped for.

When Frank asked Lee what he and Casey talked about on the evening of July 15, Lee said he asked Casey why she wouldn't let them see Caylee. Frank asked him, "What was her response?" Lee's answer was "I don't recall." With way more memory refreshers than we thought were necessary, Frank finally got Lee to say Casey had told him, "Maybe I'm just a spiteful bitch," something he had said in a previous deposition.

The same thing was true when Lee was asked about Casey's comments about Cindy. "I don't know," he told Frank. Frank again helped him find what he had said in prior statements, and Lee then remembered saying that his mother had thrown it in Casey's face that she was an unfit mother. He said Cindy told Casey that Caylee was the best mistake her daughter ever made.

During Jose's cross-examination of Lee, Baez tried to introduce some statements that Casey had made to Lee. It was the same tactic of introducing hearsay that Baez had attempted when Tony Lazzaro was on the stand. Because Baez had already been warned by the judge, we let him move forward and then sprang into action, asking the judge to allow us to introduce Casey's criminal past. I recall seeing the amusement on the judge's face as we approached the bench—Judge Perry had of course seen this coming, but Baez seemed clueless. We explained that we were requesting admission of Casey's prior convictions on check fraud. Baez looked like someone had punched him in the stomach. Judge Perry acknowledged that the prior convictions might now be admissible, but he said he wanted to consider the significance of what Baez had brought out before he ruled. Over the course of the evening, the prosecution team did the same and concluded that the statements Baez had elicited were so innocuous that it wasn't worth the risk of a postconviction incompetence claim, so we withdrew our request. Once again, the judge gave Baez a warning about the consequences of introducing hearsay. We all hoped that this time Baez would actually listen.

CHAPTER TWENTY-THREE

PROVING THE INVESTIGATION

W ith the initial testimony from Lee out of the way, we segued from the family and "friends of Casey" witnesses to the witnesses who were related to evidence from the investigation.

After Lee Anthony, jurors heard from Orange County Sheriff's officers Rendon Fletcher, Adrianna Acevedo, Amanda Macklin, and Reginald Hosey, who all testified to the arrival at the Anthony house on July 15, 2008. Yuri Melich, the lead investigator on the case, was then called to the stand to address his first interview with Casey on July 15, describing his general opinion of Casey as well as the trip they'd taken to the Sawgrass Apartments in search of Zanny. He told the jury that from this first interview he thought Casey's story about the nanny was suspect.

When the defense had its turn to cross-examine, Baez dropped a hand grenade, saying he had evidence that Melich was biased toward the prosecution. His attack was based on a blog posting the officer had once made where he referred to himself as "Dick Tracy Orlando." The court asked the defense to point out specific statements that showed bias, per its accusation. After a lot of downtime, the court found that the issue might certainly go to the professionalism of Melich, but not to his credibility.

One of my favorite courtroom moments, though, was later on during the cross-examination when Baez was asking Melich questions about his first recorded interview with Casey. Melich had asked her if she had drug problems.

"Then you asked her if she's ever committed suicide?" Jose said.

Melich paused, with a quizzical look on his face. "I don't think I could have asked her if she ever committed suicide, 'cause if she had she wouldn't be there," he intelligently replied. Everyone in the courtroom had a chuckle during that moment of levity. At the close of Yuri's first testimony, June 2, Day 8 of the trial, we let Judge Perry know that we were halfway through our case. We thought we were moving forward at a very expeditious rate. We were doing our best to be mindful of everybody's time, especially the jury's.

Our next witness was Jeff Hopkins, the subject of many of Casey's alibis. We called Hopkins to show how Casey used details from her past to craft plausible lies, and he told jurors that he and Casey had met in middle school, though they were not friends. He had worked at Universal in 2002, years before Casey had worked there, but she had referred to him as a coworker. Reiterating what we'd learned three years earlier, Hopkins said he didn't have any children, so the nanny connection was puzzling, but he did relate the story of running into Casey at a bar in Orlando in July 2008, after not having seen her for years.

Jeff Hopkins was a perfect example of the collateral damage of Casey's narcissism. He had known her as a cute kid in middle school, hadn't seen her in years, ran into her by pure coincidence in an Orlando hot spot, and now here he was three years later, practically a household name. The havoc one person spewing lies could wreak on the normal lives of so many others always amazed me.

Yuri Melich was much more seasoned in the witness box than Hopkins. When he was recalled to the stand after the Hopkins' testimony, he described the walk-through of Universal Studios. Recalling that bizarre day, Melich relayed how Casey "walked with purpose through Universal." He figured he'd let her go and see where the lie would end. During his testimony, we took an hour to play the video of the interview he had conducted with Casey right at the theme park. Just how far-reaching the scope of the search for Caylee had been came out in Melich's second testimony. He said his office had received more than six thousand tips of Caylee sightings from all over the country in the weeks and months after her disappearance. To me, this number was such a testament to how much people had invested themselves in finding Caylee alive, because there was not a chance that even one of the six thousand tips was a match.

Baez's cross-examination took the questioning to the family pool. He was curious why Melich had never questioned Casey about her mother Cindy's reference to the occasion when the pool ladder had been in the pool and the side gate was open. The detective explained to Baez that Casey had been questioned about the pool. That afternoon in the interview at Universal, Sergeant John Allen had, in fact, asked Casey about the possibility Caylee had drowned. But the defendant had been so adamant that Zanny had kidnapped the child, no one pursued it further. There was no reason to think she had drowned in the pool if her mother said she had been kidnapped.

CSI experts familiar with the evidence collected from the car, the computers, and the Dumpster followed Yuri Melich on the stand. Deputy Charity Beasley took the stand about collecting the computer from the Anthony home, Awilda McBryde introduced the trash retrieved from the Dumpster, and Gerardo Bloise testified about the Pontiac. These witnesses all provided testimony about the long and boring process of meticulously identifying and documenting the precise location and appearance of each item found. Although Frank did the questioning, my muscle was needed briefly, when help was needed to open an evidence box containing the trunk liner and spare tire cover. It was taped up pretty well, and it took us a while to coax it open. The instant it did, I could smell the decomposition. It seemed there was no escaping it.

Decomposition odor was the specialty of the cadaver dog handled by our next important witness, Jason Forgey of the Orange County Sheriff's Office canine unit. Jurors seemed genuinely interested in this testimony. When he took the stand on June 7, Deputy Forgey told the enrapt courtroom about how his cadaver dog, Gerus, had alerted on the trunk of the Pontiac and in the Anthonys' backyard. Forgey said that Gerus, whose search command was "Find Fred," was trained to find blood, bones, and human remains. After relating the dog's credentials, we played a videotape taken from a helicopter that showed an actual cadaver search conducted at night. In the video, you could see the figure of the dog handler glowing in an infrared light. He was moving back and forth through a heavily wooded area that surrounded a lake. The dog was unable to see the figure of someone in the lake, newly drowned, but the person was visible on the infrared camera. Watching the dog working his search and finally alerting near the body was totally fascinating. What a credit to their training and abilities to be able to locate a body in such conditions.

Baez had tried to block Forgey's testimony on qualifications, and later criticized him for having failed to videotape Gerus's search for Caylee's remains. Still, he made a point when he got Forgey to admit that Gerus did not alert on his second day back to search the Anthonys' yard.

Karen Lowe was also a widely respected expert in a very specialized field. She was the FBI hair analyst at the FBI lab in Quantico, Virginia, who had analyzed the nine-inch hair that was found in the trunk of the Pontiac and linked it to Caylee. In her testimony on June 4, she described the microscopic banding on it, which was termed the "band of death," explaining to jurors that only hairs that have come from a decomposing body exhibit this dark marking. Hairs with these colorations cannot have come from a living person, she said. Her testimony would later be backed up by Stephen Shaw, a hair and fiber examiner from the FBI lab. Shaw had examined the hairs from the skull itself. He testified that despite his best efforts, he could not re-create conditions under which a hair might acquire a "band of death" other than in decomposition.

The defense did not have any opposing experts on this issue, so Baez tried to challenge the finding by degrading the science on which it was based. We made the point on redirect that the hair in evidence was not a "shed" hair; it hadn't fallen out and then decomposed. Also, the hair collected from Caylee's hairbrush did not have the banding, so it was not a natural characteristic of Caylee's hair to have this band.

ON MONDAY, JUNE 6, THE time had come for Dr. Arpad Vass to take the stand. Dr. Vass was our forty-first witness in ten days. He had a very natural and professorial manner of describing even the most disgusting things, like the stages of decomposition. I loved his engaging way of looking at the jury when explaining things. The first hour with Dr. Vass was spent on the background of his work. His presented his credentials without a hitch. The physical evidence that followed was the kind of presentation that tends to be dry and boring, but Dr. Vass, like an eager intellectual, would light up and say to the jury, "Now this is the cool part." If he had lingering nerves about testifying, he didn't show them.

Dr. Vass's testimony was significant because it was scientific confirmation that what had been smelled by humans and dogs was the odor of decomposition. I wanted to demonstrate to the jury that we had incorporated all that science had to offer as we tried to understand what that smell had been. If they believed Dr. Vass's findings, they added to the overall quantum of evidence that proved there was a dead body in the car. If they found it too "cutting edge" for their liking, then they were free to ignore it and rely on all of the other witnesses and evidence proving that fact.

Confident as I was in Dr. Vass's actual testimony, when dealing with more than one hundred pieces of evidence, mistakes are bound to happen. While Vass was on the stand, I made mine. I had five metal cans, each containing a small piece of the stained carpet. I happened to hand Dr. Vass the wrong one. After we moved the can into evidence and after his testimony was done, I realized I had shown him the wrong can. The one I had shown him was the one that had been sent to the FBI, not the one he had worked on. To my embarrassment, I had to put him on the stand again to introduce the correct can. Of all the witnesses to make a mistake with, why did have to be Vass? We put the correct can into evidence and moved forward.

Dr. Vass was a foremost expert on odor mortis, the smell of death. He had asked the crime scene investigators at the Orange County Sheriff's Office to collect a carpet sample from the trunk of the Pontiac to test at his lab. There, he used a gas chromatograph mass spectrometer to analyze the samples and try to detect compounds consistent with human decomposition. He was successful. In the sample, he found forty-one such compounds, including butyric acid, one of the first compounds released by the body after death.

Dr. Vass described to the jurors how he jumped back when he first opened the can with the carpet sample, so strong was the odor. Before trial, Linda, Frank, and I had considered the possibility of giving one of the cans containing the odor to the jury to open for themselves. To make sure we didn't have an OJ Simpson moment, I had opened two of the cans in the company of Mike Vincent of the Sheriff's Office to confirm that the odor was still detectable. We agreed that the odor was both evident and recognizable. However, during the prosecution's presentation of Dr. Vass and his odor findings, we decided having the jury smell for themselves might create potential legal problems, and we didn't want to risk an appeal that challenged the can of odor.

Later on in the trial, though, when the defense was presenting its case, I actually revisited the idea. During cross-examination of a defense witness, I was showing the jurors the pieces of garbage that had been in the trunk before being retrieved from the Dumpster. I saw a juror smelling one of the garbage pieces that had been handed to her. Because the defense was claiming the odor in the trunk was from the garbage, I thought this might be my opening to say "in that case, smell the can and compare that with the garbage."

The idea of having the jury smell the evidence in this trial had originally come from Professor Andy Raum of the University of Florida, Levin College of Law, who was assisting me in the forensics aspects of the case. He mentioned that juries had been allowed to use their sense of smell in the past. These were mostly moonshine cases that had taken place back in the twenties and thirties, where the jurors were allowed to sniff liquids to decide if they were booze or not. But when I asked Judge Perry if I could introduce my cans as sniff evidence, he said no. He would not allow the jury to sniff the carpet samples from the trunk.

Dr. Vass also described his discovery of "shockingly high" levels of chloroform in the sample he tested. He told jurors the levels were 10,000 times higher than levels from a piece of carpet in the trunk of a control car, a vehicle he picked randomly from a junkyard for the purposes of testing. In his twenty years, he had never seen levels this high. In my opinion, the greater significance of Dr. Vass's testimony was in regard to the chloroform. We had the smoking gun in the duct tape, and now we had the agent that would have subdued little Caylee Marie enough for someone to use it.

RETRACING THE FOOTSTEPS OF OUR investigation into the fall of 2008, our prosecution case moved to the evidence found on the Anthonys' home computer. We called Kevin Stinger, the supervisor of the computer forensics lab for the Orange County Sheriff's Office, and John Dennis Bradley, a computer expert and software developer. Stinger confirmed that the word "chloroform" had been searched for and found in unallocated deleted space on the Anthonys' home computer. Bradley had developed software called Cache Back for his employer, the Canadian software company Site Quest. He had been provided the deleted file from the Anthonys' computer by Stinger.

It was a team effort. The sheriff's people had found references to chloroform on the computer, but they couldn't decode the exact sites or dates they were visited. Bradley had the new software, so investigators gave him the file to decode. He was then able to decode specific sites, dates, and search terms. He found that two searches that had been conducted in March 2008, one for "chloroform" and another for "how to make chloroform." Unfortunately, Bradley's software made a mistake in determining the number of searches to a particular site about "chloroform," claiming it had appeared eighty-four times on the Anthonys' home computer. The defense caught the error before we did and presented it in their case. The error overshadowed the real importance of the matter, which was that a search for chloroform had been conducted *at all*. This error certainly hurt our credibility, but our presentation of this evidence in trial was in good faith.

We moved from computer forensics and chloroform back to Casey, recalling Lee Anthony to the stand. Computers could give us mountains of techno-clues, but for those who didn't have a good handle on "unallocated

deleted space," humans held important evidence to our case as well. Frank
led Lee through the conversation the brother and sister had about Caylee
being kidnapped in Blanchard Park, what the prosecution called Casey 3.0.
We hoped that the jury would be able to see Casey's ability to spin lies from
lies. Whenever investigators had uncovered some new fact that refuted a
story of hers, she had responded by creating a new drama about what had
happened to Caylee Marie. The supposed kidnapping at Jay Blanchard Park
was a great example. Lee's testimony showed how Casey's story of the night
of July 16 had shifted. His words also provided a good transition into the
next phase of our evidence: the discovery of Caylee's remains and all the
accompanying forensics.

Dr. Jan Garavaglia, our chief medical examiner, took the stand on June
10. She testified to the findings of her autopsy of little Caylee Marie. She
had determined that the toddler was a victim of a homicide, but the manner
she died was "of undetermined means." I walked her through the steps she
had followed to reach that conclusion. I didn't take a lot of time going over
her findings, because I wanted to leave those questions for the defense. I
knew that Cheney Mason would be the one to cross-examine her, and that
he would be his usual outspoken self. I also knew that Dr. G was ready for
him. Cheney was a good attorney, but he was very predictable.

Sure enough, Cheney Mason decided to argue with Dr. Garavaglia,
and after that, it was game on. Mason would ask a question, and Dr. G
would go into an unchallengeable medical explanation. Mason would try
to interrupt, but she would ignore him. He challenged her opinion that the
death was a homicide and not an accidental drowning, and she pointed out
that in all the records of drowning by children, in 100 percent of the cases,
rescue was called. "No matter how stiff that body is, they always call 911
in the hopes that the child could be saved," she said. She pointed out that
there was no reason *not* to report the incident if it had been a drowning.
She also said that there was no other logical conclusion for the facts presented in this case other than that it was a homicide. She continued, "There
is no child that should have duct tape on its face when it dies. There is no
reason to put duct tape on the face after they die." As much as Mason tried
to out-argue her, she applied her science and experience to answer every
single one of his challenges.

Dr. Michael Warren followed Dr. G in our list of witnesses. He offered one of the most dramatic pieces of evidence in the case. He was the head of the C. A. Pound Human Identification Laboratory at the University of Florida. In order to demonstrate that the duct tape could be used as a murder weapon, we had asked him to prepare a demonstration. We provided him with three photographs: one of the skull, one of a full face of Caylee, and one of the duct tape. The tape and skull pictures had small rulers in the frame, referred to as "scales," to establish size. By matching the scales in the two photos, Dr. Warren's lab was able to magnify them enough to match them up and overlay them. Then, by comparing and aligning anatomical features like teeth and the bridge of the nose, he was able to overlay all three photos. He then created a video with a dissolve feature, making the photo of the skull transition to the photo of Caylee's live face, then back to the skull. The duct tape was overlaid in both pictures to indicate where it would have been when Caylee actually died. It was heartbreaking to watch. Once again, I was surprised at how little visible reaction I saw in the jury. Still, Dr. Warren's presentation appeared to have impacted Casey greatly. Judge Perry had to stop the trial. "Okay, ladies and gentleman of the media, Ms. Anthony is ill, we are recessing for the day," he had to announce when the proceedings abruptly came to an end.

The defense was outraged by the introduction of the video, calling it inflammatory and insisting that it presented only one of a number of possible scenarios. They had lobbied the judge to prevent it from being entered into evidence and had filed a motion for a mistrial related to its being shown to jurors. But Judge Perry agreed with our argument that it was important and "highly relevant" in determining the role of duct tape in Caylee's death.

After the trial resumed the following day, we called Dr. Neal Haskell, the prosecution's sixtieth witness. Haskell was our forensic entomology expert. He was a professor of forensic science and biology at Saint Joseph's College in Rensselaer, Indiana, and a nationally known expert in his field. Haskell testified that he had found flies related to decomposition in the trunk of the Pontiac, flies which were known familiarly as "coffin flies." According to Haskell, Caylee's body probably would have been in the trunk a very short time, based on the bug evidence. He then compared those flies to those collected at the scene where Caylee was found and described how they were consistent.

Our final forensic expert, Elizabeth Fontaine, was also testifying to a very emotional piece of evidence. She was the latent fingerprint analyst at the FBI lab, the same agent who'd seen the outline of a heart shape on the duct tape. In the minds of the public, the "heart on the duct tape" had taken on a life of its own. Images of Casey's mouth, covered with a piece of duct tape embellished with a bright red heart, flooded the Internet to the point where people thought there really was a *sticker* on the tape, not a trace of sticker residue. Such was the case in a "trial by media," where fact and fiction weren't properly separated. There wasn't much any of us could do about it, though. At least the jury was unaware.

Fontaine testified that the outline she saw resembled a heart, even though there was no photographic evidence of the heart-shaped residue. She described it as something you would see if you left a bandage on your skin for a while and then removed it, with the dirt creating an outline of the bandage.

Ever since the story of the heart sticker had first circulated, I'd felt that this evidence was not worth presenting due to its ambiguous nature. Now that the defense was saying Caylee had drowned and was trying to accuse George Anthony of being complicit in the crime, it had turned into a side issue, as far as I was concerned. There were still questions about the sticker and whether the stickers found during a search of the Anthony home were an exact match to the dime-size imprint Fontaine had seen on the duct tape. I also questioned the relevance of including a sticker that had been found thirty feet away from Caylee's remains that may or may not have been involved. I thought it was a distraction that we didn't need, but Linda wanted it included in the testimony, so I acquiesced.

Our final witness was Bobby Williams, the tattoo artist who had given Casey her *"Bella Vita"* tattoo in the weeks after Caylee disappeared. The purpose of putting him on last was that I felt that the fact that she had gotten the tattoo and what it said were the strongest pieces of evidence we had to suggest motive. I felt it would have a great deal of impact on the jury that three weeks after Caylee died, her mother had gotten an irreversible tattoo celebrating her beautiful new life.

Casey had claimed to one of the shrinks that the tattoo was an ironic commentary on the fact that her life had *not* been beautiful, but we thought that was ridiculous. The defense never really argued what the tattoo signified. Instead, Baez seemed to be mostly concerned about whether "*bella*" meant beautiful or good. A substantial legal argument ensued, whereby everyone finally agreed that "*bella*" meant beautiful.

Wednesday morning, June 15, the nineteenth day of the trial, we on the prosecution team rested our case with great confidence. We had covered everything we wanted with barely a hitch. We had ended with motive, that Casey wanted a life without Caylee, substantiated by our final witness, Bobby Williams. All our witnesses had held up well under cross-examination, and we thought we had laid it all out there as best we could for a circumstantial case. The defense's opening remarks had thrown us for a loop, but at least we knew the nuclear lie was coming. We were ready to take on Baez and all he had to offer.

CHAPTER TWENTY-FOUR

DEFENDING CASEY

Jose's dream team had forty-five witnesses on its list, mostly experts to challenge our own forensic discovery. I had reviewed everyone's reports which, by the judge's order, were supposed to contain everything a witness was going to testify to. Not included on the defense's list were the two mental health doctors, so I was unsure how the defense was going to prove their molestation premise without them. Also it was unclear how, without the molestation story, they'd be able to justify Casey's lies to everyone during the thirty-one days. Furthermore, without the therapists, there would be no evidence that Caylee had drowned, so we weren't sure how the defense was going to convince the jury of that accusation from their opening argument, either.

We didn't think Casey was going to testify, but it was still a far-fetched possibility. If she testified, she could speak to these points and more. Regardless of whether she told the truth, we knew that she would be convincing on the stand. On the other hand, Linda was eager to cross-examine her. She had been preparing for the opportunity for three years.

Looking over the witness list ahead of time, we'd thought maybe Baez's team would mount a defense focused on Casey's character, as they could claim there was no substantial evidence showing that prior to June 16, 2008, Caylee had been abused or neglected. Instead, most of the defense's case was based on evidence it claimed had *not* been found, such as fingerprints, DNA, or fibers. I was going to use my cross-examination of most of the defense witnesses to support my position that the absence of these minor corroborating clues was meaningless. You wouldn't expect there to be fingerprints or DNA under the conditions in the swamp. An absent fingerprint didn't mean a finger had never been there.

The first witness to be called by the defense was Orange County Sheriff's Deputy Gerardo Bloise. This would be Bloise's third time on the stand, having been called twice by us. He testified about places he *had* searched, the trunk of Tony Lazzaro's car, and places he *hadn't,* the master bedroom of the Anthony home. Baez's goal of calling crime scene investigator Bloise was to infer that police had spent so much time focusing on Casey as the suspect that they had overlooked other potential suspects.

Baez next brought two highly trained FBI experts to the stand in order to demonstrate some problems with the duct tape evidence. It appeared his goal was to embarrass the FBI and suggest that if such a distinguished lab could mishandle evidence, perhaps all our evidence was questionable. First up was Heather Seubert, a DNA expert. She said there was trace DNA found on the duct tape, but it turned out to be from an FBI technician who had handled it. It was an embarrassment to the FBI, but it was irrelevant to the case. Next was Lorie Gottesman, a forensic document examiner. She testified that she found no evidence of a sticker or sticker residue on the tape, contradicting the testimony of our expert, Elizabeth Fontaine. I thought these issues were irrelevant to the case, and prompted only by the defense's motive to discredit our evidence.

To refute the opinion of our bug expert, Neal Haskell, the defense called Tim Huntington. Huntington was a twenty-nine-year-old Ph.D. from Nebraska, a forensic entomologist, and an assistant professor at Concordia University. He had once studied under Dr. Haskell. He reminded me of Ichabod Crane, the schoolteacher from Washington Irving's "The Legend of Sleepy Hollow," except for being about forty years younger. He was a nice guy and tall, with very thick glasses. Before trial, I had been told by Dr. Haskell that we might expect Huntington to disagree with us, but he would be honest.

Huntington's testimony focused on the bugs that had been found in the Pontiac's trunk. He talked about the lifespan of flies and how flies might make their way into a car's trunk. The gist was that if Caylee's body had been in the car, there should have been lots of dead flies in there, and there weren't.

Haskell had already testified that the reason there weren't more bugs in the car was because the trunk was sealed and they couldn't get in. We thought this would be a simple disagreement between two experts about bugs. But Baez started moving Huntington in a direction beyond his field of expertise, asking Huntington his opinion about whether the stain in the trunk looked like the stain from a decomposing body.

I objected, based on his lack of qualifications. He said he was in a position to render an opinion, saying he had worked at a funeral home in his teenage years. When Judge Perry said he would allow testimony and leave it to the jury to determine if Huntington had the expertise, I objected again. I said Huntington's deposition did not cover opinions on the subject he was now testifying to. This would be the first of many objections on the prosecution's part regarding the testimony of defense witnesses. Over and over, Baez would lead his witnesses to areas his reports did not address, and since they weren't contained in reports or the depositions of these witnesses, our objections were sustained time and again. But what a frustrating situation for everyone, including the jury, who would have to wait for all these objections to be ironed out.

Judge Perry's admonitions to Baez about these repeated violations of procedure seemed to fall on deaf ears. These incidents were going to test even Judge Perry's patience, and he was a very patient man.

Huntington described an experiment he had performed just for the Anthony case. He took the carcass of a pig, put it in the trunk of a car, and let it decompose over time. He showed the jury pictures of the rotting pig and all the flies at various stages of decomposition. As he was making his presentation, Linda leaned over and whispered, "He didn't put his pigs in a blanket." We both laughed, and Linda dared me to actually say that during cross-examination.

So, when I was crossing Huntington, I said, "Well your experiment didn't mimic the conditions under which Caylee's body was wrapped. You didn't put your pigs in a blanket, did you?"

I immediately told the jury that someone dared me to say that. I'm not sure if the defense team was as amused as we were, but Huntington gave a little chuckle.

Huntington was the first witness to argue the idea that the garbage found in the trunk made the smell in the car. He was standing by his opinion that the flies were the result of trash in the trunk. On cross, I challenged him to show me where there was actual food in the garbage. I asked him if he had actually seen the evidence with regard to the trash and he said no, just a photo. First, I produced the picture in which he had claimed to see fly-producing garbage.

He pointed to this one Oscar Mayer salami container. "See? There is meat inside that container, and if it rotted, that could create the smell," Huntington said.

We had the garbage in evidence. Our forensics people had taken the trash, dried it out, and put each piece in its own bag. I found the evidence bag that had the salami wrapper, handed it to Mr. Huntington, and said, "Show me the piece of meat in that package."

"Oh no, it was paper," he said. What he had thought was meat in the picture was actually paper. That was the first step in the debunking of the smell in the trunk as garbage.

Dr. Werner Spitz was a forensic anthropologist who was over the age of eighty. Back in the eighties and early nineties, he was one of the leaders in his field. Over the last ten years or so, he had inserted himself into a number of high-profile cases; O.J. was one, Phil Spector was another. Now he had involved himself in this case. I felt he was desperately searching for a way to maintain some relevance in his field.

His testimony was twofold. First, Dr. Spitz attacked Dr. Garavaglia for having not opened Caylee's skull at autopsy. She had left it intact. That was a violation of basic autopsy protocol, he continued. Second, he was the only witness trying to render the opinion the skull had been removed from the crime scene. He testified that someone could have removed it, taken it home, put duct tape on it, and returned it to the scene.

When Dr. Spitz had performed his own autopsy, he had opened the skull and found some residue, which he claimed to be able to recognize from sight as the decomposition of the brain. To him, the residue indicated that the skull had been on its side when the brains decomposed. I called this the "brain dust" testimony.

On cross, I started with his criticism of Dr. Garavaglia's autopsy, about the violation of protocol claim, that Dr. G had not opened the skull. Dr. Spitz had been one of the authors of a basic textbook on forensic anthropology. I took his book up to the stand, put it down in front of him, and said, "Show me where you say it is protocol to open a skull when it is skeletonized."

He leafed through the pages and did not find any reference to his claim. I next asked him if he was familiar with any other written protocol on the opening of the skull at autopsy. And he answered no. Next, I addressed the "removal and return of the skull" theory. I went through what I thought would be necessary to carry out what he was alleging. Someone would have to take the skull and the mandible home, put them in an anatomically correct position, tape the two pieces together, and put the skull back in the exact location where it had been. Dr. Spitz argued that though it would be difficult, it could be done.

I showed him the photo taken at the medical examiner's office, showing that strands of hair were draped over the skull. I asked him how the hair could fall so perfectly back to its original position in a re-created scene. I pointed out that the manner of the hair falling on the skull was not consistent with it being on its side.

Dr. Spitz got belligerent with me, to a point where he didn't know how to answer. He said that maybe the medical examiner had staged the photo. So I showed him the photo taken at the scene with the strands of hair in exactly the same position. He then claimed that maybe the police had staged the skull. In my opinion, Dr. Spitz's testimony ended up being completely discredited.

William Rodriguez was a forensic anthropologist who worked for the U.S. Department of Defense, Armed Forces Institute of Pathology, a government body in Washington, D.C., that does all the U.S. military's pathology, such as remains found in Vietnam twenty years after the fact. I had read his report and it was not all that in conflict with what our experts were saying, so I decided not to depose him. He took the stand on a Saturday morning and recited his qualifications. One of his claims was that he was a cofounder of the Anthropological Research Facility, also known as the "Body Farm," at the University of Tennessee, where my man, Dr. Vass, had his lab. This was news to me. Being so familiar with that research facility, I was shocked that I hadn't heard about him before. However, in the days following his testimony, I received calls from people in the field who were offended that he had claimed to be a cofounder. They acknowledged he had been a grad student at the "Body Farm," but had not been credited as a cofounder.

Right off, Dr. Rodriguez started talking about the stickiness of duct tape and other areas that were not in his report and not necessarily in his area of expertise. I objected, and after a great deal of wrangling back and forth, the judge said it appeared there were new areas being discussed and authorized a recess so I could depose him. The witness had to stop testifying and the jury was dismissed. We completed his deposition that afternoon.

Unbeknownst to me, while I was sticking to the decorum of courtroom argument, chaos was breaking out outside the courthouse. The previous night, people had begun lining up for tickets to view the proceedings. The paucity of seats had caused a lot of aggressive behavior in the line. Little fights had broken out now and again, but this was a blow-out brawl. At five A.M. that Friday, two men tried to cut the line. People who had waited all night would have none of it and a shoving match erupted. The circus of this trial had officially turned violent. This was a major embarrassment to our community to have such uncivilized behavior shown on national television. I was often disgusted with the atmosphere reminiscent of the Roman Colosseum. After that, we changed the rules of ticket distribution. All tickets were handed out the night before and no one could show up the day of court without a ticket.

That evening, when I was dining with family and friends I received an urgent call from Dr. G. She had just gotten a call from Dr. Rodriguez's boss, a captain at the Armed Forces Institute of Pathology in D.C. He wanted to talk to me urgently. I excused myself from the table, and there in the lobby of the Cheesecake Factory in Winter Park, Florida, I called the captain. He told me he had seen on television that Dr. Rodriguez was a witness in the Casey Anthony trial and there was a huge problem. As a government employee, he was not authorized to testify, and if he continued to do so, he would be terminated from his employment. I was surprised by the information but did not want to become involved in any way in the decision of Dr. Rodriguez's boss, but I did not expect that he would show up on Monday to complete his testimony. It all made sense why he had pointed out at the start of his testimony that he was appearing in court in a private capacity. "I'd like to inform the court I'm here as an unpaid consultant," he had announced.

To my surprise, Dr. Rodriguez did show up in court on Monday morning, ready to testify. Before he could begin, I raised the issue about his deposition with Judge Perry. After some wrangling, the court recessed. A meeting with the judge and defense ensued in a back room. I brought up my conversation with the captain and the consequences of Dr. Rodriguez's testimony. Jose went and spoke with Dr. Rodriguez, and when he came back it sounded like Rodriguez still wanted to testify. But not long after, Jose came to us and told us that Dr. Rodriguez did not want to lose his job, and the defense was withdrawing him as a witness.

A day or two later, Jose filed a motion asking that the charges against Casey be dismissed and accused me of engineering the employment action against Rodriguez, claiming that I had contacted his employer. He was accusing me of tampering with a witness, accusing me of a crime. I was upset, but Linda was outraged. She went to the defense and told them that if they believed this was what had happened, they needed to report me to the Florida Bar, and if they didn't, she was going to report them.

"You can't say stuff like this unless you can damn well prove it!" she told them. Linda told them that this was a serious allegation and if they were saying it to cause a little trouble and it wasn't true, heads were going to roll. About two minutes later, one of Cheney Mason's young assistants came over to us and said the defense was withdrawing the motion. The bickering behind the scenes was escalating. Even Judge Perry seemed to be at his wit's end with Baez's antics.

On June 21, the defense called Jane Bock, a forensic botanist who examined the crime scene on February 1, 2009. Bock testified that "leaf litter," or fallen leaves, in the area of Caylee's remains suggested that Caylee might have been put there as recently as two weeks before the discovery. I asked her if it could have been longer, and she said yes. When I pointed out a bone that was buried four inches in the mud, she suggested a dog could have buried it there. With great effort I stifled a laugh and moved on.

Richard Eikelenboom, a "touch DNA" expert from Holland, was the third defense witness to try and testify beyond the scope of his report. Eikelenboom analyzes skin cells left behind when a person touches something, and he was going to render an opinion on whether there should have been detectable DNA on the duct tape found on little Caylee's skull.

Eikelenboom's initial report had contained only one line, stating that at the time he had no opinion about the DNA findings to which he was an expert. He had not been set for deposition since he had no opinions, so when he showed up in the hall one Friday I was surprised. The next thing I knew, the defense was calling him. Now I objected to him taking the stand until I could depose him. As with Rodriguez, we hurriedly took his deposition. I was prepared to respond to his testimony as best I could, but I was wary of investigating witnesses in the middle of trial and pursued sanctions against the defense.

Judge Perry agreed with me, seeming really annoyed with Baez. He went as far as making a specific finding that Baez had "willfully" violated the Court's order and the rules of discovery despite the number of his admonitions. This time, the judge allowed Eikelenboom's testimony but went to the extraordinary step of advising the jury about the violations by the defense. He told the jurors that they could take into account Baez's willful violations when they judged this witness's credibility. Judge Perry told Baez he would address additional sanctions against him personally after the trial. As of this writing, Judge Perry has not addressed the additional sanctions. In the end, Eikelenboom's contribution was that there "might" or "might not" have been detectable DNA on the duct tape found in the car and I was able to effectively cross-examine him. Baez's ambush tactics in this case had little effect on our ability to cross examine his witnesses. All it really accomplished was cutting into what little time I otherwise might have had with my family.

Dr. Marcus Bain Wise was the analytical chemist at Oak Ridge Laboratory who had worked with Dr. Vass on the odor evidence. I think the defense called Dr. Wise, expecting him to say that the amount of chloroform found in the air samples collected from the Pontiac could not be quantified, which he did. But, he added another level of comment to the issue. Dr. Wise had broader experience with chloroform in other contexts in various environmental testing and said he'd never seen levels that high. He also touted Vass's expertise in chemistry, even though he acknowledged that this was not Vass's area of specialty. Calling Dr. Wise appeared to have really backfired on the defense.

Kenneth Furton, a professor of chemistry at Florida International University, took the stand to testify about the chloroform and fluid found on paper towels in the trunk of the Pontiac. He was in court to refute Dr. Vass's findings on both. Dr. Vass had noted that five chemical compounds found in the trunk were associated with human decomposition. Dr. Furton agreed, but clarified that in his opinion those same five compounds could also be found in garbage and household products. He also attempted to blame the odor on the trash in the car, maybe some dried-out remnant of cheese spread. Once again, I faced him with the actual item from the garbage and he fared no better than Dr. Huntington had.

With regard to fluid found on the paper towels, Dr. Furton said it could have come from a milk fat, a cheese, or an animal fat. He mentioned the Velveeta cheese and salami wrappers as being a possible source. In my questioning of him, Dr. Furton agreed that the fluid could have come from a decomposing body, but maintained that it could have been from another source as well.

The topic of chloroform was a sensitive subject for Cindy Anthony. She was in her own chloroform hot water when she took the stand for the defense on Thursday, June 23. In my opinion, this was the point when

Cindy chose Casey over Caylee. She testified that she recalled searching for the word *chloroform* after her little Yorkie had become sick and she was researching if there was a connection between chloroform and the bamboo he had been eating. She said she did not, however, type the words "how to make chloroform."

During the cross-examination, a stern Linda Burdick asked Cindy question after question about her specific search terms. While Cindy said she had searched the word *chloroform,* she had not searched *how to make chloroform.* Linda also drilled her about where she was on the date of the search.

"So, it's your testimony today that it's possible that you were home on that day even though your work records reflect something differently? That's correct? Is that correct? On March 28, 2008, is it your testimony in front of this jury that you were home between 2:16 and 2:28 P.M.?"

"It's possible," Cindy replied, and then started to hem and haw.

Work records showed that Cindy was on her computer at the office around the time the searches for chloroform had been conducted on her home computer. Because it would have been impossible for her to be in two places at once, it was my opinion that Cindy Anthony lied to help her daughter. If she was lying and if that lie were found to be material, it could have subjected her to prosecution for perjury. Subsequent to my retirement, the State Attorney's Office chose not to pursue perjury charges against her.

Because the chloroform searches were now the topic of evidence, the defense recalled Sergeant Kevin Stenger, the head of the computer forensics division at the Sheriff's Office. In this, the defense caught something we missed, to their credit. Through computer software expert John Dennis Bradley, we had placed into evidence a computer report of the chloroform searches conducted on the Anthonys' computer. It had been prepared by Stenger, using Bradley's software. Stenger's view was that software was the most reliable. That report had indicated that one of the websites related to chloroform had been visited eighty-four times, with specific dates for those searches.

Prior to submitting the files to Bradley, Stenger had done a similar search of the file using a different software program, but felt some of the results may not have been accurate. That report reflected all of the activity in that file. Both reports were provided to the defense. As it turns out, the earlier report that Stenger had produced indicated that the particular site was only visited once and attributed the eighty-four hits to a MySpace page. The defense called Stenger and exposed the discrepancy in the two reports. We still are not completely sure which one was correct but the real effect on the case was that the error took the jury's attention away from the most important issue: that the site was visited *period*. It certainly made us all look bad. Once the discrepancy was pointed out to us, we never again argued the search number.

Stenger did an analysis of the deleted file shortly after the trial ended, using a different program, and found the same searches on the same dates, but instead of eighty-four visits to the one site, he found only one. Again, the error unfortunately detracted from the important information, which was that someone had searched for "how to make chloroform" in the first place.

During his testimony, Lee Anthony showed his allegiance to Casey much as his mother had. Perhaps the death penalty on the table was a motivating factor in their loyalty. In deposition, Lee had talked about the period of time when Casey was pregnant. He had been living at home, and said she looked like she was getting fat, so he went to talk to his mother. Cindy didn't want to talk about it. Lee had just shrugged it off, figuring it was none of his business. He said his parents were soon "over the top" about it, and had even made a nursery and thrown a baby shower.

Now on the stand, he was throwing his parents under the bus, crying and hamming it up. He blamed his mother and father for "hiding" the pregnancy and for being ashamed of it. He acted beside himself that his parents "wouldn't let him" be involved in any aspect of the pregnancy, and had even kept him away from the birth of his niece. Lee was totally playing into Baez's claim that this family had secrets and everybody was a victim.

Lee was never asked at trial about his sister's allegations of sexual misconduct, but I was told that he had denied the claims to Anthony family attorney Mark Lippman, telling the lawyer "it never happened."

THROUGH THE TESTIMONY OF ALL of these witnesses, Baez had been almost entirely on his own. Cheney Mason had joined the defense team with great hype and celebration, and throughout the six and a half weeks of trial, we had barely heard from him. He had a good reputation as an elder statesman, but made most of his money on divorce cases or high-publicity trials. He tried to project himself as larger than life. In the Anthony case, he had cross-examined only a couple of witnesses, among them Dr. G, but had done little else. Part of his role may have been funding. We had heard that Cheney was paying for hotel rooms for members of the defense team when we were picking the jury in Pinellas County.

At one point in the middle of trial Cheney had handed Frank a piece of paper with trivia information about the courtroom: how many ceiling tiles there were, how many recessed lights, and other minutiae. I think he was basically telegraphing his boredom, that he was not involved in the case and that this was Baez's case. Because he was not engaged, he had a lot of time to fill his mind with other factual nuggets. That became clear after one of our many sidebars with Judge Perry over the admission of evidence. Cheney shrugged his shoulders and said in his southern drawl, "I keep trying to teach the boy the rules of evidence." When we asked him about anything pertaining to the trial, he would often answer, "I don't know. This is Jose's show."

At the eleventh hour, however, it appeared that Cheney had decided he needed to step in. He had approached Linda about a plea. Linda told him that if Casey wanted to plead to second-degree murder for a specific sentence of thirty years, that she could do that. That she might be allowed to plead to the aggravated manslaughter charge, but she would have to give us an explanation to justify it. She would have to give us the truth about how it happened and it would have to fit. We weren't going to let her plead down without knowing what happened to Caylee.

Cheney wanted Casey to talk to him about entering a plea. At first Jose was not on board with the idea, but he had come around and was at least entertaining it. On Saturday, June 25, we approached the bench and moved to a back room with Judge Perry. There, Cheney told us that Casey refused to even listen to the idea of a plea. Every time he approached the subject with her, she would look at him blankly, like she didn't know what a plea was. He said her expression gave him concerns about her competency.

Whenever an attorney says there is a question of competency the law requires the court to take it seriously and explore the issue. Casey was being so stubborn that she would not even discuss the plea issue with Cheney. When he tried to broach it, she would not react or listen in any way. If he talked about it, she acted like he wasn't there. Though we doubted there was truly a competency concern, we agreed that a competency examination was necessary.

My take was that Cheney felt they were losing the case and Casey needed to seriously start thinking about taking a plea. I think he was frustrated with her stubbornness. We agreed to tell the press that a legal matter had come up. Casey was ordered to speak with our old friend Dr. Jeffrey Danziger and another psychiatrist, Harry McClaren, who was from Chattahoochee, a small town up near Tallahassee.

The doctors both agreed that Casey was fine and competent to stand trial. They also said that she told them that she was not interested in a plea. It never came up again.

I have never had a "competency for stubbornness" issue before. People decompensate and get worse through the stress of a trial, but this was not a real competency issue. This was addressing stubbornness.

ROY KRONK WAS THE WITNESS everybody had been waiting for and the defense called him to the stand on June 28. Cheney Mason was going to be questioning the Orange County meter reader, who we hadn't called because of his credibility issues. But he was an important witness for the defense, because they were trying to make him a scapegoat. Kronk repeated his story of seeing something suspicious at the scene where the body was found on the eleventh, twelfth, and thirteenth of August. The jury heard all three of his calls to 911. Kronk said that on the day of his final 911 call, he didn't get any closer than twenty to thirty feet of the suspicious bundle. Mostly, the defense was curious about what kind of money Kronk felt he stood to make for the discovery of Caylee's body. He said he was aware of the $50,000 reward. Cheney asked him if he had ever used the term "winning the lottery" about the body and if he had told someone he didn't want his ex-wife to know about his reward. Kronk said that he had been joking when he made those remarks.

Because the defense was alleging that Kronk had taken the Anthony's duct tape, on cross, we asked him if had ever met the Anthonys or had access to their house, car, or garage. Kronk said he didn't know the family and did not have access to their home. Kronk's estranged son, Brandon Sparks, was called to testify the following day. Sparks said his father had told him in November 2008 that he had found Caylee's skull, and he was going to be rich and famous. But Kronk told jurors the conversation with his son had never happened.

George Anthony took the stand for a fifth time on June 30. Jose started right off the top, ripping into him about why he didn't do anything if he thought the trunk of the Pontiac smelled like death, and about a statement he allegedly made that his granddaughter would be found in a swamp. Till now, George had managed to keep his composure during his prior cross examinations, but he wept openly when Baez raised questions about his attempted suicide in January 2009.

He asked George about the suicide letter and implied that it contained some expression of guilt. I didn't want Baez telling the jurors what was in the note. I wanted them to read it for themselves. To this point, I wasn't sure the judge would let the entire letter in. I had done a ton of research on the issue, and I thought I could get some of it in, but all of it would be a stretch. I objected to Baez's question, since the letter was not in evidence and pointed out that I had it in the courtroom if defense counsel wanted to place it in evidence. I don't think Baez knew I had it. He took the letter in his hand and held it as he tried again to give his version of what it said. I objected again and we approached the bench.

At the bench Judge Perry showed once again his understanding of tactics and appellate issues. During the discussion I argued that the questions already had made some portions of the letter admissible. The judge discussed the issue and seemed to agree that what Baez had done might make it admissible, rather than explicitly rule he just sort of gave his impressions on the issue but did not rule. Baez left the bench apparently under the mistaken impression that the court had decide to allow the whole letter in. He then proceeded to question George extensively, implying that the suicide attempt was a fraud.

Casey made no reaction from where she sat, as her father was forced to recount his attempt to end his own life.

George said he had purchased a gun and planned to track down and interrogate friends of Casey who he believed had information about his dead granddaughter. Even as George fought to compose himself, Baez kept hammering away at him. He came back to Casey's molestation he had used at opening arguments. "You of course would never admit to molesting your child, would you, sir?" Baez prodded.

"Sir, I would never do anything to harm my daughter in that way," George Anthony said, fighting back tears.

"Only in that way?" Baez taunted.

When I asked George to describe the way he felt the day he learned Caylee's remains had been found in the swamp off Suburban Drive, it took all he had to answer. "A deep hurt inside, tears, the whole gamut of an emotional loss, a breakdown inside of me and seeing what my wife and son went through," he sobbed.

I finally did move George's suicide note into evidence during our rebuttal case, and Baez objected. The judge pointed to his questions as the very reason that he had ruled to make the letter admissible. Judge Perry permitted jurors to read the eight-page farewell George had penned to his wife and that police had discovered in the motel room in Daytona, Florida. I felt that this heart-wrenching correspondence was the single strongest piece of evidence that established that George's involvement in the death of Caylee was unthinkable. I felt that Baez's clumsiness in handling the issue was a major mistake on his part.

George's testimony was followed by the appearance of Krystal Holloway, George Anthony's supposed mistress. Holloway went by the nickname "River Cruz." She was a volunteer for the Casey Anthony cause but she was not with Texas EquuSearch. She said the two had met at a tent set up to hand out water bottles and such. Through her volunteering, she had become friends with Cindy and George. She said that she and George had started having an affair in the fall of 2008. It ended before his suicide attempt in January of 2009.

She first spoke to police in 2010 about conversations between her and George. She claimed that George had supposedly told her that his grand-daughter's death had been an accident that had spiraled out of control. At that time, police had asked her if she and George were having an affair, and she said no. But her story changed after she sold it to *The National Enquirer* for $4,000. Then, she portrayed herself as George's mistress.

On the stand, George Anthony denied the affair, but Krystal had a text message from him that said, "Just thinking about you, I need you in my life." George admitted that he had sent the text, explaining that at the time he had needed every volunteer in his life.

On cross, Krystal said that she had lied to the police about their affair to protect George. She also said she chose *The National Enquirer* for her story, because she could trust the magazine to tell it honestly, and not because they were willing to pay her. She admitted that George referred to a *belief* that Caylee had died by accident. I got her to admit that he had never claimed any firsthand knowledge, and never indicated any involve-ment in disposing of his granddaughter's body.

George was the last witness on the defense's list. Now came the moment when Casey was either summoned to the stand or wasn't. In our opinion, Casey needed to take the stand to back up all of the sensational claims that Baez had made in opening. If she did, we would finally hear the story of the sexually-abused child trained to lie. The details would be hor-rific. Finally the public would see Casey speak and more importantly, face cross-examination. The defense requested a brief recess to consult with their client. When it returned, we learned Casey would not testify, as I had predicted five weeks earlier. Casey 4.0—that Caylee had drowned and she had lied because of her family history—would only come from Baez.

After thirteen days, the defense rested its case. They had thrown the kitchen sink at us, including theories about Roy Kronk and George Anthony, while attacking our forensics. They had never supported their outrageous opening statements. They had not put Casey on the stand. They had no evi-dence that Caylee had drowned in a pool, or that Casey was so traumatized by sexual abuse that she would not know the difference between a lie and a true story. Their forensic people put on the stand to refute our forensics people were cut to size. We were riding high. We thought the defense case was borderline ridiculous, making claims in opening that you never even supported. In my thirty years, I had never heard of such of a thing.

In all criminal trials, the State has an opportunity to offer evidence to rebut any of the defense's claims. In most cases, nothing is presented in rebuttal. Whether to rebut is always a difficult decision to make. By the end of a trial, you figure the jury is sick and tired of the case and just wants to get on to deliberations. You don't want them to perceive you as wasting their time on things that seem trivial. Rebuttal is the last thing they hear, so potentially it can be important. One of the things that we felt we needed to rebut was Cindy's testimony about the chloroform searches. Before she testified, we had already obtained her work records, which showed that she had been at the office at the times the searches had been conducted. She said it was common practice to clock in at work, then run errands and not note her time away from the office in the time records. Linda knew we needed to probe this further.

From Cindy's employer, Linda was able to get records of usage on Cindy's work computer. These showed that Cindy had been on the computer at her desk and entering data at times that would have made it impossible for her to be at home as well. A vice president from Gentiva's home office in Atlanta, John Camperlengo, was unlucky enough to be the one to come to court with the records to testify. I say unlucky because he ended up having to stay in Orlando for three days while the defense desperately tried to prevent him from testifying. They deposed him, demanded additional records, demanded to talk to the company's IT people, and ended up trying to argue to the judge that Camperlengo's testimony should be excluded because of the late disclosure of the information.

Judge Perry responded that the defense should have checked out their witness's story better before they put her on the stand. He then ruled Camperlengo's testimony admissible and allowed him testify. On the stand, Camperlengo explained how his office's record keeping procedures showed that Cindy could not have been home at the times she had claimed.

Cindy's testimony was further rebutted by the testimony of Sandra Cawn and Kevin Stenger, both of whom had searched the Anthonys' home computer and had found no evidence that a search for the term *chlorophyll* had ever been conducted.

We also spent a few moments rebutting some of Dr. Spitz's claims. We presented the testimony of Dr. Bruce Goldberger, the forensic toxicologist who had tested the washing of the interior of the skull. He said that the material that Dr. Spitz had identified as residue of brain matter was, in fact, not organic in nature, and was most likely just dirt.

Dr. Warren from the C.A. Pound Human Identification Laboratory was also called to dispute Dr. Spitz's claim that Dr. G had not followed proper protocol for examination of a skull. In response to questions, Dr. Warrant explained that the skull of a child should not have been sawed open as Spitz had done. After the rebuttal, all that was left was for Casey to be found guilty, sentenced, and I would retire on a high note.

CHAPTER TWENTY-FIVE

THE PROSECUTION RESTS

The cases had been presented. The objections had been made. I believed our case was strong. I'm sure the defense believed the same about theirs. But there was still one final drama to play out: the closing arguments.

Early on, we'd decided how we'd order our remarks. Linda, with her brilliant opening, had gotten us off on the right foot, and I would start bringing it full circle. The prosecution always went first, so I would lead off for us. Baez and Mason would close for the defense, then Linda would do our final rebuttal to address anything the defense had said. My portion would spend a lot of time reviewing the thirty-one days that Caylee was missing, connecting Casey's lies to specific purposes and driving home just how calculated her deception was.

I love closing arguments. I've loved them ever since I first began standing in front of court. Closing arguments are the cherry on the sundae, the one thing you don't give away and the best thing you get to do.

As I prepared for the closing arguments, I was thinking a lot about common sense. We'd based so much of our case on common sense. Was Casey's behavior that of a loving, caring mother? Did it make sense that she would lie to this extent having done nothing wrong? Putting aside the minutiae of the case, the forensic evidence, the detailed timelines, the intricate lies—what did common sense say about a mother who leaves her parents' home one morning with her child, and then proceeds to live a new life with her boyfriend without the child? What does common sense tell you about that mother? My common sense told me that it meant she wanted a life without her child. My common sense told me that Casey wanted to be rid of Caylee. When you hear that a few weeks after her child had last been seen, she appeared at a tattoo parlor in high spirits and got a tattoo that said "the beautiful life" in Italian, doesn't common sense say she got the tattoo because that's how she feels?

When you hear the young mother spin lie after lie after lie to everyone about her child and where she is and why no one has seen her, your common sense says she is hiding something. When you hear the manager of a tow yard, experienced crime scene technicians, an ex-cop (who happens to be the accused's father), and a scientist who spent twenty years studying an odor tell you that the smell in the trunk was that of a dead body, common sense tells you that there was a dead body in the car. When you hear that a hair from a child was found in that same trunk with evidence indicating that it came from a corpse, common sense tells you there was a child's dead body in that car.

When you find that someone has searched on a computer for instructions to make chloroform and you find chloroform in the trunk of the car, common sense puts two and two together, and concludes that someone made chloroform for some purpose.

When Casey continues to spin multiple tales to explain the child's disappearance, even in the face of questioning by law enforcement officers, and maintains the lie even in the face of arrest, doesn't your common sense tell you that what she is hiding is her own guilt?

When you find the remains of a little girl in a wooded swamp surrounded by items that tie back to one house, common sense says the child was killed by someone at the house who didn't want the body found.

Most important, when you find the skull of a two-and-a-half-year-old girl with three pieces of duct tape wrapped from one side of the jaw to the other, covering where the nose and mouth would have been, what does your common sense tell you?

While plotting out my remarks, it also didn't escape me that this was the last time I'd be standing before a jury for the State of Florida. My thirtieth anniversary with the State Attorney's Office had come and gone six months earlier. Had I chosen to sit quietly for the last couple of years, I would have been relaxing at home with my kids. Instead, I'd decided to try one last time to bring justice, to see Caylee's trial through to the end.

Regardless of the outcome, I never second-guessed my choice to be a part of this prosecution team. The last three years had encompassed everything that I'd loved about being a lawyer, as well as a few things that I hated about it, too. Win or lose, I was ending on a high note. But I sure as hell wanted to win. I believed our case was strong. I was ready to help prove that once and for all.

ON JULY 3, 2011, I arrived at court ready to deliver my closing argument in *State of Florida v. Casey Anthony*. We had finished thirty-three days of testimony, two days longer than Caylee had been missing. In all, 141 people had taken the stand, some more than once. Cindy Anthony alone had testified eight times.

As I arrived, the cameras were staked out at Camp Casey and Little Camp Casey. News trucks filled the street. My final day in front of the jury would be anything but quiet, but that was how I wanted it. From the first day I'd signed on, I'd known what I was getting myself into.

When it came time to deliver my remarks, I felt calm. I don't normally write my remarks out beforehand, but since I would be talking about the thirty-one days, something I was not as conversant in as Linda, I'd spent a good deal of time organizing my thoughts. I knew how I wanted everything to be structured and made myself a road map.

I began by emphasizing the pattern of lies Casey had demonstrated when her baby was missing. One of the things I really wanted the jury to

take away was that everything Casey had done had been deliberate. These were not delusions she was suffering from. These were lies for manipulation and gain, lies designed to disrupt and deceive.

In keeping with that idea of deliberate behavior, I returned to the idea of Casey's MySpace password, which she'd revised to "Timer55" in the days following Caylee's disappearance. Now, that could mean any number of things, it's true. But in many ways, the new password was just too coincidental for me to stomach. The "55" number has such a precise significance, the number of days between Caylee's disappearance on June 16 and her third birthday on August 9. The word "Timer" reminds her that the clock is ticking whenever she logs into her account. The end was drawing near, and she needed to have a solution to the problem that she couldn't produce Caylee. Playing off this idea of how Casey found new solutions to her lies, I brought up the "end of the hall" concept and how in each of her lies she'd reached a point where she could go no further, a point past which the truth behind the lie was inescapable, when she was officially at the end of the hall. This was the point she would reach when "Timer55" expired on Caylee's birthday, August 9. Before then she needed to have a plan, an out—specifically, one that would allow her to get away with murder.

Pushing the "end of the hall" idea one step further, I brought up the creation of Casey's final lie, Casey 4.0, the drowning story that became her version of the truth at trial. I explained how this story was yet another example of Casey reaching the end of the hall. Once the body had been connected to the house through the duct tape and laundry bag, suddenly the stranger abduction story became implausible. She had to take the lie somewhere else, and that somewhere was George Anthony.

One thing that was important to emphasize was the total absence of logic in Casey's version of the truth. Part of what I wanted to show was that even if you bought the idea that Caylee's death was an accident, there really was no way to justify Casey's behavior after the fact. Simply put, her behavior did not reflect how a mother would react to the "accidental" death of her child—unless, of course, you believed in the logic of Casey's world. In Casey's world, you didn't call 911 when your child drowns. In Casey's world, you didn't frantically bring your child to the hospital to try and revive her.

In Casey's world, you didn't grieve for weeks and months on end. Instead, in Casey's world you stuffed your little girl in a laundry bag, threw her in a swamp, and went out partying with your new boyfriend.

Turning to something that I knew Baez would feature in his closing, I brought up George Anthony. I explained all the reasons why I knew George was not involved with Caylee's death, saying his love for her was undeniable, his passive acceptance of her death unthinkable, and his disposal of her body in a swamp unimaginable. I mentioned the suicide letter, the depth of the despair that finding Caylee's body had pushed him to. George Anthony may have struggled with his own demons, but harming Caylee was not a solution.

From George I moved on to the forensics, reminding jurors of Dr. Vass, the odors he uncovered, and the chemical compounds found in the trunk, which were only present during human decomposition. I talked about Caylee's hair, which was found with the "death band" on it, a hair that could only have belonged to Caylee with a characteristic that had only been found to occur in dead bodies. But the piece of forensics that I really wanted jurors to focus on, the piece that I myself could never get past or understand, was the duct tape. I reminded jurors, in case they had some lingering thought that maybe the whole thing had been an accident spun out of control, that the duct tape proved the accident theory wrong. That was why the defense had gone to such great lengths to implicate either Roy Kronk or George Anthony with the duct tape; because it was the duct tape that showed an intent to kill. Almost certainly, it was responsible for her death. It was the duct tape that made little Caylee's death murder in the first degree.

Finally, as I wrapped up my speech, I stood in front of the court, and provided the judge, jurors, and spectators with the prosecution's version of events. I told them how we thought Caylee's murder happened, walking them point-by-point through the timeline that Linda, Frank, and I, with the help of Orange County Sheriff's Office, had spent nearly three years assembling. By the end of close, I'd been speaking for almost two hours, but it felt like only minutes. I would have stood there for another twenty-four hours if I thought it would help to prove our point. To me, the answer couldn't have been simpler: Casey wanted to live the "beautiful life," and the only problem was the beautiful life did not include a two-year-old daughter.

NEXT WAS BAEZ'S TURN. WE expected him to argue about everything we had presented, and we were spot-on. Judge Perry had ruled that Baez could not return to his molestation allegations, as he had not proven them at trial. Without that fiction in his quiver, he attacked us heavily on our forensics and George Anthony. He drilled into George's credibility and minimized Casey's lies as nothing but part of her fantasy world. At times, his argument was convincing and well-articulated. At others, it was disjointed and choppy, hard to follow, and failed to tell a cohesive story, reflecting their "throw everything against the wall and see what sticks" strategy. My hope was that the jury would see this fractured presentation as indicative of just how fractured the defense had been.

At various points in his remarks, Baez displayed fifteen poster boards with assorted, oversize fridge-magnet photos of various witnesses from throughout the trial. Two assistants were in charge of moving the photos, adding some while taking others away. It gave the proceedings a kind of *Wheel of Fortune* quality, which in my opinion was not such a good thing.

Baez stated that Casey loved Caylee, reminding jurors that all of Casey's friends and family had testified that Casey was a loving mother. No one had admitted anything less than that. In Baez's telling, it was simply impossible for this mother who, by all accounts, loved her daughter, to kill her in cold blood. From this opening concept, he then segued into what proved to be a rather solid argument about reasonable doubt and the role it played. Pushing this point in a different direction, he then attacked us for overcharging Casey for the crime, one of about a dozen rather direct attacks on our character or motives, saying that our case was not strong enough to warrant either a Murder One conviction or the possibility of the death penalty. I had to hand it to him, there were moments when he could be a very convincing lawyer. For all his faults, he was the consummate salesman.

After the reasonable doubt discussion, however, Baez moved a bit clumsily to his poster boards, showing a calendar of dates. As he discussed each date, he would put a photo of a witness who had been linked to that date on the calendar. The disarray of the presentation obscured whatever points Baez was trying to make, and to me, he seemed to be doing more harm than good with the use of the posters. I wondered if the posters were a bit of a crutch that showed a lack of confidence in the persuasiveness of his words.

As he moved to the topic of George Anthony, Baez delved into what he said was George's obvious culpability. Regarding the gas cans, Baez expressed skepticism over George's reporting them missing in the first place, asking the question of who in the world would ever report the theft of gas cans (well, I would, for one) and stating that the duct tape connection made George look guilty. Overall, the critique of George was a good one, but it was hampered by how Baez jumped between topics. His argument didn't seem as organized as it could have been. Baez went on to attack the investigators at the sheriff's office for drying out the garbage that had been in the trunk, saying that the cops didn't want the jury to know what had been in that garbage and reiterating that it had been the garbage that produced the smell in the trunk. This kind of attack levied either at the police or at us seemed to occur every fifteen minutes or so, to the point that at least once the judge actually admonished Baez for what he was saying.

Staying consistent with the case that the defense presented, Baez focused on the evidence that been found at the crime scene and hammered home his points about chloroform and the computer searches. He went after both Dr. G and Dr. Warren for their testimonies, reserving particular scorn for Dr. Warren, calling him a fantasy man for producing the video superimposition of Caylee's face, the skull, and the duct tape. He next touted his own medical witness, Dr. Spitz. Switching gears yet again, he went back to the Anthony family, hitting home the point about dysfunction, bringing in Cindy's bizarre behavior during Casey's pregnancy to show that there was something strange going on in the family.

One of the things Baez knew we'd proven conclusively was that his client was a liar. His attempt to address that included what was perhaps his most amusing linguistic flourish, rebranding Casey's lies as "fantasies." Ever the salesman, it was interesting to watch him try to sell the jury on this idea that her lies somehow did not carry the sinister nature that the word "lie" implied. Instead, these were Casey's own fantasies; a playful, almost innocent way of describing the delusions that justified Casey's repeated attempts at deception.

After levying yet another attack on the cops, Baez then went on to make what was probably his biggest rhetorical leap of the day, but also the one that got me into trouble as well. Baez returned to make this ridiculous argument that George's report of the missing gas cans on June 24, and the use of the duct tape at the Find Caylee search command post, had been an attempt to frame Casey for the crime. There was no evidence to support this in the slightest, yet Baez found himself making this argument in such an animated way that his voice went up a couple of octaves in pitch, giving him an almost Mickey Mouse–like quality. I began to smile, both at the sound of his words and the absurdity of their content. Aware that the situation was getting the best of me, I covered my mouth with my hand to hide it from the jury.

Glancing over, Baez saw my reaction, and it infuriated him. He seized on that moment to accuse me of being smug and disrespectful. Now, I can say unequivocally that my reaction was not what it should have been. As a lawyer and as a prosecutor, I demand better of myself. However, Baez also overacted to the situation.

Furthermore, what I will say in my defense is that I'd spent the last three years listening to all manner of flack from Baez. I'd taken numerous personal insults and attacks. I'd heard him spew baseless accusations at me, at my team, and at the hard-working men and women of the Orange County Sheriff's Office. None of them were justified. None of them were deserved. None of them were true. But perhaps, most important, none of it was professional. So the argument that somehow Baez had become an arbiter of professional decorum in court was simply one I was not willing to listen to so I smothered my chuckle. What I did may not have been right, but given the absolute absurdity of what Baez was arguing and the total lack of respect he'd shown me during our time as adversaries, I have forgiven myself the moment of weakness.

After calling me out for my reaction, Baez continued on George, bringing up the painful suicide note, a letter that to me marked just how wounded George had been by his granddaughter's death and his daughter's apparent involvement. Instead Baez used it to say that George had only written it and had only attempted suicide because the cops had searched the Anthony home and were closing in on him. Of course, only one half of that was actually true. The cops had indeed searched the Anthony home, but the only places where George was ever an actual suspect were the minds of Baez and Casey.

As Baez prepared to relinquish the floor to Mason, he began to thump his chest out of passion for his argument. I'd learned my lesson this time and kept my composure, but I couldn't help but wonder what impression this would leave on the jury. When Mason took the floor, he spoke mainly in vague platitudes about the U.S. Constitution, and brought in little that Baez had not already said. In all fairness, though, Baez had thrown so much out there that it would have been hard for Mason to find something that Baez had not discussed. I think Mason, who had been largely silent throughout the case, just wanted a moment in the sun. In the end Mason's contribution to the closing, like his contribution throughout the trial itself, was brief. It was unclear what, if anything, he'd said that would sway the jury one way or the other, but the defense had officially come to a close.

BECAUSE BAEZ'S CLOSING LEANED SO heavily on attacking the forensics, Linda asked me to handle part of the rebuttal. Though we'd all wanted to have Linda handle it, she knew that to do this rebuttal properly she would have to address the forensics and George, two areas that were mine. I knew it was a hard call to make. At the end of the day, this was Linda's case, and after everything she'd put in, she really deserved to have the final word. At the same time, we both knew that this material was where I had my best stuff, and in the end we decided that I would rebut the forensics, and then she would sum everything up. It was a credit to her that she was able to take herself out of it and focus on what we felt would be best for the case. That's just the kind of great team player that she is.

When it came time to present, I was in my element. I began first to discuss the comparison of the testimony of Dr. G to Dr. Spitz, and to expose the ridiculousness of his claim that the skull was moved and duct tape placed on it before it was returned. I then moved to a discussion about the significance of the duct tape to prove premeditation.

If there was one thing I had complete confidence in, it was the strength of our forensic experts compared to theirs, so I set up a direct contrast, pitting our bug guy (Haskell) vs. theirs (Huntington), and our medical examiner (Dr. G) vs. theirs (Dr. Spitz). Walking through what Baez had said about Dr. Vass point by point, I explained the unavoidable truth to Dr. Vass's findings and Dr. Vass himself: His findings were conclusive, and he was the leader in his very legitimate scientific field. I even went so far as to refer to Dr. Vass as an unapologetic science geek. (Dr. Vass told me later he received a lot of teasing from his colleagues over that, and a couple dozen pocket protectors pinned to his office door.) Everything in his experience told us that there had been a dead body in the back of Casey Anthony's car. Baez could try all day to tie the smell to nonexistent food in the trash or blame the police for drying out the trash; the bottom line was that the science was in our favor. I tried to hit that point hard. As with the forensics, I wanted to tackle Baez's claims about George's attempts to "implicate" Casey head-on. Discussing each one individually, I tried to drive home just how ridiculous it would be for someone involved in a crime to then expose himself to suspicion by bringing evidence of that crime to the attention of the police. I saved my best ridicule for the Kronk issue and how impossible it would be for Kronk to get the tape from the Anthony home even if he were perverse enough to want to in the first place.

From my three decades in criminal law, I knew full well that jurors sometimes concoct scenarios that no one has argued, so I repeated our theory but allowed that they might have imagined other scenarios and explained how those, accidental death while giving Caylee chloroform, or while using tape to silence her, would still be murder.

I ended with a discussion of George's suicide letter. I recall I actually got choked up when I was describing the pain and anguish he felt as he penned the words on those pages.

I sat down and Linda took over. She began by poking a bit of fun at the *Wheel of Fortune* moments of Jose's closing, saying that "posters and pyrotechnics" were not her style. She harkened back to the opening statements that she and Baez had given six weeks earlier, and in another jab at the defense pointedly stated, "I meant what I said," a reference to the fact that Baez had not come through on his promises in opening statements. Her next comment turned out to be prophetic:

"My biggest fear," she said, "is that common sense will be lost in all the rhetoric of the case."

She implored jurors to look at the big picture of all of the evidence and what it revealed. When discussing the original kidnapping story, Linda asked jurors to consider its genesis and what it illustrated about Casey's awareness of guilt, reminding them once again that Casey had multiple opportunities—both with investigators and with Cindy—to assert that Caylee's death had been an accident. No such claim had been made—at least not until Casey was out of all other options.

As she began to wind down, Linda played the first call Casey made to home from jail and pointed out how it showed Casey's real focus was on Tony, not Caylee. Referring to Casey as a pathological liar, Linda reminded the jury of the connection of the items found with Caylee's body in the swamp to the Anthony house.

Ending as we had discussed, Linda told the jury that the only thing they needed to ask was whose life was better without Caylee. Linda then played Cindy's frantic 911 call from when she had first learned Caylee was missing and referenced George's suicide letter. But lastly she displayed the photograph of the *"Bella Vita"* tattoo and a photo from the hot body contest at Fusian. Pointing to the screen, Linda gave everyone a moment for the images to sink in before she said, "There's your answer."

And then we were done. Judge Perry read a lengthy list of instructions to jurors, all of which were fairly standard. The only point of note was that the instructions made clear that nothing any of the attorneys said in the case was evidence. The evidence could only come from witnesses. This meant that if the jury was following these instructions properly, they were not allowed to consider the unproven statements that Baez had made in his opening remarks. He hadn't supported those points with actual evidence during the course of the trial, therefore the jury could not consider them.

The jurors stood up and filed out of the courtroom. With the instructions read, there was nothing to do but wait. If waiting for the verdict to be read is the worst part of a trial, waiting for the jury to reach a decision is second. We'd presented closing arguments on July 3 and July 4, so there was no time to enjoy the Fourth of July holiday. I spent the rest of July 4 in the office, waiting for the jury with my feet up watching TV on a set the secretaries had positioned so they could follow the trial. Toward the end of the day, I returned to the twenty-third floor so that I would be there when the judge released the jury for the day. I was sitting in a chair in the hallway playing a game on my phone when Jose approached me and we exchanged pleasantries for a bit before he said:

"You're the toughest motherfucker I've ever been up against."

I thanked him. It was good of him to say, even if the list of "motherfuckers" he'd been up against was pretty short. The gesture seemed genuine and I wish I could say it erased all the crap that I had been through in the last three years, but it didn't. I have fought ferociously against attorneys many time and left the courtroom with them as friends. But there were times when I felt Jose misled me, and that is one thing I cannot forgive.

On Tuesday, July 5, I slid into work feeling pretty good. It had been 1,085 days since Cindy Anthony first called 911. The morning was uneventful. No one was expecting anything that soon. That afternoon, Linda, Frank, and I grabbed lunch. No sooner had I returned to my office than my phone rang. The jury had reached a verdict. I hustled over to the courthouse, where I learned the jury's decision: not guilty of first-degree murder, aggravated manslaughter, and aggravated child abuse; guilty of all four counts of lying to police.

AFTER THE VERDICT, MEMBERS OF the prosecution team met in a conference room with all of the investigators and State Attorney Lawson Lamar for a private discussion before meeting with the press. The defense team also appeared before the cameras for a press conference of their own. As hard as I may have been on Jose Baez in these pages, I thought his posttrial comments showed class and professionalism, and I commend him for them. Mason, however, indulged in some rather childish comments directed toward legal commentators who had dared to point out errors committed by his team. Again, the irony was rich, since Mason himself had once been one of those commentators. I might have written it off to the adrenaline rush of a verdict that he was not expecting, but shortly thereafter the child-ishness continued as he was photographed "flipping the finger" to media folks filming him and the team in a rather unseemly champagne party at a bar across the street from the courthouse. If he had wanted privacy, per-haps he should have partied in private. I would have expected a man of his age and reputation to have shown a bit more class.

As soon as the press conference was over, I was off to New York to break the silence that we had held for three years. Since then, I haven't stopped talking about the case.

When I returned from New York, I took a few days to wrap up and pack up my desk. People throughout the office came up to me to express their frustration in the "not guilty" verdict, and to let me know that they were on my side, Caylee's side. Then, I left the office I had worked in for thirty years for the final time. Where I was headed, I couldn't say.

Disappointing though the verdict was, I refused to let it overshadow what I'd accomplished with the State Attorney's Office. As with any retire-ment, there was a bittersweet air to things. I had used every skill I'd devel-oped in my thirty years to get the jury to see the big picture. The team of investigators, prosecutors, and assistants did all that was humanly possible to do the same. Once that is done, all you can do is rest with the knowledge that you did everything anyone could do. As they say in sports, we left it all on the field.

A few weeks later, Linda and another friend, Sara Freeman, organized a retirement party for me at a local establishment. Many old friends from my homicide days in the nineties were there, men and women who had since retired. Seeing all those old and familiar faces, it was great to reminisce— not only because of how much fun it was, but also because it reminded me that this was not my only murder case. There were many other stories that I'd told to juries, many other crimes that I'd taken pride in bringing justice to. Looking at everyone from throughout my legal career gathered together, I was reminded that, in spite of all the difficulty this case had put me through, it might not have even been my hardest. And as much as it felt like an end, it might not even be my last.

During one of the rare moments I had to myself that night, I sat down at a small table on the periphery of the party. Glancing over the crowd, I thought back to that lunch with Linda three years before at the Daily News Café. In retrospect, it would have been so easy for me to simply turn her offer down, to say I wasn't interested and quietly wait out until I'd hit my thirty years. It would have been so easy for me to pass the case on to someone else and simply coasted by. I certainly would have saved myself a lot of frustration.

But I'd wanted the case then. Now, sitting at my going-away party and knowing the outcome, I still understood why. I hadn't wanted the case because of the spotlight. I hadn't wanted the case for a shot at glory. In my past cases, I'd had both of those things. Alone, neither was enough to get out of bed in the morning, and they certainly weren't enough to justify putting up with Jose Baez for three years.

No, I'd wanted the case because I thought it was worth fighting for. I was going to go out either way, and I can't think of a better way to go out, than fighting for little Caylee Marie Anthony.

EPILOGUE

I n the wake of the verdict, a lot has been said about every aspect of the Casey Anthony case. Most vocal are the people expressing outrage at how this verdict was possible, reserving a uniquely powerful ire for Casey and, in at least one poll, naming her the most hated person in America. Perhaps a bit less loudly, people have criticized the jury for the decision they reached, wondering how it was possible for them to hear the evidence and reach such a surprising conclusion.

Likewise, people have found room to criticize our efforts in the prosecution. As a prosecutor who has taken part in cases like this before, I try not to put too much stock in the Monday-morning quarterbacking that goes on, but at the same time, I know it's inevitable. In listening to the anger and the frustration that people have displayed, it's been hard for me not to chime in in agreement, but I also know that these decisions and the forces that create them never have any easy answers. People around the country who passionately believe Casey was guilty still struggle with just how this woman was able to get away with it. It's a frustration I share, and while there's nothing to alleviate that, I do have some thoughts that might help put it in perspective.

Simply put, I think Jose Baez won in spite of himself. Time and time again, I saw how his lack of procedural knowledge hampered his ability to effectively represent his client. His defense was disjointed, his presentation questionable. Even now, after reviewing three years' worth of motions, depositions, and witnesses, the defense's strategy is nearly impossible to discern. Throwing everything out there and seeing what sticks has never been a viable defense strategy, in my mind. To say it was all smoke and mirrors implies there was some grand illusion that the defense worked the whole time. I think that gives them too much credit.

In many ways I think the defense came to mirror the client they represented. Just as Casey reacted when she reached the end of the hall, Baez took each leg of the defense as far as he could, and when he finally ran out of options, he just grabbed on to the next available thing—whether that thing was Zanny, Roy Kronk, or George Anthony. Standing back from it all, it's very hard to find any aspect of their case credible when so much of it was dependent on Casey, the world's least reliable narrator.

Of course, if Baez's defense didn't lead to the verdict, then what did? In the months since the verdict was handed down, I've asked myself that question about once an hour. There are no easy answers, but in hindsight, my belief is that the evidence as well as the makeup of the jury played large roles in how this decision was shaped.

First, to the evidence. As I've said before, you can only try a case with the evidence and the facts that you get from investigators, and in this case, despite the exhaustive efforts of the investigators and our experts, the evidence we had was entirely circumstantial. Now, plenty of murder cases gain convictions with purely circumstantial evidence; however, the caveat when trying a murder case with circumstantial evidence is that you need the jury to be willing to do a lot of work.

Furthermore, we'd always known that there were a couple of spots in the evidence that were problematic for us. Chief among them was not having a cause of death, but also we on the prosecution team could never effectively say exactly how Casey went from a search for chloroform in

March to killing Caylee in June. We had our theories, of course, but there was never anything that we could say definitively and prove in court. Similarly, another barrier was that Casey, according to all the testimonies of her friends and family, had been a loving mother. If this were true, how did she become a cold-blooded killer?

Of course, there was no way for us to suddenly come up with a cause of death or prove that the events between March and June led to Casey killing her daughter, but the claim of Casey being a loving mother was an area where a more complete and candid testimony from Cindy could have been really beneficial. As Cindy's coworkers had shown in our interviews with them, Cindy had her doubts about Casey as a mother. Because these interviews were based in hearsay and therefore inadmissible, Cindy alone had the power to show this to the jury. If Cindy had chosen Caylee over Casey, we might have been able to use Cindy's testimony to make a stronger case for Casey as an irresponsible parent with more of a motive for murdering her daughter.

However, even with those shortcomings, we had an incredibly strong case. I'd always felt (and still do) that the presence of the duct tape showed clearly that this was first-degree murder. Couple that with Casey's pattern of lies, her total lack of emotional response to the "accidental" death of her child, the smell in the trunk, Caylee's hair, and the cadaver dog's reactions, and I feel this demonstrates an undeniable level of guilt on Casey's part.

While I believe that the evidence proves Casey is guilty of first-degree murder, it is possible to see why the jury might have disagreed with that specific charge. Perhaps they felt the burden of proof was just too high for murder one, which would carry the possibility of the death penalty. If that were the argument, I'd beg to differ with it, but on some level I could at least understand that response. But there were lesser charges the jury could have convicted on that would still have reflected Casey's responsibility for her daughter's death. What I find truly baffling though is that somehow they did not see the proof enough to convict her of a lesser murder charge or even manslaughter.

In the wake of the verdict, a frequent criticism has been that the state attorney should not have made this a capital case. Without the death penalty, the thinking goes, the jury would have almost certainly returned a "guilty" verdict, because they just couldn't bring themselves to rob George and Cindy of their only daughter when they'd already lost their grand-daughter. Of course, the obvious problem with this logic is that the jury would have been fully within its right to reject first-degree murder in favor of a lesser murder conviction that did not carry the death penalty. If they'd really felt she was guilty but did not want to award the death penalty, a lesser murder charge would have conveyed that point quite well. This ver-dict, however, was not the work of a jury that was concerned about the punishment; instead, this decision was the work of a jury who didn't believe she deserved to be punished at all. To me the biggest legacy of this decision is not that Casey wasn't convicted of first-degree murder, but that she got away scot-free.

Ultimately, it is this piece of the jury's decision that I absolutely cannot understand: how could they disregard so much evidence showing that Casey had played a large role in Caylee's death? Looking through the tes-timonies that we presented at trial, one thing that seems quite apparent is that, either through her own deliberate actions or through some kind of negligence, Casey was involved in her daughter's death. There is simply too much evidence tying Caylee's dead body to the car Casey was driving for me to believe that Casey herself was completely uninvolved.

Our case was not a slam dunk; we knew that from the start. It required work from us, it required work from the witnesses we'd called to present our evidence, and it required work, not to mention common sense, from the jury. From the moment our jury had been fielded back in May, we'd had concerns over their apparent absence of strong opinions as well as over the amount of effort they seemed willing to expend on this. In retrospect, I think those concerns were justified.

My worst fears from jury selection manifested themselves in the ver-dict. This jury needed someone to tell them exactly how Caylee died. Piec-ing it together from circumstantial evidence was not good enough for them. They wanted the answers on a silver platter, but we didn't have the evidence to serve it that way. It's not just the verdict that tells me this, but also the manner in which it was reached. The fact that they didn't request any materials to review. The fact that they didn't have any questions for the judge. If the statements that the foreman of the jury made to the media are true, ten of these twelve jurors felt that ninety minutes of deliberation was sufficient to fully weigh, consider, and reject four weeks' worth of testimony that we on the prosecution used to establish that this was first-degree murder. The rest of the thirteen hours of deliberation had been spent trying to convince the two holdout jurors of the decision.

Juror Jennifer Ford, the only juror to identify herself, later said in an interview that "no one showed them how Caylee died." My question would be: How hard in those ninety minutes did you look for it? The jurors had to put the pieces together and apply some common sense to the notion of how people do and don't act. This jury was not willing to do that, so in a sense we lost before we started.

I AM FIRST AND FOREMOST a lawyer, and as such I believe in the system of trial by jury. It's the best we have. That system can't work if jurors aren't free to follow their consciences and do what they think is right, without fear of condemnation. The system can't work without it. But at the same time they take a sacred oath to honestly try the case and follow the law. We expect them to take that obligation seriously, and we entrust them to do their very best. The system can't work without that, either.

We will never know if the jury followed the law in this case. We weren't in the jury room with them. Judge Perry told them that George's statement to River Cruz could not be used as evidence of how Caylee died. Did they follow that instruction and ignore that piece of evidence? Similarly, the Judge told them that what the attorneys say is not evidence, so they should have ignored most of the defense's opening statement. Did they ignore the unsubstantiated idea that George had abused Casey? Absent some strong evidence to the contrary, I believe they followed the law.

Three of the jurors have given statements to the media, two anonymously and one by name. Having reviewed them all, I am pleased that it appears they did follow the court's instructions. None of them seemed to give any thought to the unproven allegations of molestation or any of the other outlandish claims made by the defense in their opening statements.

Along the same line, the defense's repeated attempts to paint Casey as a victim ultimately fell on deaf ears, and no one seemed to believe Roy Kronk was seriously involved in anything beyond his discovery of the body.

Assuming they did follow the instructions, the question becomes one of reasonable doubt. We tell jurors that burden of proof is beyond a reasonable doubt, but defining that term is difficult. A reasonable doubt is not a speculative, imaginary, or forced doubt. We use concepts like "abiding conviction of guilt," which ultimately means that the definition of "reasonable" is up to them. They must apply common sense, that knowledge of how people act by having lived in the world, to reach their own conclusion.

They presumably felt it was reasonable to believe that a mother would react to the accidental drowning of her young daughter by making no effort to revive her. They presumably felt it made sense that the mother's next act would be to stuff her in a garbage bag and throw her in a swamp. If the jurors felt that those were "reasonable" reactions in keeping with what they knew about human behavior, then they had every right to feel that way and we have every right to disagree with them. I'd always said that if the jury saw the photograph of Caylee's remains with duct tape over her nose and mouth and didn't see in it what I did, then so be it. To me the duct tape was the one thing that could never be lied away, the one thing that said murder beyond a reasonable doubt, the one thing for which the defense had no explanation, and the one thing for which none of the jurors had any explanation in their post-trial interviews. Clearly, though, they disagreed, and we have no right to condemn them, no matter how angry the outcome may make us.

Throughout the weeks of the trial, I kept thinking that justice for Caylee would be sufficient to make the jury work harder and care enough to really think through what was reasonable. From the instant we showed the photo of Caylee's remains with the duct tape and were met with no discernible emotion from the jury, I knew that it would be a struggle to make them care. Maybe there is something we could have done to make them care more or motivated them to think a bit harder about the evidence that we did have, but if there is I can't think of it. We just couldn't make them care more.

And perhaps that is the saddest part of all of this, that right up until the end so few people were willing to care about Caylee. Caylee got lost. I believe she was lost to Casey when she got in the way of the *"Bella Vita."* She was lost to Cindy when Cindy chose to get behind Casey rather than lose her. And finally, I fear she was lost in the trial and never made it into the hearts of the jury members in the deliberation room.

There have been many cases in the past where juries have convicted people of murder based on less evidence, cases where the exact cause of death was unknown, or even cases where the body was never found. Part of it always comes down to the random and unpredictable variable of who shows up for jury duty. I do think that the outcome was influenced by the publicity and the difficulties it created for us in jury selection that I talked about before. I remember a conversation I had when we were debating whether to try and pick a jury here in Orlando and I said, "You might be able to get a jury here, but you're not gonna like what you end up with." I guess what applied to Orlando applied to Pinellas County as well. Maybe we should have gone farther away. Maybe to the moon.

IN SEPTEMBER, GEORGE AND CINDY Anthony gave their first televised interview since the verdict when they appeared on *Dr. Phil.* Watching both of them together, I found myself thinking of that day at our office when they came in, and we'd explained to them via their lawyer what Casey would be accusing George of at trial.

I thought about the look on George's face then, and how utterly eviscerated he'd been by both the accusation itself and the idea that his daughter would make up such an outrageous claim. I remembered the sound of Cindy's voice as she leaned over to him and said, "I don't know what's wrong with her," echoing a sentiment that everyone associated with this case had wondered at one point or another, yet it was the first time we'd heard Cindy say it. I recalled how sorry I felt for them in that moment—because they'd lost their granddaughter, but also because I could see just how hard it was for them to accept the reality of what their daughter had become.

In some ways that day at our office had changed everything and in other ways it changed nothing. While George's demeanor toward us shifted for the better after that, Cindy's remained largely the same. Now, months after that day, their disconnect appeared to have only grown more entrenched, and it was on full display on *Dr. Phil*. For anyone watching the segments, it was obvious that they were still going in opposite directions. Cindy was as rooted in her denial as ever, even going so far as to test out a brand-new "theory" about a seizure playing a role in Casey's decision-making and Casey's ability to help or protect Caylee. Meanwhile, George, in some of his strongest statements to date, appeared as though he was finally facing the reality he'd spent three years ignoring, saying that he felt Casey had played a role in Caylee's death, though he could not say precisely what.

Replaying all of my various interactions with them over the years, it was hard not to feel frustrated all over again by the behavior each of them had displayed throughout this case. Difficult as they had been, though, neither of them deserved what Casey had put them through. I'm not sure how any parent bounces back from what they've experienced. My hope for them is that whatever their beliefs may be—whether it's complete denial or tacit acceptance—they are able to heal and move on. To find a way to make themselves whole again. And perhaps someday, a while down the line, maybe even Cindy will finally have the fortitude and the hindsight to pick Caylee.

AS A PROSECUTOR, ONE OF the things that you never want to get good at is losing. I'm a competitive person and I like to win, but in a case like this the loss always feels worse, because the stakes are so much higher.

In many ways, it's been strange for me during the months since the verdict to see such a high level of frustration with the verdict, one that's usually reserved for the actual losing participants, spread across the country. On one hand it's helpful to know that I'm far from alone in thinking that this verdict was the wrong decision. On the other hand, though, it's odd how personally people took the decision. While I applaud everyone's passionate support of justice for Caylee, it's important to remember that as unsatisfying as this may be, this is how the system works. In general, you put your faith in the system, and usually it treats you right. Sometimes there is a case that manages to expose the flaws that exist, but that doesn't mean the system is broken—just that it's not something we can simply bend to our will.

Looking to the future, the trick for me, as well as for everyone else who finds themselves angry and frustrated, is how do we let go? How do those of us who haven't forgotten Caylee in our hearts move on? Forgive? Not possible. Forget? No way.

There are no easy answers to these questions, but the one thing I've learned in my years as a trial lawyer is that you must accept the verdict. The law will not punish Casey. We have to come to terms with that. What we can all hope for instead is to turn that anger we feel into something positive. In the past, when faced with an outcome like this, I've always channeled my frustration into another case. I did this not because I wanted another chance at winning, but because I wanted to turn my frustration into something positive. And that is the best that those of us who want to remember Caylee can do. Turn your anger into something positive—hug your child, help someone else, keep a little closer eye out for the little ones you see running around. Justice is not just about what gets decided in the courtroom, it's about how we should go about our lives and respect others. And in the end, that's what it really means to remember Caylee.

ACKNOWLEDGMENTS

I would like to acknowledge some people without whom my career, this case, and this book would not have been possible. First and foremost, my mother and father, Barbara and Richard Ashton. Mom, everything I have accomplished in my life has been for one single purpose: to make you and Dad proud of me. We talked many times about how much he enjoyed watching me work and how much we both wished he could have been around to see this one. Love you, Mom.

Now to my wife, Rita. Thank you for putting up with me, listening to me bitch on the bad days and brag on the good ones. You were a single parent a lot this summer, and I know it was tough at times. I couldn't have done any of this without you. We found each other later in life, but sometimes the best is saved for last. I love you.

To my kids, Adam, Jon, Becky, Alex , David, and Emma, I am proud of you all and love having you in my life. To David and Emma, sorry Daddy didn't have much time to play this summer.

To Linda Drane Burdick, trial partner, work wife, and friend. This has been the best professional partnership of my career. You are truly one of the best lawyers I have ever worked with. I will forever be in your debt for bringing me in on this case.

Frank George, it was truly an honor to finally get to work with you. Your level head and sense of humor were a perfect complement to the team. Your skill and professionalism are your great assets and will serve you well in what will be a stellar career in law.

Lawson Lamar, thank you so much for allowing me to serve you once again on this case. Your constant support of our efforts is greatly appreciated.

Mario Perez and Arlene Zayas, your tireless support was the key to our ability to present this case in a competent and professional manner

Professor Bernard "Andy" Raum, thank you so much for all of the advice and assistance in the case.

To Yuri, John, and Eric, the investigative team from the sheriff's office that I have spoken of so often in these pages, and Nick Savage and Karen Cowan of the FBI. You guys are amazing; you put heart and soul into the case. You did everything you could. You should be proud.

To the ladies and gentleman of the crime scene unit, who spent countless hours of work sometimes braving snakes and poison ivy to find Caylee and give her remains the respect they deserved. I salute you all.

My thanks to Mark NeJame, whose behind-the-scenes assistance in dealing with the EquuSearch issues really made our job so much easier.

To Lisa Pulitzer, thanks for helping me tell this story and making me sound halfway intelligent. Thanks to Martha Smith for pitching in as well. We would have been at this till Christmas without you. To my editor at HarperCollins, Matt Harper, thanks for staying on me and putting the final polish to our words.

Last, to all the well-wishers and supporters who sent us their kind words—my eternal thanks.